DEFYING CONVENTIONAL WISDOM:
POLITICAL MOVEMENTS AND POPULAR CONTENTION
AGAINST NORTH AMERICAN FREE TRADE

This book offers a crisp and thoughtful account of political phenomena still fresh in the minds of Canadians and still relevant to policy-making processes. As the first major work on the origins, strategies, and activities of movements and coalitions that arose in Canada and spread across North America to oppose free trade, it captures an important developmental period in Canadian political life.

Focusing on an analysis of the Action Canada Network, Jeffrey Ayres adopts a political-process model to link the emergence of popular sector movements and transnational networks to constraints posed by the Canada–U.S. FTA and NAFTA. His extensive use of popular writings and interviews highlights the personal reflections of coalition members and provides an intimate perspective on their strategies and actions. As a contribution both to the study of recent developments in Canadian politics and to our understanding of emerging transnational contention in North America, *Defying Conventional Wisdom* will appeal to readers across a wide spectrum of interests and backgrounds.

JEFFREY AYRES is Assistant Professor in the Department of Political Science, Saint Michael's College, Winooski Park, Colchester, Vermont.

STUDIES IN COMPARATIVE POLITICAL ECONOMY AND PUBLIC POLICY

Editors: MICHAEL HOWLETT, DAVID LAYCOCK, STEPHEN MCBRIDE
Simon Fraser University

JEFFREY M. AYRES

Defying Conventional Wisdom: Political Movements and Popular Contention against North American Free Trade

UNIVERSITY OF TORONTO PRESS
Toronto   Buffalo   London

© University of Toronto Press Incorporated 1998
Toronto Buffalo London
Printed in Canada

ISBN 0-8020-4246-5 (cloth)
ISBN 0-8020-8089-8 (paper)

Printed on acid-free paper

Canadian Cataloguing in Publication Data

Ayres, Jeffrey McKelvey
  Defying conventional wisdom : political movements and popular contention against
  North American free trade

  (Studies in comparative political economy and public policy)
  Includes bibliographical references and index.
  ISBN 0-8020-4246-5 (bound)   ISBN 0-8020-8089-8 (pbk.)

  1. Political participation – Canada   2. Social movements – Canada.   3. Foreign
  trade regulation – Canada – Citizen participation.   I. Title.   II. Series.

  JL186.5.A97 1998   322.4'0971   C97-932406-8

The publication of this book has been made possible by a grant from the Association for
Canadian Studies in the United States (ACSUS) and the assistance of the Government
of Canada.

University of Toronto Press acknowledges the financial assistance to its publishing
program of the Canada Council for the Arts and the Ontario Arts Council.

To my parents

Contents

List of Tables

Acknowledgments

In the course of researching, writing, and subsequently revising this book I have been supported and encouraged by many individuals and institutions. I owe a great deal of professional and personal thanks to colleagues in the academic community, including Graham Wilson, Pamela Oliver, Richard Merelman, Crawford Young, and Mark Beissinger, all of whom read this manuscript at various stages of revision. William Reno was especially helpful, enlightening me on the various nuances of editing, rewriting, and revision in matters of both content and appearance. Sidney Tarrow provided key advice during the study's early stages, and Charles Franklin gave helpful tips to prod the entire process of revision along as smoothly as possible.

In carrying out the initial field research in Canada I benefited from the financial support provided by a grant from the Canadian Studies Fellowship Program of the Canadian Embassy in Washington, D.C. Tim Ryan, of the Canadian Consulate General in Chicago, helped especially in the acquisition of this grant and in sorting out the initial logistical challenges when I arrived in Ottawa. A subsequent visit to Ottawa was supported by a Vilas travel grant from the University of Wisconsin-Madison.

The publication subvention committee of the Association for Canadian Studies in the United States awarded a generous grant to help offset the cost of publication; without it this book might not in fact have been published. I thank David Biette, executive director of ACSUS, for his most helpful advice. I also wish to thank Dennis Moore, public affairs officer at the Canadian Consulate General in Detroit, who was instrumental in procuring an additional grant from the Canadian Consulate General in support of publication.

My editor at the University of Toronto Press, Rob Ferguson, was extremely helpful during the publishing process in guiding me through what was, for me, uncharted terrain. Thanks as well to Virgil Duff, who encouraged me to submit the manuscript in the first place. Others at the Press who deserve my thanks include Darlene Zeleney and Rosmarie Gadzovski. My copy-editor, Henri Pilon, provided an excellent and sound reading of the manuscript. Finally, the anonymous readers procured by the Press also provided helpful criticisms of the manuscript, prompting me to rework it and extend its scope in many areas. Of course, any remaining errors are mine alone.

I want especially to thank John Trent, who invited me to be a visiting researcher with the Department of Political Science at the University of Ottawa during my period of fieldwork in Canada. The office, staff, and other institutional support provided by his department were immensely useful in helping me to become quickly acclimatized to the Ottawa milieu. I thank John for his advice, criticism, and support, as well as for the many valuable contacts he enabled me to make in the academic, government, and activist communities in Canada.

So many Canadians were generous with their time and support during my fieldwork that it would be impossible for me to thank them all. I owe a great debt to the staff of the Council of Canadians, especially Peter Bleyer, Ann Boys, and Maude Barlow, who provided me with extensive access to their files and led me to further contacts in the activist community. Thanks go as well to the people at the Ecumenical Coalition for Economic Justice in Toronto, especially Dennis Howlett; the Action Canada Network in Ottawa, especially Tony Clarke; and the Canadian Centre for Policy Alternatives, especially Sandra Sorenson, Bruce Campbell, and Duncan Cameron. Additional helpful advice was provided by Sylvia Bashevkin, Brian Tomlin, and Lawrence LeDuc, and by the many other academics, activists, politicians, and government officials who took the time to respond to questions and to provide the information needed to complete this study.

The institution at which I was employed during the writing of this book, Lake Superior State University, provided a stimulating academic and intellectual environment in which to work. My colleagues there, especially in the School of Arts, Letters, and Social Sciences, were very supportive of my interests and efforts in the field of Canadian studies. The School was particularly helpful in subsidizing my participation in various Canadian Studies conferences, which, in the long run, helped facilitate the publication of this book. I wish also to thank Susan Gadzinski for her help in preparing the index.

Finally, I thank my wife, Denyse Butler Ayres, for her support and patience during the entire process. She kept me going when I thought that I had had enough and prevented me from losing sight of the broader picture. She has provided me, during the last three years, with the greatest possible source of support and incentive, our daughters Virginia Margaret and McKelvey Catherine.

Parts of two chapters of this book were published previously. Part of chapter 1 appeared as 'From Competitive Theorizing Towards a Synthesis in the Global Study of Political Movements: Revisiting the Political Process Model' in *International Sociology* (March 1997), and part of chapter 4 appeared as 'Political Process and Popular Protest: The Mobilization against Free Trade in Canada,' in the *American Journal of Economics and Sociology* (October 1996). Portions of chapter 7 appeared as 'From National to Popular Sovereignty: The Evolving Globalization of Protest Activity in Canada,' in the *International Journal of Canadian Studies* (fall 1997).

JEFFREY M. AYRES

Abbreviations

ACN	Action Canada Network
BCNI	Business Council on National Issues
CAFT	Coalition Against Free Trade (Toronto)
CATJO	Canadian Alliance for Trade and Job Opportunities
CAW	Canadian Auto Workers
CBC	Canadian Broadcasting Corporation
CCAFT	Citizens Concerned About Free Trade
CCPA	Canadian Centre for Policy Alternatives
CCU	Confederation of Canadian Unions
CEQ	Centrale de l'enseignement du Québec
CIC	Committee for an Independent Canada
CLC	Canadian Labour Congress
CMA	Canadian Manufacturers' Association
COC	Council of Canadians
CSN	Confédération des syndicats nationaux
CUPE	Canadian Union of Public Employees
ECEJ	Ecumenical Coalition for Economic Justice
FIRA	Foreign Investment Review Agency
FTA	Free Trade Agreement
FTQ	La Fédération des travailleurs et travailleuses du Québec
GST	Goods and Services Tax
NAC	National Action Committee on the Status of Women
NAFTA	North American Free Trade Agreement
NDP	New Democratic Party
NEC	National Economic Conference
NEP	National Energy Policy

PCN   Pro-Canada Network
SDI   Strategic Defense Initiative
UPA   L'Union des producteurs agricoles du Québec

DEFYING CONVENTIONAL WISDOM

Introduction

This is a book about mobilization and contention. It examines a remarkable set of challenges to the conventional wisdom that privileges the primacy of the market and free trade, as well as party and parliamentary politics, over other forms of economic policy and political behaviour. It specifically links the rise in Canada of cross-sectoral coalition building and of the mobilization of political movements to the economic and political upheaval the country has experienced in the past fifteen years, especially through the implementation of the Canada–U.S. Free Trade Agreement (FTA) and the North American Free Trade Agreement (NAFTA). This political activity – an unprecedented mobilization of nationalist, women's, church, student, artistic, labour, Native, farmer, environmentalist, and other groups – significantly challenged the content and style of Canadian politics over the past fifteen years.

The emergence of the Council of Canadians (COC) and of the Pro-Canada Network (PCN), later the Action Canada Network (ACN), as well as of other community-based coalitions, has marked an important development in political movements in Canada. The COC, initially viewed as a centrist rehashing of the older Committee for an Independent Canada (CIC), continues to experience a vitality and a growth in membership commensurate with its status in the late 1990s as one of the few alternative, pan-Canadian political vehicles remaining in the political vacuum of recent federal elections. The PCN/ACN, moreover, represents the most significant example to date of national cross-sectoral coalition building.

The PCN first arose to oppose the FTA and it and its successor subsequently intervened in the debates over the Goods and Services Tax, the constitutional talks leading up to the failed Charlottetown Accord, and the discussions over ratification of NAFTA. This coalition tapped into the historical and widespread public unease in Canada over the notion of a continental free trade agreement with the United States and it mobilized a broad-based movement that built a public consensus against free trade and that nearly succeeded in defeating it during the 1988 federal election campaign. While subsequent cross-country coalition building has met with less success in recent years, this book suggests that familiar images of Canadian politics should be revised to one that allows for more scope for the role played by non-traditional, extraparliamentary actors.

In particular, greater attention needs to be paid to the record of popular-sector coalition-building activity in Canada. The term 'popular sector' initially emerged to describe a broad cross-section of groups that had struggled through the 1981–2 recession, including trade unions, women's groups, social agencies, Native peoples, and farmers. Duncan Cameron and Daniel Drache, in their book published in the mid-1980s, *The Other Macdonald Report*, apply the label 'popular sector' specifically to the variety of progressive and social welfare groups that developed briefs for presentation to the Royal Commission on the Economic Union and Development Prospects for Canada, chaired by Donald S. Macdonald. These groups shared broad characteristics of economic and political marginalization from the major decision-making institutions in Canada, including a rank and file that was not drawn from the elite or establishment levels of Canadian society.[1]

This umbrella term became widely used in the years following the release of the commission's report to describe the groups that mobilized in contention against established elites and particularly against the policy of continental free trade. Various church, Native peoples', women's, labour, seniors', youth, farmers', and anti-poverty groups found commonality within this 'popular sector,' linked by a shared unconventional counter-discourse on Canadian political economy. From the perspective of many such groups, the neo-conservative tenets of the 1980s and 1990s – privatization, downsizing, free trade, deregulation – represented ill-conceived, if not ideological, responses to the mounting social and economic problems facing not only Canada but also many marginalized groups around the world.[2] In consequence, the FTA and NAFTA, as significant public policy responses to global economic stagnation, were met by protests employing particularly the strategy of popular-sector coalition building to defy the conventional wisdom that encouraged free trade and unfettered markets.

The strategy of coalition building sought to bring together a cross-section of groups with common goals whose resources could be more effectively maximized through cooperation and sharing. Conceptualized as a 'new style of politics,' popular-sector coalition building sought to build links between groups based on non-hierarchical, consultative, and democratic relationships.[3] Coalitions pooled the unique skills of various groups for research, membership, and leadership towards the achievement of more generalized goals shared across sectors. As a result, coalitions served as vehicles for political contestation and change to challenge the deferential and hierarchical networks of political access and influence that were current in Canada's parliamentary democracy.

The term 'popular sector,' then, is employed throughout this book to capture a central theme of analysis: the ebb and flow of contentious politics against continental free trade in Canada. The popular contention studied here characteristically involved broad-based coalitions of community groups engaged in various forms of collective activity to protest against North American free trade. As McAdam, Tarrow, and Tilly argue, 'contention begins when people collectively make claims on other people, claims which if realized would affect those others' interests.'[4] The contentious politics analysed in this book involve popular-sector interactions with the government, institutions, the state, and other social and political actors, interactions that sought to prevent the implementation of continental free trade. The interactions were popular in that those represented under this rubric were largely located outside the traditional party or parliamentary system, and contentious in that the means employed by these groups to seek and secure goals often relied upon non-institutional, collective protest activities.

In addition to providing a much-needed empirical account of the dynamics of popular-sector coalition building in Canada, a major purpose of this book is to put forth an integrative political perspective on movements.[5] The political model I apply builds on the work of McAdam, Tarrow, Tilly, and others who directly link the dynamics of movements to the political process. Moreover, as opposed to the divergent, competitive models that are often employed, this book seeks to incorporate systematically other strands in the literature on movements to offer an inclusive model. This model also fleshes out the role of domestic and international political processes – international economic constraints, political institutions, political opportunities, electoral instability, and social and political organization – on the emergence and mobilization of movements in Canada over the past fifteen years.

The exercise in updating and synthesizing theory that this book represents is called for because the literature on social movements is inconsistent and at times simply confusing. There remains a need for studies that systematically organize and highlight the role of political processes in the mobilization of social movements through a clearly demarcated political model. Many reviews of the literature of movements have placed proponents of the political-process model under the alternative 'resource mobilization' or 'new social movement' paradigms, and have thus muddled the way in which political processes often provide the most consistent explanation for the outcome of the mobilization of movements.[6] For example, where does the obviously useful concept of political opportunity structures fall analytically? Is it within the paradigms for resource mobilization or for new social movements, as has sometimes been suggested? Or can these variables bolster a more explicitly political model of movements? Much scholarly value can be gained in untangling these different concepts and in attempting to delineate the boundaries of the political-movement model in particular.

A political-process approach, such as the one employed in this book, analyses protest and mobilization through three core conceptual tools: changes in the strength and resources of organizations, changes in political opportunities, and changes or transformations in the subjective consciousness of participants in movements.[7] This approach is extended to the interesting phenomena of popular-sector coalition building and mobilization in Canada, and thus provides a useful addition to research in cross-national movements.[8] It draws on interviews with members of the political elite and with activists, as well as on primary documentary and archival sources to describe the impact that various political processes have had on the fortunes of popular-sector politics in Canada.[9]

Specifically, this analysis also links the rise of popular coalitions to pre-existing social, personal, and organizational networks and, in particular, to the emergence of several favourable political-opportunity structures in the Canadian political system in the 1980s. The availability of allies within the political party system, electoral instability, and divisions among the elite provided a supportive context for popular mobilization. In contrast, a declining set of political opportunities in the 1990s, prompted in part by the constraints imposed by economic globalization and in part also by the election in 1993 of a Liberal Party majority and the electoral and political decline of the federal New Democratic Party, has undermined the potential of the popular sector. While many of the popular-sector organizations that were previously active have not disbanded, much of the coalition work has been reduced to ad hoc relationships through having been absorbed and institutionalized into ordinary politics.

On the other hand, the post-NAFTA reality of near-hemispheric free trade has encouraged new forms of community-based resistance and anti-corporate campaigns, with social groups across Canada rethinking traditional, national methods of protest in an era of shrinking government power and resources. Increasingly, groups have begun to mount broader collective campaigns that transcend both the concept of national sovereignty and national borders to focus on transnational and popular democracy. In this light, the book also reflects on the lessons learned by movements and the prospects for future popular-sector coalition building and for social solidarity both in Canada and within the larger North American political economy under the constraints of globalization.

The chapters that follow analyse various stages of popular-sector coalition building and mobilization from the early 1980s to the late 1990s through the lens of a political-process approach. Chapter 1 considers recent developments in the theory of social movements, outlining the resource-mobilization, new social movement, and political-process perspectives. It then discusses some potential limitations in the first two approaches – chiefly their apolitical nature – and then calls for greater consideration of the role of the political aspects in movement mobilization. Chapter 2 analyses the shifting and unsettled political context of the early 1980s in Canada, which set the stage for the rise of popular-sector coalition building and mobilization. It frames the 1981–2 recession, the turn towards privatization and marketization, and the Progressive Conservative landslide in the federal election in 1984 as critical political events that dramatically shifted the Canadian political status quo and created political opportunities for popular mobilization. Chapter 3 studies the structures that facilitated the coalition-building style of movement politics that emerged from the fusing of popular-sector and nationalist currents, with particular attention given to the emergence of the Pro-Canada Network.

The fourth chapter links critical organizational developments, political opportunities, and the strong sense of political efficacy among activists to the anti–free trade protest campaign. The intervention of the popular movement in the parliamentary debates on free trade is examined, along with the impact that it had on the positions of the two opposition political parties, the Liberal and New Democratic parties. Chapter 5 examines the high and low points of popular-sector mobilization in the run-up to and during the 1988 federal election. It describes the constraints that electoral politics posed for the popular-sector campaigns, detailing the closure of political opportunity, the weakening of organizations, and the decline in the sense of the political efficacy of collective action that occurred. It also highlights occasions of mutual political opportunity – a situation of popular-sector–political party symbiosis – when both sets of actors benefited from the tactics employed to rally the public against the free trade agreement and the Progressive Conservative government. In addition, it analyses the declining fortunes of the popular sector amidst an inspired counter-mobilization and a declining set of political opportunities in the latter half of the election campaign.

Chapter 6 analyses how the constraints imposed by economic globalization – and continental free trade in particular – helped to structure new forms of transnational political opportunity. As the mobilizing potential of the Canadian national political-opportunity structure declined, Canadian, U.S., and Mexican groups cultivated cross-national ties and developed joint coalitions and protest strategies to counter the evolving international negotiations for a North American free trade agreement. The chapter also underscores how partisanship and the collapse of political allies within the political system by the time of the 1993 federal election took a heavy toll on the popular coalitions, particularly the federal NDP, the only pan-Canadian political party on the left. Chapter 7 looks at the more recent, post-NAFTA strategy of transnational coalition building and assesses the subtle shift in strategy employed by some popular-sector groups in the struggle for both national and popular sovereignty.

Finally, the book concludes with some thoughts on the lessons learned from a study of over fifteen years of popular-sector politics. It summarizes this study's findings, and considers their implications both for an understanding of current Canadian political behaviour and for the study of political movements. Although popular-sector activity on the Canadian domestic front remains primarily in a defensive position, in the context of the constraints imposed by the continental free trade agreements transnational networking and coalition building present interesting possibilities for the emergence of transnational social movements.

1

Studying Movements Politically

The globalization of the world's economy has sparked a great deal of unrest, protest, and mobilization of political movements. Movements protesting economic integration have arisen to contest the Maastricht Treaty on European Union in France, Denmark, and Norway, while popular opposition to this project has manifested itself in Great Britain and Sweden as well. The push for continental economic integration in North America via the Canada–U.S. free trade agreement provoked popular-sector coalition building in both countries. In addition, the uprising of indigenous people in Chiapas, Mexico, had a similar, if less well analysed, link to the disruptions wrought by the emerging global economy. Yet, if there can be little doubt about the rightful place for the empirical study of the link between globalization and protests, there is much less certainty regarding the availability of reliable theoretical tools for systematically understanding and explaining the phenomenon.

This chapter addresses the problem and describes an approach that makes use of the political-process model for overcoming ongoing competition between various theories at the expense of analytic clarity and understanding. The discussion specifically responds to both the overcompetitive nature of the theoretical literature and the need for greater conceptualization of the role played by politics in movement mobilization. Towards this goal, the chapter is divided into three sections. The first critically reviews recent cross-national research on socio-political movements, highlighting the growing body of literature that confirms the frequently determinant mobilizing role played by political processes. The second briefly looks at the essential propositions presented by the three major approaches – the new social movement, resource mobilization, and political process – and discusses the ability of each to account for the role that politics plays in the mobilization of movements. Finally, the third suggests that of the three models, a reconceptualized, integrative political process approach represents a more inclusive alternative for arriving at a general understanding of the important interplay between movements and politics.

The Link between Politics and Mobilization

Over the past two decades the study of socio-political movements has 'gone global' and produced an expanding and productive debate across the disciplines of the social sciences. A number of social scientists took the lead during the 1970s in linking politics to collective action,[1] providing what McAdam has called the 'reassertion of the political' into research on social movements.[2] In the 1980s and 1990s case studies have provided rich empirical detail to highlight the conditioning of the dynamics of movements by national political institutions. European scholars have linked the rise of protest movements to national political-opportunity structures in Finland,[3] Italy,[4] and the Netherlands.[5] In addition, other cross-national European comparisons of social movements have given scholars a more general understanding of the political factors essential to movement formation.[6]

These important findings that link politics to collective action have by no means been limited to the parliamentary systems of Western Europe. Social scientists who have focused on North America have also brought political variables into play for explaining the ebb and flow of the activity of movements in the United States and Canada. Several scholars have pointed to the turbulent changes in the American political environment during the 1960s to explain the rise and success of farm workers' movements, especially changes in electoral realignments and the availability of political allies.[7] Other examples have tied expanding forms of political opportunity in the United States to the rise of the Townsend movement,[8] to extensive protest by the unemployed during the Depression of the 1930s,[9] and perhaps most notably to the rise and decline of the American civil rights movement.[10] Recent research has also linked the rise of popular-sector protest in Canada in the 1980s and 1990s to expanding political opportunity in the wake of the integration of the North American economy.[11]

Research on movements in underdeveloped countries has also uncovered the conditioning role political systems have played in collective mobilization. Brockett and Cuzan have both linked the expanding structure of political opportunities – especially the fragmentation of the elite, conflict within it, and the existence of support groups – to widespread popular mobilizations of peasants throughout Central America.[12] Other works that discuss the political context of the mobilization of peasants include Skocpol's, which focuses on the fragmentation of the repressive agencies of the state;[13] McClintock's, which looks at the mobilizing impact of public policy;[14] and Midlarsky's and Roberts's, which examines the impact of relationships between the state and its elite.[15]

In light of these outcomes in collective mobilization that highlight the impact of politics across varying contexts and countries, movement analysts have called for a more precise theoretical interpretation of the political context of the emergence and mobilization of movements.[16] Tarrow has argued that what is now required 'is a theory of the political situations in which states become vulnerable to collective action, when ordinary people amass the resources to overcome their disorganization, and gain knowledge of when and how to use their resources.'[17] The next section discusses how well the three major models – resource mobilization, new social movement, and political process – have responded to this need, and will evaluate and compare the extent to which each one can account for the increasingly critical role of politics in collective mobilization.

Resource-Mobilization Theory

For the school that favours the resource-mobilization theory, the central differentiating and determining factor in the emergence and sustainability of social movements has been the variability in the level of available resources. More specifically, as the organizational-entrepreneurial variant of this theory asserts, organizational resources hold the key to the success or failure of social movements.[18] This perspective also argues that these resources frequently originate from outside the insurgent, mobilizing groups, in other words, that movements thrive by tapping support among the elite and other outside sources. As McCarthy and Zald argue, 'in accounting for a movement's successes and failures there is an explicit recognition of the crucial importance of involvement on the part of individuals and organizations from outside the collectivity which a social movement represents.'[19]

In particular, movements draw support from the affluent middle classes and from so-called 'conscience constituents' – 'direct supporters of social movement organizations who do not stand to benefit directly from [their] success in goal accomplishment.'[20] Accordingly, affluent societies give rise to conscience constituents who donate their time and discretionary income to movements and whose rewards derive less from direct involvement than from 'siding with the underdog.'[21] This argument also suggests that the support provided by conscience constituents counters a reduction in mass participation. In sum, then, modern movements emerge less in reaction to individual grievances and societal strains than in response to the guidance of professional organizations and entrepreneurs; they rely on a very small membership base and gather resources and support through outside contributions of money and resources from conscience constituents and other members of the elite.

Focused as the resource-mobilization school has been on the role of resources, there have nonetheless been attempts by some scholars to formulate more politically potent versions of this theory. Jenkins has introduced what he calls a more 'multifaceted model' of movement formation, including consideration of the availability of resources, organization, and political opportunities.[22] Tilly's 'polity model' and McAdam's own version of the political-process model have also been lumped into the resource-mobilization theory as 'political-interactive' versions of it.[23] However, the last two scholars have both rejected this categorization of their work, claiming that the resource-mobilization theory fails to capture crucial aspects of their approaches.

In fact, some scholars have selectively critiqued the resource-mobilization theory and instead focused on the dominant organizational-entrepreneurial variant and ignored attempts to give the theory a more political edge. As Tarrow has pointed out, the 'emphasis on entrepreneurship and external sponsorship in the critical reception of resource-mobilization theory obscured its rich political potential.'[24] Yet critics can be excused for their oversights given that the dominant formulation of the theory has remained focused on the internal dynamics of social movements – their organizations and resources – at the expense of its political possibilities. For the most part, the theory's political implications have remained underdeveloped, creating what Mayer has called a 'systematic lack of the resource mobilization approach concerning the relationship between social movements and the political system.'[25] As Mayer has further argued, 'there are political conditions outside the organizational and resource capacities of movements that influence and shape mobilization dynamics.'[26] Yet efforts to address this weakness within the resource-mobilization school have been largely ineffective, forcing scholars to develop a research program that more directly links politics to collective action.

New Social-Movement Theory

In part, the dissatisfaction some scholars have felt towards the theoretical emphasis of the resource-mobilization school has contributed to the development of the alternative new social-movement perspective. The resource-mobilization theory has been attacked by scholars for not taking into consideration the supposedly 'new' aspects of the movements that have emerged since the late 1970s. In particular, scholars have argued that the resource-mobilization theory has overlooked the cultural and ideological content of new movements, which for some scholars represents the crucial element in creating a 'qualitatively new aspect of contemporary democratic politics.'[27] Scholars have complained that the resource-mobilization approach is indifferent to the type of insurgency, the kind of praxis, or the substance of the ideology and the idea of society envisioned by movements – variables that have all been closely identified by the new social-movement school as central to the emergence of modern social movements.

The origins of the new social-movement theory lie in the so-called incongruities of advanced capitalist society and in the anti-institutional and counter-cultural focus of its proponents. New social-movement theorists argue that movements arise in protest against increasingly technocratic and bureaucratic socio-political systems that are based on the prerogatives of material consumption and the assumed benefits of perpetual growth.[28] Such movements present an alternative world view, one with new cultural and ideological norms, political tactics, organizational structures, and aspirations that challenge the existing modes of interest intermediation in advanced industrial societies.[29]

Scholars of new social movements have also tended to emphasize the remoteness of recent movements from established political institutions, including parties, interest groups, and political elites. This discontinuity of movements from mainstream political institutions, with social protests reflecting the disaffection of a growing proportion of the population in advanced industrial societies from 'politics as usual,' represents a central characteristic of the theory. As Dalton and Kuechler suggest, this detachment may be due in part to the adoption of unconventional political tactics, including sit-ins, protests and riots, and other acts of civil disobedience, that alienate more conventional political groups from these movements.[30] Other theorists have argued, moreover, that movements have intentionally distanced themselves from the mainstream political process simply because their aims are cultural rather than political. New social movements have sought to construct new 'life-spaces' or alternative life styles that are incompatible with established political institutions.[31] Accordingly, participants in a movement seek to create a counter-culture. The values they hold are supposedly inimical to the values of the large, bureaucratized political institutions of the modern advanced industrial state.

However, it is precisely the propensity for scholars of the new social-movement school to stress the marginalized nature of recent movements that has come under scrutiny by researchers who question this view as an oversimplification. As Scott has argued, new social-movement theorists mistakenly treat all new movements as reflections of a single crisis in capitalism – they wrongly assume a similarity of interests between the movements.[32] Empirical studies on the women's movement, the European peace movement, the American civil rights movement, and the anti-nuclear protest movements in Europe have helped fuel concerns regarding the adequacy of the new social-movement approach.[33] The various movements examined in these empirical studies were found to have interacted and actively cooperated with an assortment of established political groups and institutions.

As a result of these and of the other studies mentioned earlier, critics have called for greater analytical attention to be paid to the political conditions surrounding the emergence of movements. 'What is new about new social movements,' argues Klandermans, 'cannot be defined in terms of marginality or detachment from existing social and political institutions.'[34] In fact, in no country studied and presented in the cross-Atlantic volume edited by Klandermans and others have movements existed in a total void – 'everywhere they took place alongside traditional lobbies and interest associations, parties and elites, stimulating conflict and cooperation.'[35] As a result of the growing evidence, then, the mobilization and dynamics of social movements must be linked to politics.

The Political-Process Model

For scholars whose work is in the political-process mould the study of movements is the study of political processes and the collective action these generate. As Charles Tilly has argued in his formulation of the 'polity model' of the political-process approach, it is the fight for power between members and challengers of the polity and the various political realities and political alignments facing the challengers that give rise to collective action.[36] McAdam more specifically unpacks the meaning behind the term 'political process': 'a social movement is held to be above all else a political rather than a psychological phenomenon. That is, the factors shaping institutionalized political processes are argued to be of equal analytic utility in accounting for social insurgency.'[37]

The political-process model specifically points to changes in the political environment as the central distinguishing and determining factors in the emergence and success of movements. Social movements arise, expand significantly, and have their greatest impact during periods marked by a profound increase in the vulnerability of the political establishment to pressure from protest groups. Thus, under destabilized political conditions, groups or challengers that were excluded from routine decision-making arenas during otherwise normal political conditions suddenly find the opportunity for collective action and protest greatly enhanced.

For adherents to the political-process model, then, such antecedent political shifts disrupt the status quo, remove political advantages, and weaken the position of powerful groups to create the potential for mobilization. The actual process of mobilization – the means by which groups secure collective control over the resources needed for collective action[38] – further requires the favourable interplay of three crucial factors. First, a suitable structure of political opportunities must exist within a political system to aid in the building of political alliances and to encourage the reception of a movement's goals by established political groups and elites. Second, a movement must have sufficient pre-existing organization and indigenous resources to take advantage of opportunities. Third, the existence of solidarity and moral commitment to a movement on the part of individual activists ensures loyalty to a movement's cause and it supports and sustains its collective identity. According to this model, therefore, variations in the level of political opportunities, organization, and related subjective factors affect the dynamics of movements.

The Structure of Political Opportunities

The absence of a systematic approach to the analysis of the mobilizing role played by political factors initially inhibited the development of a framework that could separate secondary phenomena and concentrate on identifying a generalizable set of political variables. However, the notion of political-opportunity structures has successfully addressed this concern. As Neidhardt and Rucht suggest, the concept of a political-opportunity structure 'can be seen as a tool for concretizing and differentiating environmental, and particularly political conditions, that may be favorable or unfavorable for social movements and their activities.'[39] Tarrow concurs, and he adds that 'the aspects of opportunity structure are not in themselves explanations of protest movements, but rather conceptual tools which facilitate the focusing of research on the political process.'[40] Proponents of the concept have generally followed Tarrow's lead in focusing on three variables of the political-opportunity structure that have permitted a great degree of generalization across cases: divisions and conflicts between political elites, the stability or instability of political alignments, and the existence or absence of allies and support groups.

A cohesive and unsympathetic political and economic elite that dominates the state obviously presents challengers and their demands with minimal opportunity for access and reform. Conversely, studies have confirmed that when elites fragment or come into conflict many opportunities begin to open for movements to mobilize and to press their demands. For Jenkins, 'major dislocations simultaneously weaken previously dominant groups and exacerbate cleavages among national elites, thereby increasing the likelihood of an elite division that could lead to elite support for movements.'[41] Tilly argues further that elites often take the risky step of admitting movements into the political system 'when the polity is closely divided, or when no coalition partners are available within the polity, or when its own membership is in jeopardy for want of resources.'[42]

Examples of divisions within the elite that can spur protest include those within a ruling coalition, between the government and other elites, or within the business and religious communities. Major political upheavals, such as depressions, deep recessions, and wars, can exacerbate cleavages between political elites. Divisions in the elite have benefited movements in a variety of diverse contexts, including the Nicaraguan Revolution, farm worker, civil rights, and nuclear freeze protests in the United States, and the peace movement in the Netherlands.[43]

In addition to divisions within the elite, major changes in political alignments, frequently brought about by electoral instability or realignment, have also facilitated the entry of groups challenging the elite into the political system. Broad electoral changes connected to shifts in government coalitions have also expanded opportunities; reform movements have especially benefited from the rise to power of centre-left governing coalitions, which generally refrain from repression and support the goals of movements.

Piven and Cloward have argued that the political climate is especially favourable to movements when political alignments are in disarray and new ones have not yet been formed.[44] The political realignments within Nicaragua's political and economic elite of the 1970s, for example, created a political environment conducive to the mass demonstrations and protests that led to the fall of the Somoza regime.[45] Similarly, Siisiainen has documented how radical shifts in alignments in Finland, both during the advent of a system of universal suffrage in 1906 and after the end of the Second World War, allowed for the entry of previously excluded popular groups into the polity.[46] Tilly has also focused on the opportunities that arise for mobilization from highly contested elections when the electoral needs of political actors and parties can stimulate cooperation with movements and cause them to acquiesce to their demands.[47]

The availability and strategic posture of potential partners for alliances represent a third highly supportive political-opportunity structure. Tilly has argued in his polity model that forging alliances with members of the polity is a central ingredient in the success of any insurgent movement, while for Jenkins access to the polity 'creates a qualitative increment in the returns to collective action and shelters the movement against repression.'[48] Klandermans has usefully labelled the potential structure of an alliance in a movement its 'multi-organizational field.' Within such multi-organizational fields there exist 'support structures' – 'the total possible number of organizations with which the focal movement organization might establish linkages' based on 'common interests, ideologies, audiences, or other shared characteristics.'[49] The mobilizing role played by these alliances has been illustrated in protests by Central American peasants, insurgencies among farm workers, and in the United States civil rights movement.[50]

Pre-existing Organization

The political-process model, as its name implies, emphasizes the importance of a conducive political environment and of political opportunities in the emergence and growth of protest movements. Yet, as McAdam points out, a conducive environment only provides an insurgent population with the opportunity for successful protest; 'it is the resources of the minority community that enable insurgent groups to exploit these opportunities.'[51] In fact, the literature strongly confirms the need for a high degree of 'organizational readiness' and strength to convert existing political opportunities into an organized, sustained protest campaign.

Specifically, the potential for the mobilization of a group has been shown to be strongly determined by the degree of pre-existing organization in that group. Supportive organizations that supply a movement with the reservoir of resources needed for rapid mobilization have taken many forms: social networks, an autonomous infrastructure, a so-called social movement sector, indigenous organizations, and established institutions and movements. Yet the specific form of an organization has been found to be less of an issue in the mobilization process than the level of internal structure and resources. Three core resources of central importance to movement mobilization have surfaced in empirical studies: leaders, membership, and a communications network.[52]

Micromobilization Processes

The political-process model also identifies a third necessary theoretical level of processes that interact between political and organizational factors and decisions by individuals to participate in movements. According to Mayer, 'mediating between opportunity and action are people and the subjective meanings they attach to their situation.'[53] This so-called 'micromobilization' level, according to Mueller, describes a variety of contexts in which 'face-to-face interaction is the social setting from which meanings critical to the interpretation of collective identities, grievances, and opportunities are created, interpreted and transformed.'[54] Such contexts include recruitment meetings, internal organizational meetings, and encounters with allies and opponents of the movement – interactions where people process information, discuss their experiences, and learn about their situations.

Scholars working in the political-process mould have framed these subjective mobilization processes in a variety of ways. McAdam focuses on what he calls 'cognitive liberation,' the transformation in the consciousness of participants in movements that he sees as crucial for successful collective action. He links such a transformation in consciousness directly not only to a shifting political environment that provides 'cues' to the vulnerability of the political status quo to mobilized challenges, but also to the existence of a pre-existing organization and of networks that provide stable group settings where cognitive liberation is most likely to occur.[55] In a slightly different vein, Jenkins argues that micromobilization processes provide interactions that fuse personal and collective interests to generate moral commitments and solidarity to a movement's actors.[56] Significantly, such processes provide 'group solidarity incentives' or collective incentives for participation in movements, which help to overcome the perennial problem of 'free-rider' for activity and growth in movements. Klandermans's notion of 'consensus mobilization,'[57] Fantasia's 'consciousness raising,'[58] and Snow's emphasis on 'frame alignment'[59] all similarly link the subjective interpretation of events and political conditions to the potential mobilization of participants and the wider public.

Towards an Integrative Study of Political Movements

The resource-mobilization and the new social-movement theories have both contributed valuable insights into the origins and mobilization dynamics of many social movements since the 1960s. The resource-mobilization theory has focused the attention of scholars on the rational, goal-oriented characteristics of the women's, student, and civil rights movements, emphasizing the mobilizing role played by resources and organization. Meanwhile, the new social movement school has brought to light the new lines of cleavage emerging in European societies based on so-called post-materialist values and antimodernist, counter-cultural ideologies that have encouraged new forms of citizen action and movement activity, such as the environmental, peace, and anti-nuclear movements. However, both theories remain incomplete in the face of the expanding body of empirical studies that highlight the emergence and mobilization of political movements. Instead, for these movements, which seek access to the polity, want to influence the policy process, or attempt to change fundamentally existing institutions, the political-process model presents a more viable, multifaceted synthesis.

The political-process model systematically accounts for the relationship between political processes and collective action. As an explicitly political model, it puts political processes at the centre by positing that shifting political conditions and a structure of expanding political opportunities represent the central determining factors in the successful emergence and growth of social movements. Unlike the new social movement approach, it does not overdraw the contrast between movements and political institutions and view movements as anti-institutional and marginalized from the formal political process. Rather, the political-process model asserts that movements frequently interact with established parties, elites, and interest groups to achieve political goals. On the other hand, it also does not view movements as simple extensions of conventional politics as does the resource-mobilization approach. Tilly has, in fact, complained that the resource-mobilization theory 'identifies the amassing or spending of resources as the absolutely central phenomenon, and to that extent, distracts attention away from power struggles and from group organization.'[60] In contrast, the political-process model focuses directly on the power struggles between the members and the challengers of the polity.

While the political-process model distinguishes itself by linking the rise and expansion of movements to the political and institutional environment, it nevertheless remains indebted to its resource-mobilization predecessor. In fact, the political-process model is more inclusive than exclusive because it profitably borrows the important emphasis that the resource-mobilization school places on the mobilizing role of resources and organization. Therefore, it is potentially a powerful analytic tool as a result of its synthetic quality. Rather than focusing exclusively on processes that are internal or external to the development of movements, the model presents movements as products of both.

The political-process model also shares analytic properties with the new social-movement school by including consciousness-raising, solidarity-building, and identity-formation as important micromobilization processes. Resource-mobilization theorists have traditionally overemphasized the rationality of movements and of their participants, disregarding subjective, socio-psychological factors central to the mobilizing process.[61] The political-process school, on the other hand, argues that a crucial aspect of the mobilization process is the manner in which people perceive changing political, resource, and organizational conditions as favourable for collective action and protest. Campaigns may appear rational, strategic, and goal-oriented, but the political-process model factors people, and the subjective meanings they attach to their situation, into its theoretical equation.

Thus, in light of the mounting evidence from the empirical literature, it is clear that the political-process model holds great potential for accounting for those variables, especially the political, that scholars have found to have made the greatest difference in the outcome of political movements. It is more comprehensive than the resource-mobilization and new social-movement approaches. On the other hand it does not identify so many factors as relevant to movement mobilization that it becomes difficult to specify those that are most central.

In short, by reflecting the diverse contributions of both the resource-mobilization and the new social-movement theories and by reducing at the same time the conceptual overlap and competition between purportedly different theoretical models, it holds a high potential of providing a synthesis of the two theories. In recent years the theoretical debate among scholars in the social movement field has become so competitive as to encourage a growth industry in the number of models that attempt to explain the definitive cause of the emergence and mobilization of movements. Yet the amount of interplay between empirical conditions encouraging movements has been shrouded by the false dichotomy between the models. Thus, although recent research has provided a lengthy inventory of conditions that matter in the rise of movements, frequently what is left is a growing array of models whose differences reflect more the divergent interests of scholars than empirical factors. The political-process model can bridge the concepts in these models by resting on the interplay of three core factors: favourable developments in political opportunities, organizational strength and resource capacities, and the mediating influence of subjective, micromobilization processes such as consciousness-raising and solidarity-building. The next chapter illustrates how the interplay of these three factors encouraged the emergence of the anti–free trade movement in Canada.

2

The Origins of a Movement

The period between the massive victory of the Progressive Conservative Party in the September 1984 Canadian federal election and the initiation of formal comprehensive free trade negotiations between Canada and the United States in December 1985 represented a watershed in Canadian political history. It marked the emergence of anti–free trade coalitions and in particular the consolidation of organizations in the anti–free trade movement. Free trade emerged as the dominant policy item on the Progressive Conservatives Party's agenda, developing from one of several policy options to an issue of paramount importance. Significantly, it was during this period that the structures of political opportunity for anti–free trade organizations expanded in conjunction with the fate of the free trade option. As negotiations for a comprehensive agreement between Canada and the United States became an increasingly greater possibility, the arenas for discussion, criticism, and protest actions against the impending deal greatly multiplied.

The Politics of 'Free Trade'

Canadian opposition to closer integration with the United States is not a recent phenomenon; rather, Canada was founded in part on the basis of opposition to integration, with its original architects desiring to carve out a political community that was separate from the United States.[1] Opposition to integration has played a fundamental part in Canadian political history since the time of the so-called 'counter-revolution' of the 1770s, with, for example, the British North America Act and the founding of the Dominion of Canada in 1867, Sir John A. Macdonald's National Policy in the 1870s, and the Liberal government's quasi-nationalistic policies of the 1960s and 1970s.[2] In fact, until recently Canada's federal government accepted the challenge of maintaining a distinct polity and society and of asserting a national agenda against the ever-present continental dynamic.

The historical sense that closer economic integration with the United States would threaten Canada's political independence was linked to a perception that emphasizing freer markets instead of state intervention would weaken Canada's federal government. Many nationalists argued that a strong, central, interventionist state had been crucial to the development and maintenance of the fragile Canadian identity.[3] The state had subsidized the railway system, the Royal Canadian Mounted Police, the Canadian Broadcasting Corporation, and the social welfare state, all symbols that cut to the heart of the Canadian political identity. Opponents of free trade criticized those who preferred unrestricted markets over a strong, interventionist state; in their view, to weaken or dismantle the state would strike a blow to the Canadian national identity. Thus, opponents of a proposed free trade agreement with the United States argued that it would be less involved with trade and markets than with sensitive political issues.[4]

Specifically, concerns about Canadian identity were related to a broad cultural fear of closer integration with the United States. Canadians worried that the uniquely constructed Canadian way of life would be at stake should Canadian economic and trade policies be harmonized with those of what was viewed as the economic behemoth to the south. This fear of the potential loss of identity had at least two dimensions: first, that Canadian culture would be placed in danger if government support and subsidization of cultural programs were phased out under the rules of a free trade agreement and independent Canadian culture (art, literature, television, theatre, film) were left unprotected against competition from the larger U.S. market; and second, and more subtly, that the harmonization of the economies of the two countries would bring with it the values of the 'American way of life,' characterized as winner-take-all capitalism and with an overriding concern for profit, would drown out the Canadian penchant for mixed public and private enterprise and for the interventionist role traditionally played by the government.[5] In short, free trade might place Canadian sovereignty and identity in a precarious position when the more than century-old struggle to build a country from the east to the west succumbed to what U.S. business interests considered was a natural direction for the flow of goods and services, from north to south.

Thus, by the time the Progressive Conservative government announced in the fall of 1985 that it intended to negotiate a free trade agreement with the United States, a disjuncture in the vision of the Canadian political community had begun to emerge. On the one hand, business, governmental, and bureaucratic interests argued forcefully that Canada's future in an increasingly globalized economy depended on a more streamlined state with preferential access to the U.S. market through a bilateral free trade agreement.[6] A deal would allow Canadian industry to specialize in those goods it produced most cheaply, would generate cheaper products for Canadian consumers, would promote domestic job growth, and would protect Canadian industry from what were perceived as the unfair trade practices that the United States Congress often relied on.

On the other hand, many social and political groups saw the deal as a threat and a break from tradition, one that would raise questions about the viability of an independent Canadian political community. The traditional mixed economy fostered by an interventionist state would have to be abandoned, many argued, in favour of a leaner and meaner adherence to the free market. The vision of the free trade advocates for the future lay precipitously close to a more global economic community, one that might lead to wholesale economic integration with the United States. Out of this division – a political conjuncture of competing visions of the Canadian community – emerged a country-wide coalition against an impending free trade agreement.

Opportunity Knocks: The Tories' Free Trade Initiative

On 9 September 1985 Prime Minister Brian Mulroney rose in the House of Commons during question period and announced his government's intention to pursue a free trade agreement with the United States. With this announcement he both concluded one of the most dramatic policy shifts by a government in modern Canadian politics and set in motion a chain of events that would drag Canada through one of the most wrenching public and political debates in its history. Over the next three years Canadians from all walks of life became enmeshed in a debate over the merits of free trade – the promise by its proponents that it represented the dawn of a new Canadian economic confidence, and the warning by its opponents that it signalled a cession of Canadian sovereignty to the United States.

The voyage of free trade, from one of many policy choices facing the Progressive Conservatives at the beginning of their mandate to the initiation of free trade discussions in December 1985, was a political drama that greatly encouraged the development of protest and collective action. The speeches, debates, parliamentary committees, and official meetings that aired the issue during the time leading up to formal negotiations provided activists with an array of mobilization points around which to develop and frame their critique of free trade and of the Mulroney agenda. In particular, the disruptive political conditions that evolved in this period stimulated the development of central anti–free trade organizations.

Of course, free trade with the United States was not a new idea ushered in by the September 1984 landslide election of the Progressive Conservative Party. The federal Liberal Party had, in fact, recently broken with its traditionally interventionist approach to fiscal and economic issues during the recession of 1981–2 with a less than discreet monetarist turn. Also, the Liberals had come under increasing pressure during these years from American investors who were furious with Canada's National Energy Program and Foreign Investment Review Agency, which sought to extend greater national control over Canada's natural resources, especially in its energy industry, and over direct foreign investment in Canada. In the context of what was Canada's worst recession since the 1930s and under increasing pressure from the Reagan administration in the United States to back off its nationalist proclivities, the Liberals undertook a major shift in policy direction with the start of a review of its trade options with the United States. The result of this policy review[7] would be increased interest in some form of limited sectoral free trade with the United States.

However, despite this germ of the idea of free trade during the waning years of the Liberal reign, the activists who would soon mobilize against the proposed accord viewed free trade as more or less the brainchild of the newly elected Mulroney government. In fact, the emergence of the anti–free trade coalitions owed much to the threat that the confluence of the election of the Progressive Conservatives in September 1984 and of the free trade option was perceived to represent for the future of Canada. As the political and economic agenda of Mulroney became increasingly apparent, the campaign to defeat free trade melded with the campaign to defeat the Progressive Conservatives, regardless of the actual origin of free trade during the latter part of the Trudeau Liberals' tenuous hold on power.

Certainly, connecting the Mulroney government with free trade was a natural conclusion to draw because of what appeared to be the government's overall tilt towards continentalism in economic and political matters. In reality, the broader agenda of the Progressive Conservative Party did differ dramatically from that of the Liberal Party, which had held power for most of the previous seventeen years.[8] The differences included the Conservatives' preference for privatizing crown corporations, less government interference in the market (seen in the government's decisions early in its term to cut FIRA and the NEP), cuts in the CBC and to a variety of social programs, and a shift away from the so-called 'third option' in foreign policy. Thus, while the free trade option was not the brainchild of the Tories, it would eventually be seen to complement the broader Mulroney agenda for economic renewal and national reconciliation.

Nevertheless, the decision to pursue a comprehensive free trade agreement with the United States represented a fundamental shift in policy on the part of the Progressive Conservative government. The 1891 and 1911 federal elections had been waged between the free trade Liberals led by Wilfrid Laurier and protectionist Conservatives, and in both cases the Liberals were rebuffed, granting the anti–free trade Conservatives a victory. In the late 1940s Washington initiated a free trade proposal but was deflected at the last minute by an uncertain Liberal prime minister, Mackenzie King, who was wary of a repetition of the fate that had awaited the Liberals in the 1891 and 1911 elections. Finally, Mulroney himself had seemed to signal continuity with his party's historic posture when, during his campaign for the leadership in 1983, he stated: 'Don't talk to me about free trade, that issue was decided in 1911. Free trade is a danger to Canadian sovereignty, and you'll hear none of it from me now during this leadership campaign or at any other time in the future.'[9]

The Mulroney government was not the only major actor to break with a historical stance on free trade with the United States. The Canadian business community had also been traditionally sceptical of the option and had held a fairly united stance against free trade into the 1980s. Influential sectors of the business community had provided the backbone of the opposition to free trade in 1911, and the position of the business community had changed little over the course of the decades that followed.[10] In fact, many in the business community had supported such Liberal government initiatives as the creation of FIRA and NEP, believing that such actions were necessary to resist the north–south continental pull in the market. Even as late as 1975 protectionist attitudes prevailed in the business sector, as shown in the label 'treasonous' applied to a commercial policy study carried out by the Economic Council of Canada that recommended the liberalization of trade.[11]

By the early 1980s several international and domestic factors had prompted the Canadian business community to switch its stance on free trade.[12] First, it generally felt more confident of its ability to compete internationally, given that it had accumulated assets and productive capabilities that exceeded the needs of Canada for goods and services. Second, this newly found confidence, which ignited a desire for outward expansion, in turn created the need for secure access to international markets. In particular, increasing numbers of business firms felt that with over three-quarter's of Canada's exports going to the United States, unimpeded access to its markets would be a necessary precondition for eventual world-wide competitiveness. The third reason for supporting free trade extended logically from the first two: the fear of potential U.S. protectionism, which might hamper expansion and growth, convinced

Canadian corporations that guaranteed access to the United States via free trade was of the utmost and pressing importance.

In addition to the business community, some influential provincial governments had recently jumped on the free trade bandwagon. Provincial governments and their constituencies had interests at stake, and some, particularly the governments of Alberta and Quebec, came to see free trade with the United States as a means of potentially enhancing and promoting these interests. In fact, in no province was the shift in support for free trade more profound than in Quebec. Historically its stand on free trade paralleled that of Canada's business community – it supported nationalist and semi-protectionist policies to ward off the pull of continentalism, and it also feared for the survival of its French cultural heritage. In the 1960s and 1970s, with the realization of the goals of the 'Quiet Revolution,' substantial provincial governmental leadership and support facilitated the economic development of Quebec. Most notably, this period of modernization nurtured the growth of the French-Canadian managerial and technical class and a francophone bourgeoisie, developments that would have been severely hampered without the leverage that protectionist measures afforded.

Ironically, the policies that emerged out of the Quiet Revolution and the changes they engendered on the Quebec landscape found a manifestation in the province's shift in support for free trade with the United States. The province's nationalistic economic policies in the 1960s and 1970s produced two key changes, a rise to dominance of a Québécois entrepreneurial class and an alliance between the provincial government and capital, the latter deeply influencing the former. Thus, by the early 1980s Quebec had experienced a dramatic growth in the number of francophone entrepreneurs – 90 per cent of entrepreneurs in Quebec were French Canadian and 50 per cent were women – all of whom had begun to demand access to a larger market. This desire to expand was coupled with confidence in what free trade might bring with it, which was greater access to the United States, Quebec's key trading partner, where it annually exported over three-quarters of its products.

It was in fact the fear that access to the U.S. market was shrinking in the face of rising protectionism that solidified both Quebec's and the broader Canadian business community's new-found support for a comprehensive trade agreement. There was a genuine sense in the business community and within Quebec that the protectionist trend would only worsen as the decade progressed. Thus, Canada had to take advantage of any window of opportunity that might exist for gaining preferred and guaranteed access to the U.S. market.

With the advent of 1985 the prospects that the Mulroney government would adopt a comprehensive free trade position became more likely. Following the initiation of a government review of its trade policy options in the fall of 1984, trade minister James Kelleher released a report in January suggesting that some kind of agreement between the United States and Canada should be considered.[13] Moreover, business interests were lobbying hard for this option because of their worry over the threat of American protectionism. It was in this context that the March 1985 'Shamrock Summit' was held.

The meeting on 17 March in Quebec City between Prime Minister Brian Mulroney and President Ronald Reagan, dubbed the 'Shamrock Summit' in light of the date and the Irish backgrounds of the two major participants, was taken over by the trade concerns of both countries. While it did not specifically call for free trade, a joint declaration issued by the two leaders seemed to point in that direction. It called for 'an examination of ways to reduce and eliminate existing barriers to trade,' and asked each country's trade officials to 'report in six months on mechanisms to achieve this end.'[14] In the eyes of many Canadians the summit seemed to confirm suspicions about the continentalist tilt of the Mulroney government, and it would also be a factor in the emergence of one of the two most significant organizations against free trade, the Council of Canadians.

It is worth pointing out that the government's plans and goals regarding the free trade issue were marked by a lack of direction from the start. The uncertainty, lack of preparedness, and limited public relations and damage control over discussions of the issue left the government's position wide open for criticism and scepticism. The contradictory statements issued by Mulroney – did he want 'free trade,' 'freer trade,' or 'comprehensive trade' – and by his ministers, provincial leaders, and ultimately the Canadian negotiating team itself presented golden opportunities for the critics of free trade to stoke the general public's growing doubts about the wisdom and benefits of entering into a comprehensive accord with the United States. The climate of uncertainty would plague the free trade debate from its infancy until the November 1988 election and it created important political space where critics and sceptics could work to mobilize opposition to an accord.

The confusion, fortunately for opponents to free trade, began almost immediately after the Shamrock Summit. The near admission by its participants that free trade was a working possibility launched the issue into the public eye without there being any indication of how the government might position itself for the eventual negotiations. This climate of uncertainty offered the elements of doubt that critics of a deal desperately needed to bolster their case. The New Democratic Party, for example, released a policy statement in March 1985 entitled 'An Alternative Strategy: Fair Trade vs. Free Trade' in response to the Kelleher report and the Shamrock Summit. In it the NDP critiqued the comprehensive free trade option – and the likelihood that it would tie Canada irrevocably to the United States – and suggested instead an industrial strategy geared to ensuring greater self-reliance for Canada.

Moreover, the various public forums subsequently held by the government in the spring and summer on the issue presented extraparliamentary opponents with an opportunity to air their criticisms. Beginning with a cross-country tour by Kelleher in March, these forums heard pro– and anti–free trade views. Business and labour groups immediately found themselves on opposites sides of the issue, with labour particularly unenthusiastic about a comprehensive accord. The business community, however, continued to voice strong support across the country for an accord.

The business support provided the Mulroney government with the confidence it needed to move ahead. This confidence was reflected in the release of the government's green paper, drafted by Joe Clark, on foreign policy in May.[15] Designed to provide a general overview of Canada's foreign policy, it addressed specifically the questions of free trade and Canada's potential involvement with the United States in the Strategic Defense Initiative. Confident that the government's position in support of both policies would carry the day, external affairs minister Joe Clark decided to convene a special joint Senate–House of Commons committee to review them. The committee held public hearings on SDI and free trade in seven cities across Canada throughout the summer and invited various groups to provide their views. The government's pretext for the hearings was based on its assertion that rising American protectionism threatened Canada's prosperity and the security of thousands of jobs. Within six months of the conclusion of the consultations, the government's trade ministers would report on possible means of reducing barriers to trade.[16]

However, the results of the hearings were somewhat less than the government had hoped. In fact, the creation of the committee gave the opposition a golden opportunity for publicly criticizing the emerging free trade policy. The committee members from opposition parties, led by such figures as Steven Langdon and Lloyd Axworthy, trade critics for the New Democratic and Liberal parties respectively, demanded that the hearings on free trade be held separately from those on the question of the government's participation in SDI. Conceding that it had breached parliamentary procedure, the government obliged, thus providing the opposition parties and anti–free trade groups with the opportunity of airing their concerns about the government's increasingly obvious direction in trade policy in a very public, media-saturated environment.[17] Axworthy noted, for example, that the brief by the nationalist COC before the parliamentary committee succeeded in discarding 'free trade now from the vocabulary ... there has been a small victory won even by our mere presence alone. We are now talking about comprehensive trade agreements.'[18]

The doubts expressed in public forums such as the parliamentary committee by the opposition and by groups critical of the government's policy had spread into various media channels by that summer as well. Media attention to free trade concerns, especially in the coverage given to extraparliamentary groups lacking formal institutional channels for expression, helped disseminate anti–free trade views to a wide audience. The *Toronto Star*, which over the course of the next three and a half years leading up to the election would become the anti–free trade movement's staunchest mainstream media ally,[19] picked up on the nationalist COC's anti–free trade refrain on the eve of the committee hearings. In an editorial entitled 'Do we want to be Americans?' the newspaper first blasted the Mulroney government for dismantling of FIRA and the NEP, and then, repeating its question, asked Canadians if 'we need to become Americans, in all but name, in order to improve our living standards? Make no mistake about it, that is precisely what a free trade deal would mean.'[20]

Despite the growing criticism the government was receiving from both parliamentary and extraparliamentary opposition groups, events towards the end of the summer pushed it further down the road towards the adoption of a comprehensive free trade position. In August the special joint parliamentary committee released its report,[21] which cautiously recommended that the government begin preliminary trade negotiations with the United States. Most significant, however, was the release of the final report of the Royal Commission on the Economic Union and Development Prospects for Canada (known as the Macdonald Commission) on 5 September 1985.[22] The commission rejected both the industrial strategy and the sectoral approaches to economic development, and instead gave its full support to the negotiation of a comprehensive free trade agreement with the United States. Taking this cue, Mulroney told the House of Commons on 9 September that his government had decided to adopt the commission's recommendation. Following the announcement, Mulroney telephoned President Reagan on 26 September to announce formally that his government wanted to negotiate 'the broadest possible package of mutually beneficial reductions in tariff and non-tariff barriers between our two countries.'[23] Thus, with its self-declared six-month deadline for exploring its trade options that it had set during the Shamrock Summit expired, the Mulroney government finally ended speculation concerning its intentions and submitted its written request for negotiations to Washington on 1 October.

No sooner had the government seemingly regained the political and public relations high ground on the trade issue than events opened new ground for free trade's opponents. On 20 September, in the midst of the government's diplomatic signal to Washington, the *Toronto Star* had printed a front-page story based on a leaked government document on its free trade strategy. The document predicted that public support for the free trade option would likely be weak and it suggested that the government would have to make a substantial effort in maintaining control of the debate in order to head off the likely development of a 'major coalition on the negative side of the issue.'[24] The government denied that the document represented official government policy, but refrained from confirming or denying its authenticity as a cabinet paper.[25]

Few critics of free trade doubted that the document had in fact originated within the hierarchy of the Progressive Conservative Party. For many, its contents betrayed a lack of faith in the free trade option and in the degree of public support that existed for the policy. Critics also gained a degree of confidence as it revealed that the government was unsure of its ability to maintain control of the issue and was fearful of the support it might receive should the general public become educated on the issue. The document could thus potentially be turned on its head because it revealed the vulnerable underside of the government's free trade position and hinted at what would become central strategies for its critics, coalition building and public education. Finally, it would also prove to be a remarkably accurate foreshadowing of the troubles the government experienced in handling the issue.

In the months of October and November the government did little to dispel the aura of uncertainty and contradiction surrounding its free trade negotiating position. Now that it had 'committed' itself to the comprehensive free trade option it had a difficult time deciding which issues it wanted – or could have – on the negotiating table. Only days after external affairs minister Joe Clark suggested that cultural industries 'might' be negotiable,[26] Mulroney argued that culture would not be included in the talks.[27] In the meantime American statements continued to frustrate the Mulroney government with their repeated insistence that Canada's social programs, subsidies, agriculture, and culture, as well as the Auto Pact, would all be open for discussion. Thus, during the fall the government stumbled along, trying to limit the appetites of the American trade officials and allaying the general public's fear that everything would be on the negotiating table while trying to convince the Americans that they would be assured of getting a fair return for their efforts.

Other obstacles to a smooth and quick start to negotiations included federal-provincial disputes over participation in the talks and an increasingly protectionist mood in the United States Congress. Because provincial governments assumed that free trade would have an impact on their jurisdictions they wanted to be equal partners with the federal government at the upcoming talks. Yet the

Mulroney government insisted that, while provincial governments would be consulted at every step of the way, only the federal government would be present at the table; the issue remained unsettled throughout the fall. In addition, Canada–U.S. trade relations were increasingly burdened by a softwood lumber dispute, in which American lumber interests and the Congressmen from states represented by these interests complained about Canadian subsidies to its softwood industry. When the U.S. Trade Commission released a study of the Canadian lumber industry which American interests interpreted as providing evidence of unfair subsidies, pressure increased for some sort of punitive response from Congress. From the Canadian point of view, these moves endangered the prospects for reaching a free trade accord and suggested that the United States might tolerate free trade only to the extent that American interests were not harmed by Canadian competition.

On 10 December President Reagan finally responded to Canada's request to start negotiations for a free trade accord with Canada by informing Congress and asking for its authority to do so. Thus marked the end of the pre-negotiations stage of the free trade drama. The Canadian government still had not settled on the items it wanted on the negotiating table. There was no guarantee that a protectionist Congress would grant Reagan the 'fast-track' authority to negotiate that he requested. Public support in Canada for free trade had slipped somewhat from a high of 65 per cent in June to 58 per cent in December.[28] Finally, and perhaps most ominously, the anti–free trade coalitions that the government so feared might coalesce should it mishandle the issue were now taking form.

The Development of Popular Movement Organizations

The pre-negotiations stage of the free trade drama was a defining period for the development of key anti–free trade organizations and coalitions. The fumblings and contradictions in the Mulroney government's position and the delays involved in getting to the negotiation stage provided critics with the opportunity to mobilize, build alliances, and present their case to the Canadian public. The two most prominent constituencies to provide organizational precursors to the anti–free trade movement during this period were the nationalist and the popular sector. These two constituencies, each containing distinct social organizations, were demarcated by their distinctive ideological orientations and concerns, policy prescriptions, organizational histories, mass base, and resources. While the nationalist current was represented fairly tightly within the organization called the Council of Canadians, many different organizations stood for the popular sector, including major church, women's, and labour groups. Yet it was during this period that the rather disparate groups would begin to find common ground and coalesce as a result of the expanding political opportunities created by the free trade debate.

The Council of Canadians

The major embodiment of nationalist sentiment in what would become the anti–free trade movement was the Council of Canadians. Formed in March 1985, by the start of preliminary negotiations in December it was the most thoroughly focused organization devoted specifically to opposing a bilateral free trade agreement between Canada and the United States. The COC brought a wealth of organizational experience, leadership, and resources that would prove invaluable to the anti–free trade movement because the overall orientation of the movement – despite its many organizational and ideological cleavages – was nationalist. Nationalism was, as one leading activist reflected, 'the common denominator for the popular movement – what brought everyone together ... the desire to preserve Canada.'[29]

The COC was inspired by a precursor with a nationalist network that was known as the Committee for an Independent Canada.[30] The CIC had been a charitable, non-partisan organization founded on 3 February 1970 by three renowned Canadian nationalists: the Honourable Walter Gordon, a former finance minister under Liberal prime minister Lester B. Pearson who had tabled a controversial budget in 1965; Peter Newman, then editor-in-chief of the *Toronto Star*; and University of Toronto economist Abraham Rotstein. It was initially formed to generate public awareness about the growth of foreign ownership, particularly American, in Canada. Its emergence coincided with increased government attention on foreign ownership, as exemplified in several semi-nationalist official reports.[31]

The CIC's push for government policies that would promote Canadian control, both public and private, over the Canadian economy, in conjunction with a Canadian public that was increasingly sensitive to its concerns, coincided with the federal Liberal Party's adoption of fairly nationalist economic policies.[32] In fact, when the CIC disbanded in 1981 the degree of foreign ownership in Canada had decreased from an all-time high of 37 per cent to 27 per cent, the federal Liberal Party was controlled by a strongly nationalist caucus, and the CIC and its members felt relatively confident about the security of Canada's economic sovereignty. Within this seemingly supportive context, then, the CIC disbanded at the height of the nationalist wing's power in the Liberal caucus.

By 1984, however, the political environment had shifted radically. Brian Mulroney and his Progressive Conservative Party had won the federal election that fall by one of the largest majorities in Canadian history. Garnering over 50 per cent of the popular vote, the Tories felt that they had earned a mandate for fundamental change. The government immediately gave plenty of signals that it intended to dissociate itself swiftly from its predecessors. Finance minister Michael Wilson's first budget took aim at such semi-nationalist programs as the CBC and at crown corporations, many of which the Tories planned to privatize. And in his speech on 10 December to members of the Economic Club of New York Mulroney declared to an audience of corporate and Wall Street interests that 'Canada [was] open for business.'[33] In this speech Mulroney announced his intention to replace FIRA with Investment Canada, which for many nationalists confirmed their suspicions about the government's continentalist tilt.

The government's agenda presented highly combustible material to nationalists and to the left, both groups that increasingly perceived their hard-earned political gains of the 1970s to be under attack. Moreover, with business and influential provinces throwing their weight behind comprehensive free trade and the Macdonald Commission leaning towards recommending that option, it became increasingly obvious by the beginning of 1985 that the Tories might embrace free trade as well. Such a significant policy shift could only add to the angst felt by many nationalists across Canada.

It was this shift in power and apprehension over the continentalist policies of the Mulroney government that encouraged the rise of a new organization. Many activists who attended the inaugural meeting of the COC in March 1985 viewed the election of the Tories and the emerging free trade issue as a critical combination.[34] In the words of one activist, 'suddenly the Conservatives and Mulroney were elected – and it appeared that Canada was now for sale.'[35] The shift in the political environment, particularly the weakening or eradication of the instruments that Canada used for securing control over its economy and that were espoused by the nationalists both within and outside of the old CIC network, provided the spark for the mobilization of nationalists.

A sample of the hundreds of letters sent to Mel Hurtig, an Edmonton businessman, publisher, former CIC member, and central COC organizer, in late 1984 and early 1985 provides many interesting examples of the growing concern among the public about the election of Mulroney and the political shift the election engendered vis-à-vis political relations between Canada and the United States:

Like many Canadians, I am concerned with the direction in which our country is being taken. Does the Prime Minister want us all to become Americans? Mulroney must speak up for Canada. We must say 'no' to some things. We must learn to paddle our own canoe.

Or another:

I am pleased to see that you are still putting some energy into the problem of the loss of Canadian independence, which should be a concern of every Canadian. Like you, I cringe every time I think of the policies which, it would appear, we will experience now that Brian Mulroney and the Conservatives have come to power.

Of particular note is the cross-Canada nature of concern:

I was indeed pleased to learn that you are convening a meeting to consider the irrational economic policies being adopted by our new Federal government. I am becoming increasingly concerned with their obsession with 'Foreign Investment' as a means for solving all of Canada's economic problems, contrary to both logic and all factual evidence. (Victoria, British Columbia)

I'm about the most apolitical person I know, but I didn't immigrate to Canada to become an economic or political surrogate of the United States. (Banff, Alberta)

I strongly protest the financial cuts imposed on the CBC and on all other cultural institutions by the newly elected Conservative government of Canada. (Saskatoon, Saskatchewan)

As I look around I see a consciousness of Canadian identity that extends not much beyond the Stanley Cup, a declining awareness of our origins and founding principles that distinguish our society from that of the U.S., and the pervasive penetration of American values, via television. The political parties offer no relief from these anxieties. (Regina, Saskatchewan)

I am quite appalled at the direction that the present government is taking us and, if unchecked, it seems that in a relatively short time we will be completely absorbed by the United States. (Ottawa, Ontario)[36]

The direction the government was taking in economic and trade policy, namely towards a bilateral free trade agreement with the United States, was the subject of the greatest amount of public concern. In letter after letter, citizens expressed to Hurtig their fears over the potential ramifications of a free trade agreement with the United States. Thus, although the COC dedicated itself broadly to the preservation of Canadian sovereignty, it made opposition to any free trade deal its priority. With the release of the Kelleher report in January and with the Shamrock Summit only days away, the COC pointedly articulated its concerns at a news conference on 11 March 1985 to announce its formation. The press release stated that 'the COC has been formed because of a growing apprehension across the country to the continentalism of the federal Conservative government, in some sectors of the business community, and in some research and economic institutions.'[37] In the 'Statement of Purpose' it released shortly afterwards, the COC followed this up by noting that it 'came into existence because its founding members believe that there are now strong pressures to change fundamental aspects of national policy in ways which will seriously erode and weaken Canadian sovereignty.'[38]

Initially, the fate of the COC depended a great deal on key actors from the earlier CIC network of sympathetic nationalists. These people provided the money, leadership skills, political influence, and organizational experience necessary to transform the genuine public concern that was mounting into a sizeable nationwide organization with local chapters in most major cities across Canada. Of particular importance was Hurtig, whose leadership and network of resourceful friends were invaluable to the formation and early growth of the COC. In response to the letters pouring into his office during the fall of 1984 and the spring of 1985, Hurtig contacted many of his allies from the defunct CIC in the hopes of loosening purse strings and encouraging them to recommit themselves to a struggle to defend Canadian economic, political, and cultural sovereignty.

Yet, although the COC inherited some of the organizational infrastructure of the CIC, it was different in fundamental respects. First, the COC had a more ambitious agenda, having broadened its interests to include not only foreign ownership of Canadian industry but political, social, cultural, and territorial sovereignty. Whereas the CIC had emphasized foreign ownership and energy policy, throughout 1985 the COC expanded the focal points to include free trade, the proposed 'Star Wars' defence system of the United States, the territorial integrity of Canada's Arctic waters, and cultural issues. Instead of the CIC's emphasis on independence, the COC embraced the concept of a secure place for Canada within the global community, and it supported a multilateral approach to decision-making in foreign policy.

In addition to expanding its objectives, the COC also sought to broaden its membership. While at first some of the more active members of the COC had ties to the old CIC, there was an explicit attempt to build a more grass-roots organization, in contrast to the relatively elitist, male, and wealthy ranks of the CIC. Whereas critics had poked fun at the CIC for being a bastion of the privileged, anglophone, Toronto establishment, many of whose members stood to gain from protectionism,[39] the COC drew people from beyond the confines of Canada's wealthy elite. Representatives from women's organizations, labour unions, and community and non-profit organizations added a more popular flavour to the COC. Complementing familiar CIC stalwarts such as writer Pierre Berton and journalist Peter Newman were a broad range of new participants, including Bob White, president of the Canadian Auto Workers, Maude Barlow, the former chief adviser on women's issues to Prime Minister Pierre Trudeau, and Sheila Copps, an outspoken nationalist Liberal member of Parliament from Hamilton, Ontario.

The COC also sought to expand beyond the CIC's much maligned anglophone roots. In its first year of existence, the CIC had attracted a strong francophone contingent that had been concerned about the effects of Americanization not just on Canada but also on Quebec.[40] However, the October Crisis of 1970, when Trudeau enacted the War Measures Act to clamp down on the terrorist activities of the Front de Libération du Québec, discouraged any long-term participation of francophones within the supposedly Canadian nationalist movement. Throughout the decade of the 1970s the CIC failed to regain a strong francophone component, with events in Quebec in 1976 and 1980 serving to dampen the prospects for a joint Québécois–English-Canadian nationalist movement.

In 1985 and the beginning of 1986 the COC expanded rapidly as regional and local chapters sprouted across the country. In little over a year the COC grew from a small exploratory meeting in March 1985 to an organization with chapters in eight provinces and with approximately 2,500 members from Vancouver in British Columbia to St John's in Newfoundland.[41] Significantly, the spread of chapters meant that the arenas in which free trade concerns could be expressed and debated multiplied. Chapters in Victoria, Vancouver, Edmonton, and Halifax presented lecture series and held debates on free trade, conferences were held on foreign and defence policy, and COC members appeared before local, provincial, and federal government bodies to present briefs on a variety of sovereignty-related issues.

National political events during its first year conditioned the COC's protest activities and also aided in the mobilization of new members. In order to sustain the public debate about issues relating to Canadian sovereignty, especially free trade, COC strategists targeted political events, which became opportunities for national exposure and mobilization, or, in other words, 'mobilization points' for the COC.[42] Examples of such mobilization points included having the inaugural press conference and meeting to coincide with the Shamrock Summit; appearing before and making presentations to the Special Joint Committee on Canada's International Relations in July 1985, at which the COC stated its position and expressed its concerns over potential Canadian involvement in the Strategic Defense Initiative and in a bilateral free trade agreement;[43] protesting against the sale of the Canadian aircraft manufacturer de Havilland to Boeing (the Toronto chapter held a symbolic midnight vigil at the de Havilland plant); and directing attention to voyage of the *Polar Sea*.

The so-called *Polar Sea* incident, which represented the COC's most successful protest in its first year,[44] arose over a disagreement between the United States and Canada over questions of sovereignty in the Arctic.[45] While Canada claimed control over the waters around its Arctic islands, the United States argued that the Northwest Passage was an international strait and therefore part of the high seas. Thus, the United States did not ask for Canada's permission before sending the U.S. Coast Guard ice-breaker *Polar Sea* through the Northwest Passage. The Canadian government issued a statement on the eve of the *Polar Sea*'s voyage reaffirming its view that the Northwest Passage was a Canadian internal waterway, but it appeared to accept its impotence in stopping the expedition.

No official diplomatic protest issued from Ottawa when the *Polar Sea* left the American naval base in Thule, Greenland, on 1 August. However, in response to complaints from experts in international law, opposition party members, and the Inuit from the Northwest Territories who claimed the land and waters of the Arctic as their homeland,[46] the COC organized an expedition to protest the incursion.[47] After chartering a Twin Otter airplane, two COC members and two representatives of the 28,000 Inuit dropped Canadian flags and leaflets onto the decks of the *Polar Sea*. The leaflets, printed on COC letterhead, proclaimed that 'Canadians consider our Arctic waters, islands, and ice to be Canadian territory under Canadian jurisdiction. Your failure to request advance permission to sail the Northwest Passage is insulting and demeaning to our citizens and a threat to our sovereignty.'[48] Later, the airplane landed on a nearby island, where the group planted fifteen Canadian flags and erected a small tent to dramatize the fact that unauthorized incursions threatened the fishing and trapping culture of the North.[49]

For COC members, the behaviour of the United States betrayed an attitude about Canada that demanded a response. Yet the facts of the *Polar Sea* incident – the unauthorized breaching of Canadian territory by the United States – was of less concern for the COC and the nearly one thousand Canadians who responded to its protest by becoming members than its symbolic meaning. The incident highlighted the sense that Canada's political sovereignty – the area and scope of Canada's independent political action – was at risk, and it ultimately helped to attach a greater sense of urgency to the COC's criticisms of the impending free trade agreement.

Following on the heels of the release of the Macdonald Commission's report and of the Mulroney government's announcement of its intention of pursuing the route of free trade, the COC held its first annual conference in October 1985. By that time the climate of political instability fanned by the issue of free trade had created opportunities for cooperation between the COC and members of the opposition in Parliament. Some members of the Liberal and New Democratic parties had become increasingly receptive to the critique articulated by the COC and were offering to help start regional chapters, had participated at the COC's inaugural meeting, and had even became members.[50] The trade critics for the two opposition parties shared the COC's concerns,[51] as did other nationalist MPs.[52] Some MPs exchanged research and information with the COC, and the COC frequently contacted MPs to channel critiques or information to the Canadian public.[53] Question period in the House of Commons emerged as an especially successful strategy. When the COC desired wider national coverage of an issue, it called upon Liberal and NDP sympathizers on Parliament Hill and asked them to present relevant questions to the government.[54]

Such alliances between the COC and the members of the Opposition proved critical in expanding the breadth of the discussion on free trade. With members of the opposition, especially the trade critics for the Liberals and the NDP, increasingly raising the alarm in question period over the government's plans to negotiate a free trade deal with the United States, media coverage of the issue significantly expanded. This pattern of cultivating allies within the political system set the tone for what would eventually become one of the cornerstones of the strategy for directly influencing parliamentary debate. Thus, as the year wound down, the COC had established itself as a major extraparliamentary player in the debate, lacking only the cross-sectoral alliances that would develop with the mobilization of the popular sector.

The Popular Sector

The other significant development of an anti–free trade organization during the tumultuous pre-negotiations period occurred with the emergence of the so-called popular sector as an actor. The popular sector encompassed a broad cross-section of groups that had experienced the brunt of the 1981–2 recession. These included churches, trade unions, women's groups, social agencies, Native peoples, and farmers. The mass base of these groups shared certain characteristics: their members originated primarily from outside the Canadian social establishment, and most felt marginalized both economically and politically from the major decision-making institutions. Moreover, as the 1980s progressed and the shift towards a more purely market-oriented, monetarist economic policy took hold in the latter days of the federal Liberal Party's tenure, these groups increasingly found themselves sharing and articulating a counter-discourse on Canada's political economy. Rejecting neo-conservative responses to economic and social problems, the mobilization points of the popular sector centred on full employment, national self-reliance, and democratizing the decision-making processes.[55]

Several segments within the popular sector had been active during the recession and continued afterwards to develop various strategies for popular mobilization in the period leading up to and during the policy shift of the Liberals. Church groups, especially the Canadian Conference of Catholic Bishops, had been at the forefront of developing a new model of progressive activism. The New Year's statement from the bishops in 1983, *Ethical Reflections on the Economic Crisis*, was an unprecedented response by a church to the ravages of the recession and a critique of the monetarist policies adopted to counter it. It struck a chord among popular-sector groups at a critical juncture when many were searching for an alternative vision and for leadership.[56] Many government and business leaders and economists chastised the bishops for intervening in issues that were beyond the realm of theology. However, for many activists the statement served as a catalyst around which people from the popular sector could gather. They used the document as a discussion tool for carving out a new vision of a self-reliant Canada.[57]

A meeting sponsored by the Canadian Centre for Policy Alternatives in March 1983 represented one such gathering to discuss the themes brought out by the statement of the bishops.[58] This meeting brought together leaders from labour, church, and welfare groups to articulate and disseminate a strategy of cross-national coalition building. This strategy brought to the fore a new style of politics, one that involved tolerance for building links that were based on non-hierarchical, consultative, and democratic relationships between groups, and it would become one of the popular sector's major contributions to the anti–free trade movement. As Bishop Remi De Roo explained at the CCPA conference,

what we hope to do through 'Ethical Reflections on the Economic Crisis' is to contribute to the building of a social movement for economic justice in Canada. And there are signs of great hope, signs that people from so many walks of life and such a cross-section of interests can come together to look at what can be done – in solidarity and co-operation – to build this kind of social movement.[59]

While church groups worked to disseminate the coalition-building strategy to other popular-sector groups, labour and women's groups mobilized as the 1980s progressed in order to agitate for social and economic welfare concerns in the face of mounting cutbacks. Labour had actually been cultivating an opposition to continentalism since the late 1970s and it increasingly viewed American investment and multinationals in Canada as counter-productive to Canadian economic development and full employment.[60] Women's groups, most of which existed under the umbrella of the major national feminist organization, the National Action Committee on the Status of Women, had also forcefully intervened in economic policy debates. Members of NAC increasingly argued during the early 1980s that the organization had to move beyond pressing for reforms on women's issues within the policy-making process and demand as well reform of the process itself.[61] NAC projected an image of this new activism during the Macdonald Commission's hearings, where thirty-four women's groups made presentations demanding greater economic equality and access to the political process.

These and other related protest activities represented stepping stones towards the confrontation between the popular sector and the government that erupted with the electoral victory in the fall of 1984 of the Progressive Conservatives. This election, an important political conjuncture for the popular sector, paved the way for a new style of political activity. Many popular-sector groups that were accustomed to struggling in advancing their agendas suddenly saw in the Mulroney election the incentive to forge cross-sectoral alliances. The Mulroney agenda appeared to be blatantly Reaganite and Thatcherite, and to have as its goal that of aligning Canada's social and economic policies in a neo-conservative direction. The combination of the huge parliamentary majority obtained by the Tories and of the party's unsympathetic policy direction convinced popular-sector groups that the polity was now closed to their concerns. On the other hand their interests would be increasingly pursued through extraparliamentary channels.[62]

Most specifically, the intimation that free trade might be on the agenda of the Mulroney government convinced many within the popular sector to promote the church-inspired strategy of coalition building. Increasingly, free trade emerged as a strategic issue for advancing a coalition-building agenda because it adversely affected many different groups. Thus, while popular-sector groups rejected all facets of the Mulroney government's neo-conservative outlook, many viewed free trade as the major political opportunity for collective action.

A variety of initiatives by the Mulroney government in the fall of 1984 pushed various groups towards a consolidation of their strategy for building a coalition. The tabling of finance minister Michael Wilson's first budget in October 1984, for example, provoked a sharp response. Church groups responded to the proposed budget cuts with a series of workshops and exchanges during that fall and into the spring that were designed to disseminate coalition-building strategies to the grass roots. Labour also reacted to the budget and to the shelving of FIRA by the Tories in December 1984 with a shift in strategy.[63] It rejected government invitations for tripartite consultations between business, labour, and government in the spring, and began to seek new allies from within the popular sector.[64]

The women's movement also underwent a significant change in leadership and strategy during the initial months of the Tory reign. The election of the Progressive Conservatives coincided with a shift in NAC's leadership after many within its dominant liberal-feminist wing were appointed to posts in the new government. These departures created crucial political space within NAC for the rise of socialist and radical grass-roots feminists to positions of leadership.[65] The new people adopted a much more adversarial relationship with the Tories, while at the same time they began forging links with other popular-sector groups.[66]

Much as they had for the COC, political events during the 1985 free trade political roller-coaster ride greatly accelerated the consolidation of the anti–free trade positions of the popular-sector groups. Many of them, including the Canadian Labour Congress and NAC, took advantage of the committee hearings to voice their opposition to the comprehensive free trade proposal. The CLC presented a brief to the committee hearings; its stance on free trade further distanced it from any tripartite consultations in the near future. NAC, for its part, went on record as opposing the free trade option at an early date by means of a resolution at its 1984 annual convention.[67] It bolstered this stance throughout the spring and summer of 1985 by making known its view that free trade would be particularly damaging to women in vulnerable manufacturing jobs and to immigrant women.[68]

The release on 5 September of the Macdonald Commission report was perhaps the single most dramatic event in forging the consolidation of the first major anti–free trade coalition. Prior to its release most popular-sector groups had assumed that the report's recommendations would ignore their calls for full-employment strategies to promote a more self-reliant Canada. The commission's hearings had provided them with an important forum for the articulation of economic alternatives. However, the popular sector's disenchantment with the process as well as with the general thrust of the commission was made fully evident with the release of a collection of briefs to the commission entitled *The Other Macdonald Report: The Consensus on Canada's Future that the Macdonald Commission Left Out*.[69] NAC's frustration with the whole process was evident when it pre-empted by one day the formal release of the commission's report. At a press conference in Ottawa NAC condemned the report's obvious free trade leanings and presented its main criticisms of that policy.

For many in the popular sector, the report drew a clear public line between a neo-conservative corporate vision of Canada and a popular-sector perspective.[70] The commission's recommendations ignored the many dozens of briefs presented by popular-sector groups, which reinforced the sense of marginalization from the policy process felt by many popular-sector groups that had begun with the Tory election. It also signalled, in their view, a definitive closure of the polity to their concerns. Yet, most importantly the commission unwittingly presented the popular sector with the glue it needed to cement alliances. The commission's strong embrace of the free trade option provided a common point of concern; it represented a threat that would hasten efforts to unite despite remaining areas of disagreement.

Emerging Solidarity and Collective Political Efficacy

The two months following the release of the commission's recommendations witnessed a rapid expansion of activity in bringing together an anti–free trade coalition. The impetus for the development of the coalition came from NAC, whose members had been extremely active on the issue. Representatives from NAC presented a feminist perspective on issues of Canadian sovereignty and free trade to the inaugural meeting of the COC and released a paper in November re-emphasizing the dangers facing women in the Macdonald Commission's recommendations.[71] In a meeting of the COC on 14 November the president of a union consisting mainly of female immigrant textile workers that was part of an independent umbrella group called the Confederation of Canadian Unions, reiterated the dangers free trade posed to women and called for a recognition of the strong role women could play in pulling together an anti–free trade coalition. She specifically argued for a change in strategy:

we need another vision, one of self-sufficiency, the ability to build a socially responsible society, one that trades with a variety of nations, one that sees a role for government and not the law of the jungle, a vision of sovereignty. For this we need coalitions. Women's groups must be a key component of any coalition. It will give power to the analysis and the effectiveness of the new popular movement which is developing.[72]

She also recognized that the various popular-sector groups still clung to separate agendas, a potential roadblock to coalition building:

some organizations, like farming, peace, professional, and church groups, are beginning to develop their positions. Others like NAC, with its 400 member groups across Canada; labour centrals including the CLC and others such as the CNTU [Confédération des syndicats nationaux] and CCU; the cultural community and anti-poverty groups have already taken positions. We need true coalitions. We can not have various organizations vying to control the rest. We can not afford to spend our energies thusly. We have our very survival at stake.[73]

NAC ultimately played a critical role in convincing many groups to set aside sectoral ambitions and to focus instead on the development of coalitions against the impending deal. On 11 December the first anti–free trade coalition was formed. A meeting held in the Toronto office of NAC drew people from the women's movement, the farming community, the seniors' network, the peace and immigrant communities, and other segments of the popular sector.[74] While all of the groups represented viewed free trade as a threat to their particular interests, few had formed links prior to the meeting across sectoral boundaries. In fact, some groups greatly disliked each other and had never had representatives in the same room together. Yet, as representatives from the various sectors discussed their concerns about free trade, a critical shift in the collective outlook took place. As one participant reflected:

what happened in there was that people started out with a narrow view and then started broadening it. It was a very moving experience ... to sit around and have people suddenly look at free trade from a big perspective – how it would shape all aspects of our economic and social life – people now had a sense of it being a larger project – a long-term project. We recognized that we had been isolated and that there was no need to be – we had a sense of us all being in the same spot and there was a transformation in consciousness in that room that night.[75]

The birth of the Coalition Against Free Trade thus marked an important stage in the development of the anti–free trade movement. The sense of optimism that emerged from the meeting greatly enhanced each sector's assessment of the potential for successful collective action and education. The meeting stimulated a sense of harmonious cooperation among all the potential coalition members, and a movement to debate and to try to defeat an agreement took shape. The threat of mass disruption and dislocation that free trade held for the sectors that were represented thus cleared a political space in which many different groups could coalesce. It was no coincidence that the CAFT emerged one day after President Reagan's affirmative reply to Prime

Minister Mulroney, indicating that his administration would seek to negotiate a comprehensive free trade deal with Canada. The pre-negotiations stage of the evolution of a free trade policy thus correlated neatly with the emergence and consolidation of anti–free trade positions by the two major organizational currents of the budding movement. A structure for an anti–free trade alliance had been established by both the COC and the popular sector. A two-year period of expanding political opportunities for the anti–free trade movement – of building coalitions across the country – that would coincide with the two years of haggling, stalemate, deadlock, and impasse between the American and Canadian negotiating teams, lay ahead.

Summary

The perspective offered by the political-process model nicely frames the early organizational stage of the developing popular-sector movement against free trade. The period between 1981 and 1985 marked a critical period of expanding political opportunity for the nascent anti–free trade movement. Protest and mobilization by disaffected and marginalized groups across Canada increased, putting pressure on an increasingly vulnerable Canadian political establishment. The effects of the deep recession, the election of the neo-conservative Mulroney government, the brewing free trade issue, and the confusion and division among free trade advocates, combined to create 'situations of exclusion' described by Tilly as conducive to extraparliamentary mobilization and protest.[76] Warnock's description of this period also nicely fits with political-process assumptions:

When we enter into a period of general breakdown and structural change, as we are now doing, it becomes possible for the popular forces to contest the established order ... Working people, through their organizations, can begin to move in a new political direction. Class alliances are shifting, and coalitions can be formed with other disadvantaged groups ... Real political change becomes a possibility.[77]

In addition, both the nationalist and the popular-sector currents experienced an upsurge in their sense of political efficacy by December 1985. The COC's Arctic mission, its well-attended inaugural conference, and the continued rapid growth of new chapters across the country bolstered the confidence of nationalists who felt vindicated in their anti–free trade cause. Moreover, the sense of optimism and harmonious cooperation that emerged from the first meeting of the CAFT greatly bolstered the assessment this popular-sector group made of its prospects for successful collective protest against the negotiations that were set to begin in early 1986.

Specifically, the emergence of the nationalist COC and the CAFT has been shown to be directly linked to the dramatic shifts in the Canadian political environment that began occurring in the early 1980s and continued until December 1985 with the agreement between the United States and Canada to negotiate a free trade accord. A series of external political factors facilitated the growth of the two movements during the pre-negotiations period by sustaining the supportive political context that had already begun to develop with the 1981–2 recession. Mulroney's election ushered in a new conservative agenda in Canada, one clashing furiously with that of the Liberal Party during its nearly twenty-year rule. The election can be likened to the event or broad social process that McAdam argues can 'undermine the calculations and assumptions on which the political establishment is structured,' promoting a shift in the political-economic environment and encouraging the development of political opportunities for protest and mobilization.[78] The election of the Progressive Conservative Party and its agenda ignited both nationalists who had supported the interventionist policies of the Liberals and the popular-sector groups which saw the election as a symbolic closure of the polity to their concerns.

Related to this burgeoning protest activity were the structures of political opportunity that emerged with the rise of the free trade issue. Free trade with the United States had historically been a powder-keg issue, and various societal actors had stood firmly behind their respective positions for the first eight decades of the twentieth century. Therefore, the sudden and dramatic shift in support in favour of free trade within Canada's business community, in the province of Quebec, and in the traditionally protectionist Progressive Conservative Party further exacerbated the political disequilibrium set off by the Tory landslide election. This political conjuncture, therefore, created crucial opportunities for the development and expansion of anti–free trade protest organizations and activities.

Among the resulting favourable political opportunities for the anti–free trade movement were the divisions between various levels of the political establishment that kept the free trade issue alive and of questionable merit in the minds of the Canadian public. The contradictory statements regarding free trade issued at all levels of the Mulroney government, the divisions between federal and provincial actors over negotiating roles, and the disagreements between the United States and Canada concerning the issues for negotiation left an aura of doubt and insecurity in Canada that critics could exploit. Moreover, the free trade issue also promoted the formation of alliances among opposition groups and with influential and sympathetic members of Parliament. The resulting political interactions gave weight to the concerns voiced by the critics of free trade, and the coalitions that emerged represented a significant increase in the degree of organizational sophistication mobilized to confront the Tories and the free trade issue.

3

The Politics of Coalition Building

Between the spring of 1986 and the fall of 1987 anti–free trade groups coalesced into a broad, nation-wide network and gained collective control over the resources needed to sustain a protest movement. Two developments relevant to the concepts of the political-process argument shaped this period of movement building. First, anti–free trade groups employed a strategy of coalition building to bind groups of many different colours and interests under the broad umbrella of a network known as the Pro-Canada Network. Second, expanding political opportunities, sparked especially by deadlocks in the negotiations for a free trade accord, critically delayed the issue in the political timetable. These delays, and the questions and controversies surrounding the reasons for them, sensitized the Canadian public to the uncertainties of the deal, provided opposition groups with ample time to consolidate their coalition-building strategy, and pushed free trade into an election period, when it became a central issue in the campaign.

The Strategy and Resources of Coalition Building

The political-process model reveals that several conditions shaped the development of the campaign to build an anti–free trade coalition. First, the model identifies a coordinated strategy required for initiating insurgencies as central for collectively pooling the resources necessary for successful mobilization. Organizers adopt strategies of mobilization to provide direction to members and to assemble and manage the resources needed for collective action. A protest movement may arise without strategic direction, but it will generally remain isolated or die out unless a concerted strategy of mobilization is applied. As Jenkins points out, although spontaneous processes are often sufficient to initiate insurgency, concerted and deliberate organizing strategies are necessary to sustain challenges.[1]

The political-process approach also suggests that a successful campaign of mobilization depends upon the existence of a high degree of organization and of resources within the dissident community. High levels of organization in the indigenous or internal group are directly linked to a greater potential for mobilization. As McAdam has shown in a study of the U.S. civil rights movement, in the absence of indigenous resources a community is likely to be unable to respond when granted the opportunity to do so.[2] Jenkins, in a study of farmworker movements, has linked the success of nascent mobilization campaigns to the existence of resources for organizing. These include the presence of skilled organizers, prominent leaders, and methods of communication such as newspapers and facilities for meetings.[3] N. and S. Fainstein, Gamson, and Tilly, moreover, all agree that the components of formal movements – professional staff, membership lists, and facilities for meetings – help sustain interest and activity.[4] For Tilly, the higher the level of these resources for organizing that are internal to a group challenging other parts of society, the more readily mobilized it will be in the early, uncertain stage of a campaign.[5]

In fact, the adoption of protest strategies proved essential to the efforts of many anti–free trade groups in building a movement against the proposed deal. The federal government's decision to initiate negotiations spurred into action many of the popular-sector groups that already opposed free trade. To be sure, significant advances had been made in the anti–free trade effort: the COC filled an important vacuum in nationalist discourse by raising concerns about the diminuition in Canadian sovereignty they feared as a result of a free trade deal between Canada and the United States. Along a parallel line, popular-sector groups had mobilized to fight economic and social welfare cutbacks introduced by the Mulroney government, as well as to argue against the market-oriented recommendations of the Macdonald Commission. Like the COC, popular-sector groups saw their broader concerns threatened by a free trade agreement. The emergence of the Toronto-based Coalition Against Free Trade (CAFT) in late 1985 had, in fact, presaged a broader effort at popular-sector anti–free trade coalition building.

Yet, despite these advances, activists recognized the necessity of a concerted, country-wide strategy of coalition building across the popular and nationalist sectors in order to create and sustain an organized movement against a free trade deal. By early 1986 the federal government had moved to isolate organized labour as the principal opposition to a free trade agreement by feeding off public antipathy towards unions and by splintering popular-sector groups along sectoral lines. Moreover, the leaked communications document reported in the *Toronto Star* in September 1985 betrayed the federal government's fear that a major coalition opposed to a bilateral deal might emerge to overcome the historical tendency for popular sectors not joining forces in Canada. In fact, the CAFT soon developed a strategy to bring together the widest coalition of groups possible to oppose free trade. In its second meeting, the CAFT concluded:

to counter this strategy every effort must be made to bring together the widest coalition of groups possible to oppose free trade. Every sector of the Canadian economy will be affected by a free trade agreement. Given an opportunity, those whose livelihood is threatened can point out the dangers of a free trade deal based on intimate knowledge of their particular sectors. By multiplying opportunities for affected groups to voice their concerns and to present alternatives, coalitions can bring the debate down to practical matters. At the same time, the broader issues of Canadian independence and sovereignty should be addressed.[6]

This early articulation of the coalition-building approach accurately presaged the successful forging of a national coalition of the two major anti–free trade currents, the popular and the nationalist sectors.[7]

Various church, women's, and labour organizations provided the bulk of the resources for organizing that shaped the early coalition-building efforts. Organizational networks, resources, and grass-roots activists from these sectors played an especially crucial role by convening conferences and meetings to discuss strategy and by issuing statements and pamphlets through their individual media outlets. Church and women's groups had a history of activity in coalition building to draw upon and they would speak out more forcefully than organized labour in advocating an intersectoral approach at the early period of the campaign.[8]

The coalition-building strategy centred specifically around simple goals: to forge cross-sectoral alliances by persuading groups to see beyond their own parochial concerns; to pool and manage existing sectoral resources; and to convince groups that a free trade agreement would negatively affect so many different groups that it represented the common denominator for cooperation across ideological and cultural divides. Free trade could thus be the issue around which manifestations of solidarity across sectors could be built.

Precursors to the Anti–Free Trade Coalition

While the policies of the Mulroney government, and free trade in particular, created the specific political conjuncture for the development of a coalition in the spring of 1986, activity had begun much earlier in Canada. In fact, organizers of the anti–free trade coalition-building strategy built on the work of their precursors in initiating their campaign. The Pro-Canada Network would not have materialized without a solid foundation of intersectoral cooperation. In fact, coalition building as a strategy for social change had been employed by an increasing number of groups in the ten years preceding the free trade debate.

Popular-sector groups had been articulating strategies and building coalitions across Canada since the mid-1970s. In 1975 church groups, especially the Toronto-based Gatt-Fly (later known as the Ecumenical Coalition for Economic Justice), employed the so-called 'Ah-hah' popular education technique to stimulate cross-sectoral coalition building at the community level.[9] Taught through seminars, the Ah-hah technique helped groups engage in critical analysis in order to enhance the effectiveness of their actions for achieving social justice. Through coalition building, Gatt-Fly argued, workers could knit together a holistic vision to enable them to critique and challenge barriers to improving their collective well-being.

The 1970s saw the emergence across Canada of a wide range of sectoral coalition-building activity. The National Action Committee on the Status of Women developed into perhaps the most notable and successful political coalition in Canadian history. Formed in 1972, it grew to represent over five hundred different women's organizations from across Canada by the mid-1980s. Coalitions had also formed around peace issues since the early 1960s with the Canadian Campaign for Nuclear Disarmament and the Canadian Peace Pledge Campaign – a coalition of over five hundred peace groups. Other related coalitions included the Canadian Environmental network, consisting of hundreds of environmental groups, and the ecumenical movement, including Gatt-Fly, which brought together five major Christian churches in Canada.[10]

Significantly, intersectoral coalitions also emerged in the 1970s at the provincial level. A number of them arose to oppose the privatization and social service cutbacks of several newly elected provincial governments. These included the Coalition for Equality in Newfoundland, Saskatchewan's Coalition for Social Justice, Solidarité populaire in Quebec, and British Columbia's Solidarity Coalition.[11] In fact, at least until the advent of the anti–free trade movement, British Columbia's experience represented a well-known cross-sectoral coalition effort in Canada.

In the summer of 1983 British Columbia, still reeling from the 1981–2 recession, elected a Social Credit (Socred) government on a platform of fiscal restraint and public service downsizing.[12] Moreover, as described by Warnock, the government presented a budget and twenty-six pieces of legislation geared towards a neo-conservative agenda; it included 'taxation shifts, raising grants to corporations, cutting basic services, cutbacks in education, eliminating programs which aided the poor and other disadvantaged groups, and a broad attack on traditional trade union collective bargaining rights.'[13] Public opinion polls showed that a large majority of British Columbians felt the Socreds lacked a mandate to enact this program and disagreed with the government's methods. Yet the NDP, which was the official opposition, also lacked the ability to stop the legislation. From this political conjuncture of mass opposition and parliamentary weakness emerged a collective resistance to the Socred budget.

Officially known as the Solidarity Coalition, it principally melded the trade union movement and a provincial-wide gathering of community groups.[14] Encompassing some fifty organizations, citizen advocacy groups, unions, and political bodies, the Solidarity Coalition launched a broad popular-mobilization campaign against the budget and the Socred government's policies. Specifically it adopted a two-point program designed to defeat the restraint program and to develop a 'humane and democratic alternative.'[15] It is important to note that the Solidarity Coalition backed its demands with mass demonstrations and meetings of collective action that were unprecedented in British Columbia history. Demonstrations of 20,000 in Vancouver on 23 July, of 25,000 on the lawn of the provincial legislature on 27 July, and of 50,000 on 10 August at Vancouver's Empire Stadium showed the muscle of the coalition's organization.[16] A demonstration on 15 October of 60,000 at the Socred Party convention – the largest ever against a British Columbia government – provided an impressive illustration of the coalition's strength, and it suggested the growing support for a general strike by the labour component of the mass membership of the Solidarity Coalition.

However, in rapid sequence the Solidarity Coalition failed to achieve its objectives and then splintered along various sectoral lines. Organized labour marginalized the coalition's left-wing members when it settled with the Socred government in return for minimal wage increases. This settlement was described by the left as a 'sellout' because it did not repeal the wage-restraint package, made no concessions to the broader demands of the popular sector, and tainted the whole coalition-building experience. The aftermath saw the dissolution of the Solidarity Coalition, the marginalization by union bureaucrats of the popular sector represented by the left, and a return to a reliance on social democratic electoralism through an ineffective NDP.

The experience of the ill-fated Solidarity Coalition provided some important lessons on intersectoral coalition-building that would prove to be especially useful to anti–free trade activists. Five flaws in particular in the coalition-building strategy provided the labour hierarchy with the ability to push the popular mobilization movement aside.[17] First, the popular sector, particularly its left-wing segment, failed to be consistently and openly critical of labour leaders and bureaucracy.[18] Second, the Solidarity Coalition depended heavily upon the trade union movement for financial resources.[19] Thus, because it supplied the bulk of the leadership and of the finances, labour had a strong influence over the direction of its strategy. Palmer argues that as a result, 'one group did have the capacity to push the entire mobilization aside when the decisive moment arrived, and that was the very small but ultimately all-powerful labour bureaucracy.'[20]

The strength of the labour bureaucracy revealed a third major flaw in the Solidarity Coalition, the lack of a strong opposition group within the trade union movement that could have pressured the bureaucracy to take more uncompromising stands.[21] A fourth flaw was the product of the undemocratic, vertical decision-making structures within the Solidarity Coalition. Popular community groups had little say in decisions over a possible general strike or over the labour-Socred compromise.[22] Palmer succinctly points out that 'the structure of Solidarity was anything but democratic. It was a wholly owned subsidiary of the top layers of the B.C. Federation of Labour.'[23] Finally, the lures and temptations of social democratic electoralism also damaged the extraparliamentary coalition.[24] The close relationship between labour leaders and a provincial NDP unsympathetic to the Solidarity Coalition's designs for a strike led the union leaders to abandon the approach of forging an extraparliamentary coalition in exchange for the hope of electing the labour-friendly NDP. In fact, the eventual outcome was less than the spectacular NDP victory labour had predicted. The Solidarity Coalition dispersed, the NDP lost the provincial election, and in 1987 the new Socred government enacted some of the most repressive anti-union legislation in British Columbia's history.[25]

It is evident that the Solidarity Coalition dissolved precisely because it lacked a leadership dedicated to sustained mobilization rather than to containment and compromise. Its members, especially the left-wing components of the popular sector, had demonstrated their strength with mass protest and action. Yet at the precise moment when the members supported the extra step of an all-out general strike – when a concerted strategy was needed to direct the members to sustain the challenge against the provincial government – the union bureaucracy settled for piecemeal concessions for their sector only. As a result, the labour leaders isolated popular-sector community groups and the protests died out without the necessary strategy of sustained mobilization.

The lessons of the experience of the Solidarity Coalition – issues of bureaucratic control, finance, decision-making structure, and the temptations of electoralism – were not lost on those organizers who were developing an anti–free trade coalition-building strategy in the spring of 1986. It provided a good learning model, a coalition-building 'prototype,' as one activist called it, which influenced the specific strategies adopted in the approach to free trade.[26]

In addition, activists also had to consider some of the more general limitations that had undercut other previous attempts at coalition building in Canada. Organizers were confronted with a history of sectoral fragmentation in most previous coalition-building efforts and with the reality that few national, intersectoral coalitions had survived for long. The sectoral fragmentation limited the political power of many social groups and had allowed the federal government in the past to resist pressure from coalitions by dividing and defining their members as 'isolated special interest groups.'[27] Moreover, the tradition of federal government funding for many social movement groups also hindered efforts at cross-sectoral coalition building that sought radical rather than simply reformist change.[28]

The New Year's declaration by Canadian bishops in 1983 radically reversed the trend in less than successful coalition building.[29] This critique of Canada's economic recession and of the efforts of governments and business to counter it struck a chord with its fresh, clear, structural analysis of the shift in the capitalist economy towards globalization.[30] It created vision and leadership at a crucial moment, when labour and other parts of the popular sector were lacking dynamism and had failed to respond to the devastating blows inflicted on them by the 1981–2 recession. Out of the vacuum that existed within the popular sector emerged the statement's call for a coalition-building strategy for building a social movement for economic and social justice.

The Canadian Centre for Policy Alternatives conference in January 1983 brought popular-sector and labour groups together to respond to the declaration of the bishops and to develop a strategy for intersectoral coalition building.[31] Specifically, church and labour emerged from the conference agreeing to work together in a 'new social movement' that would develop more equitable and workable economic policies and represent marginalized groups in Canadian society. The conference subsequently produced a plan for building coalitions around economic and social issues, which included a proposal for bringing together popular-sector groups and institutional allies. The plan specified the strategy for 'creating an organizational vehicle that would sustain ongoing action and commitment by the coalition partners and their allies ... building solidarity links with other popular groups or coalitions already involved in the struggle for social justice.'[32] While it was not apparent at the time, these points provided the framework for the eventual emergence of the movement against the free trade agreement. It would take four years of concerted mobilization and coalition building.

The Implementation of the Anti–Free Trade Strategy

The development and gradual articulation of a coalition-building strategy helped to meet a key condition relevant to the mobilization potential of the anti–free trade forces. Yet this mobilization potential also hinged on a second important condition, the role to be played by various resources to assist in organizing those forces. A look at the research on the role played by organizing resources indicates that the potential existed for a successful coalition-building campaign in the spring of 1986. Tilly defines the level of internal organization resources as the degree in which a group of people sharing an interest in common become aware of this interest and are joined together by interpersonal bonds of solidarity networks.[33] As Jenkins notes, the networks can often be the result of previous activities in movements or of mobilization efforts.[34] The presence of such networks, especially within church and women's groups, and the important facilitative role that they played in providing the resources needed to jump-start the coalition-building campaign fit well with the conceptual expectations. Church and women's groups had a high degree of internal organization and experience in mobilizing, much of it drawn from their own coalition-building efforts over the previous decade. This experience included organizing NAC's coalition and Gatt-Fly's 'Ah-hah' popular education campaign, as well as the construction of the broad ecumenical movement. The churches and women's groups provided many of the facilities for meetings, the channels for communication, and the seasoned leadership at the key early stage of the campaign. One church activist implicitly recognized the mobilizing role played by these internal resources:

we had the church media, the labour media, and the women's organizations newsletters, as well as the ability through these different networks to hold workshops and public meetings across the country. Even though our efforts were not getting much media attention, across the country it was happening, and we were reaching thousands of people.[35]

Along the same line of argument, the potential for successful, sustained mobilization also increases with the density of internal organization.[36] That there was a high degree of internal organization helps explain the success of activists in launching the anti–free trade coalition-building campaign at the early, vulnerable stage of mobilization. Especially important were the informal networks of friends that had been established between activists who had been seasoned through years of activity within the independent left in Canada. One church activist emphasized the importance to the coalition-building process of the informal dynamics that were at work:

you can't overestimate the importance of personal relationships. Many people had gone into different sectors and worked things out – cooperated on different issues over the years and got to know different people. So having that personal trust and confidence just allowed us to move on stuff in a way that wouldn't have been possible in a formal organizational structure sort of way.[37]

While the depth of personal ties and the high levels of existing, organizational resources played an instrumental role in stimulating the coalition-building strategy, the bureaucratic priorities of the individual organizations often severely tested the strength of the ties and nearly undermined the efforts of committed activists. A collapse of the anti–free trade coalition would have fitted well with the research on coalitions that has shown that their lifespan is frequently short, often because coalition building can be threatening to the organizations that are involved. As James Q. Wilson has argued, 'resources, autonomy, and purposes can be jeopardized if the organization must share the credit for victory and the blame for defeat.'[38] Moreover, the tenuous bonds of coalitions can disintegrate over conflicts about ideology, goals, or strategy, or simply when the priorities of an organization take precedence over the needs of the coalition.[39]

The organizations involved in the preliminary efforts at popular-sector coalition building in the spring of 1986 found that these very issues threatened to derail an anti–free trade coalition even before it had the opportunity to gain any significant momentum. Specifically, an important gap existed between church and women's organizations on one side and labour on the other over questions of leadership, decision-making, and strategy. The differences of opinion and of organizational structure reflected a tension in the political traditions of the groups. The tradition of coalition building, especially as it had been practised by church and women's groups, reinforced an inclusive and free consultative stance concerning issues of decision-making and alliance-building. In contrast, labour, or to be more specific, the Canadian Labour Congress (CLC), displayed a more hierarchical structure, whose bureaucratic priorities and allegiances had traditionally precluded alliance-building in favour of consultative strategies with state and business as a means of securing policy gains from the state. As late as the early 1980s, for example, and even into the first years of the Mulroney government, the CLC participated in so-called tripartite consultative exercises with government and business in the Tier I and Tier II committees on sectoral policy and in the Major Projects Task Force.[40]

Many activists involved in building the anti–free trade coalition characterized the differences as a conflict between 'new politics' and 'old politics.'[41] The 'old politics,' as thought practised by the CLC, depended on social democratic electoralism, bread-and-butter issues such as collective bargaining, and reinforced deference to the hierarchical leadership and vertical decision-making structures of the labour bureaucracy. The 'new politics' of church, women's, and environmental groups in particular, centred on developing an extraparliamentary stance, especially one focusing on coalition building within the popular sector and one displaying a more horizontal, democratic decision-making and organizational structure. In due course, some church and women's groups played a critical role in the adoption by the anti–free trade forces of the new style of politics in the coalition-building efforts.

Dialogue '86

Organizational tensions came to a head early in the anti–free trade coalition-building efforts at the Dialogue '86 conference. Held in January 1986, it was the first major national gathering of popular-sector community groups and labour where free trade was a central issue of debate. Initially conceived as a follow-up to the National Economic Conference called by Prime Minister Mulroney in March 1985, Dialogue '86 aimed to bring government, business, labour, and community groups together to discuss shared economic and social concerns. However, many of the same conflicts and obstacles that had undercut the Solidarity Coalition campaign in British Columbia surfaced in the planning and implementation of this conference. Like in the British Columbia experience, Dialogue '86 nearly saw the CLC consolidate its bureaucratic hegemony over the incipient efforts at building an anti–free trade coalition. Instead, Dialogue '86 set a crucial precedent for the direction and strategy of the mobilization campaign.

Specifically, tensions surfaced between prospective participants in Dialogue '86 over differences in expectations and goals. The CLC intended the conference to be a straightforward extension of the NEC, that is, a similar exercise in government, business, and labour consultation where labour might exact sectoral policy gains.[42] For their part, popular-sector groups, especially church and women's organizations, had reservations about the proposed agenda, partly because of their dissatisfaction over the outcome of the previous year's NEC. According to a report issued by the Canadian Conference of Catholic Bishops, community groups were dissatisfied with the actions of the Progressive Conservative government after NEC, which, from their point of view, were based 'on the policy directions outlined by the country's major corporate and business associations rather than those proposed by labour and community groups.'[43] Instead of another round of consultations in which, it was feared, government might in the end listen only to business, popular-sector groups wanted to pursue an alternative model and strategy at Dialogue '86. NAC's representative argued that 'a conference like this lets us focus on goals and real, viable alternatives to those the government wants. We hope in the next few days to form stronger coalitions around the economic issue we see as particularly threatening to women in the coming year – namely free trade and more reliance on only the market as the arbiter of our future.'[44]

Bishop Adolphe Proulx, on behalf of the Canadian Council of Churches, further argued that 'the time has come for labour unions and community groups to develop new strategies for building solidarity and generating social change in this country. This conference could, if we put our minds and hearts to it, mark a beginning. We could begin the process by reaching out to help build grassroots coalitions around critical issues at local, regional, and national levels.'[45] In short, while labour saw Dialogue '86 as another venue for consultation, popular-sector groups saw it as an important opportunity, in light of the specific political conjuncture of neo-conservatism and free trade, for advancing a strategy of coalition building to confront the state and the business community over their disagreeable policy directions.

The CLC approached the conference as it had approached the broader economic and social problems afflicting labour in the mid-1980s context of restructuring and globalization – it straddled the political fence. It consulted with potential popular-sector allies, but held out an olive branch to government and the business sector for a possible rapprochement that might result in piecemeal policy gains. In a detailed analysis of labour's strategy during the conference, Smith points out that,

a mobilization and alliance-building strategy allowed the CLC to leave the table when the game was too clearly stacked against labour, and at the same time recoup legitimacy with affiliates skeptical of the gains of consultation and participation. Nonetheless, the CLC's participation in popular sector alliances did not mean that consultative strategies with the state and business had been surrendered.[46]

To many popular-sector groups the experience of British Columbia's Solidarity Coalition, where the labour bureaucracy had abandoned a vulnerable popular-sector community and chosen instead a path of consultation and compromise with the provincial government, weighed heavily on the Dialogue '86 conference. Wary of another similar move by labour and eager to seize the moment, popular-sector groups outflanked a CLC bureaucracy that was unwilling to deviate from the prepared list of policy themes. Thus, when the CLC hierarchy refused to discuss free trade, popular-sector and sympathetic labour delegates met on an ad hoc basis to share their concerns.[47] Finally, in the face of pressure from the popular sector and despite considerable resistance from the CLC hierarchy, a session on free trade was held. One NAC participant summed up the importance of this moment by saying, 'this is really where the seeds for the anti–free trade movement began, and it began in opposition to the desires of the CLC.'[48]

The outcome of the Dialogue '86 conference thus differed critically from the ill-fated Solidarity Coalition experience. It set a precedent for the rest of the mobilization campaign against free trade, both in terms of the relationships established between labour and the popular sector and of the strategies and organizational forms ultimately adopted in the coalition-building process. Three points in particular stand out as having been crucial in avoiding the weakness of the alliances between labour and the popular sector struck within the Solidarity Coalition.

First, unlike their counterparts at the Solidarity Coalition, church and women's groups challenged the CLC leaders. Whereas the British Columbia experiment failed partly because popular-sector groups were not openly critical of labour's leadership and bureaucracy, leaders of the popular sector at Dialogue '86 brought cross-sectoral pressure to bear on the CLC hierarchy, and they continued to do so. By drawing upon cross-support from personal networks and grass-roots coalitions the popular sector was able to outflank people on the right-wing of the CLC.[49] As one church activist reflected, Dialogue '86 was 'a turning point':

people stood up to the CLC – called them on it – and said that coalition building would have to take a different position, posture, and direction. Popular-sector groups gave a signal that things would not be able to operate along established models in the future – that new models would have to be created for working in coalition politics in the future.[50]

The existence of an opposition to the CLC's hierarchy that was rooted in several key unions, as well as the consultative strategies of this opposition, represented a second key force for change in the relationship between labour and the popular sector. The Solidarity Coalition failed in part because a left opposition movement did not exist within labour that could challenge the bureaucracy. With Dialogue '86, on the other hand, the sympathies of at least two key unions, the Canadian Union of Public Employees and the Canadian Auto Workers, were much more clearly in line with the coalition-building efforts of the popular sector. CUPE and the CAW represented radical, left-wing elements of the CLC, and certainly their leaders, ideology, and actions challenged and perhaps threatened the more right-wing tendencies within the CLC bureaucracy. CUPE had recently established a radical approach to the economic crisis by adopting a platform similar to the Alternative Economic Strategy put forward by the left-wing of the British Labour Party.[51] The CAW had also recently staked out a confrontational, nationalist position by breaking from the United Auto Workers based in the United States.[52] These two elements within the CLC advocated a broader shift by the labour movement towards social unionism as well, and took a critical approach towards the political and social conventions in Canada. CUPE and the CAW and their skilled leaders opened up political space within which popular-sector leaders could work cooperatively to pressure the CLC bureaucracy to adopt an anti–free trade stance. Thus, key unions and their leaders played a mobilizing role and prevented the CLC bureaucracy from pushing aside the coalition-building efforts of the popular sector in favour of consultation on the status quo.

Finally, the seeds of a new, non-hierarchical style of cooperation between labour and the popular sector emerged from the Dialogue '86 conference. Whereas the links between such groups within the Solidarity Coalition were undemocratically structured and wholly controlled by the labour bureaucracy, working relationships based on trust and solidarity were built up between labour and popular-sector groups during the Dialogue '86 conference and in subsequent coalition-building meetings.[53] These working relationships would prove to be crucial in allaying the suspicions held by other potential partners of an alliance in the budding anti–free trade coalition-building campaign. To be sure, counter-tendencies within the labour movement, as well as within other popular-sector groups such as the church, survived the Dialogue '86 conference and persisted throughout the entire campaign.[54] However, this conference injected a looser and more decentralized structure of working relationships between labour and the popular sector, a style that would indelibly mark the coalition-building efforts.

Anti–Free Trade Coalition-Building Blocks

Anti–free trade coalition building gained considerable momentum following the Dialogue '86 conference. Existing organizations, personal networks, and indigenous resources continued to play the central role in expanding and sustaining coalitions throughout 1986 and into the spring of 1987. Within the popular-sector and nationalist camps, several parallel campaigns of coalition building got under way by the spring of 1986. One coalition that ultimately contributed form and substance to the broader campaign was the Working Committee for Social Solidarity.[55]

Formed initially to fight against cuts to social programs by the federal Progressive Conservative government after the 1984 election, Social Solidarity by 1986 had developed a broad critique of the 'market priorities' of the Tory government. It argued for both social and economic alternatives and for further coalition building by the popular sector. Its Declaration on Social and Economic Policy, officially released in November 1987 on the eve of the culmination of the free trade negotiations, combined the language and vision of different sectors. It argued for

an alternative vision of society and economy, one based on social solidarity rather than market values and priorities. In a society based on solidarity, the economy is people-oriented in the sense that resources, capital, labour, and markets are organized to provide for the basic life needs of the population.[56]

The Declaration was a product of much give and take between women's, labour, and church groups, and cross-sector pressure was brought to bear on labour to hammer out this alternative vision.

In addition to the activities of the Working Committee for Social Solidarity, CAFT and the COC had begun to employ cultural events successfully in order to raise public awareness to their coalitions and the anti–free trade cause. Grass-roots cultural events fitted well with the populist anti–free trade approach. For example, a rally and a theatrical event, the 'Against Free Trade Revue' at Toronto's Massey Hall in March 1986 drew a large response, gained a great deal of media attention, and was even grudgingly given respect by outspoken supporters of free trade.[57] The rally strategically combined theatre and musical entertainment with an array of speakers, including well-known personalities such as the writer Pierre Berton and Roman Catholic Bishop Remi De Roo. Members of the Canadian cultural community figured prominently in rallies and demonstrations. Such figures as the writers Margaret Atwood, Farley Mowat, John Ralston Saul, and Rick Salutin provided prominent names and national exposure to the anti–free trade mobilization.[58] The active involvement of members of Canada's cultural community and the success of cultural events in the free trade debate, in fact, fitted well with the cultural community's long-term effort to secure a separate existence from the U.S. cultural market.

Cultural nationalism had existed in Canada since Confederation in 1867 but its modern expression emerged in the 1950s and 1960s alongside the growing concerns in Canadian economic and political circles about excessive U.S. ownership, control, and media spillover. Having exerted pressure on questions of cultural policy for several decades through several government commissions, the cultural community and its supporters had seen greater regulation of Canadian television content, the prohibition of new Canadian editions of U.S. magazines, and the elimination of tax exemptions for firms advertising in Canadian editions of foreign publications. As Bashevkin points out in her broad study of Canadian nationalism, one of the most influential statements of Canadian cultural nationalist thought in the modern period emerged from Margaret Atwood's 1972 study of Canadian literature, *Survival*, where she argued that

Canada is an unknown territory for the people who live in it ... I'm talking about Canada as a state of mind, as the space you inhabit not just with your body but with your head ... For the members of a country or a culture, shared knowledge of their place, their here, is not a luxury but a necessity. Without that knowledge, we will not survive.[59]

For many in Canada's cultural community, then, this shared knowledge, promulgated through the arts, media, and other communications outlets, could only be maintained through a concerted effort by the federal government and through policies geared towards limiting American influence. Free trade threatened the basis for such federal action, and it spurred the cultural community to action and involvement in coalitions to counter it. David Peterson, the premier of Ontario, captured the concerns of the cultural community vis-à-vis free trade when he remarked in November 1985 at the annual conference of first ministers in Halifax, Nova Scotia:

Nor can we trade away Canada's soul. Cultural sovereignty cannot be separated from political sovereignty. We must maintain our ability to develop and support our own cultural and communication industries. We must maintain our ability to publish books and magazines, produce records and films, and create television and radio programming that help us define our hopes and dreams, our way of seeing ourselves and the world.[60]

The Emergence of the Pro-Canada Network

After nearly a year of concerted organizing and mobilization, beginning with the milestone Dialogue '86 conference, efforts at anti–free trade coalition building culminated in April 1987 with the creation of the Pro-Canada Network. Its emergence as the focal, national anti–free trade coalition is a clear validation of the emphasis placed by the political-process argument on the mobilization potential that is inherent in existing indigenous resources and organizations. Formal organizations, with their organizing resources of skilled organizers, leaders, professional staff, and facilities for meetings, played the key role in the formation of the PCN. In fact, because the PCN provided a loose umbrella structure to house the emerging extraparliamentary movement, the mode of recruitment for membership in the movement fits well with a dominant pattern of recruitment evident in empirical accounts of mobilization.

First, by the spring of 1987 the many formal and personal organizations and networks opposed to the free trade deal in existence provided the necessary individual interactions to promote the recruitment of members to the broader anti–free trade movement. A person involved in such coalitions as the COC, the Toronto CAFT, or the Working Committee for Social Solidarity was much more likely to participate in the protest activities of the anti–free trade movement. As Gerlach and Hine have argued, 'no matter how a typical participant describes his reasons for joining the movement ... it is clear that the original decision to join required some contact with the movement.'[61] Interaction at the level of the anti–free trade coalitions thus created the necessary contact.

Second, the broad range of anti–free trade indigenous organizations provided the core source of recruitment to the movement through what Oberschall has called 'bloc recruitment.'[62] As McAdam has suggested, through this type of process, 'movements do not so much emerge out of established organizations as they represent a merger of such groups.'[63] From this pattern, movements emerge from previously established coalitions of organizations; they retain their organizational structure and status while at the same time they share their resources with other similar coalitions. Through this process, then, the role of pre-existing indigenous organizations is clear. 'Mobilization does not occur through recruitment of large numbers of isolated and solitary individuals,' concludes Oberschall, but 'occurs as a result of recruiting blocs of people who are already highly organized and participants.'[64]

The PCN, as a self-described 'coalition of coalitions,' drew upon this solid pattern of movement recruitment and participation. Delegates from several well-established coalitions and groups attended the 4 April 1987 Canada Summit from which the PCN emerged.[65] During the next six months the pattern of bloc recruitment saw the PCN expand from its initial six founding members to over twenty national organizations and coalitions in nearly every province and territory. Significantly, and in line with bloc recruitment patterns, these groups joined the PCN on the condition that they would not dissolve their formal pre-existing functions and identities.

According to those involved in the PCN coalition-building process leading up to the April conference, groups were brought on board by the concept of a cooperative network structure. For many groups, joining and participating in a national anti–free trade organization implied joint responsibility and a lack of autonomous control, an unattractive alternative to many groups in light of their ongoing commitments to their sectoral coalitions. A national network, however, attracted groups because it implied cooperation and coordination while simultaneously allowing them to maintain their structural integrity and control over their resources. Thus, every meeting organized by the COC, the principal instigator of the PCN coalition, in the fall and winter of 1986–7 witnessed a growing number of interested organizations in attendance that were committed to creating a national anti–free trade network. 'It was a snowball effect,' reflected one leading COC organizer; 'we brought increasing numbers of groups in on their own merits, without regard to ideological, national, or professional differences. We united in opposition to the free trade deal.'[66]

This 'united opposition' met over the weekend of 4 April 1987 with the convening of the Canada Summit organized by the COC. The timing of this counter-summit coincided with President Ronald Reagan's visit to Ottawa and was designed as a mobilization point to demonstrate the broad-based and growing opposition to the free trade negotiations and the impending deal. The event included speeches by representatives of over thirty organizations concerned about the issue, and they directed their addresses to a panel symbolically representative of ordinary Canadians, people in business, labour, science, culture, sport, and agriculture.[67] Following the speeches and a press conference that included testimonials from individual Canadians who felt personally threatened by a free trade agreement, a 'Declaration of Canadian Independence' was circulated and endorsed by all the participating organizations. The summit concluded with a protest march to Parliament Hill, where the demonstrators, in a self-consciously Martin Lutheresque fashion, Scotch-taped the Declaration to the doors of Parliament.[68]

The groups involved in the Canada Summit came together that weekend to form the PCN for several reasons. First, anti–free trade organizations and coalitions recognized the strategic need for a national network to counter the Tory government's attempts to curb and control the debate over the FTA, as well as the lobbying efforts of the newly created pro–free trade coalition, the Canadian Alliance for Trade and Job Opportunities.[69] Second, organizers wanted to keep their members better informed about the impending FTA as the debate over it intensified. The PCN would be especially valuable in its capacity as a national communications clearing house, where all participating organizations could draw upon and exchange knowledge and research from the various affected sectors.

PCN founders were also sceptical about relying on political parties as the avenue through which to pursue an anti–free trade campaign. The groups affiliated with the PCN were especially concerned that the opposition NDP and Liberal parties would be less concerned with running an all-out campaign to defeat the FTA than with winning the next election at all costs. Finally, the common denominator for many of the groups that came together was not so much anxiety over the impact that the abolition of tariffs might have on, for example, the trade in beer or machine parts, but a broader concern for preserving the 'Canadian way of life.' This was what drew the diverse collection of speakers at the Canada Summit. For a representative of the National Federation of Nurses' Unions free trade threatened Canada's health care system; for another from the Canadian Teachers' Federation it was the limiting of political choice in Canada through a possible harmonization of social and economic policies; while for the director of the Association for Native Development in the Performing Arts it was the threat to the survival of Canadian culture.

All of the meetings leading up to the Canada Summit, and the Summit itself, took advantage of existing networks and organizations in mobilizing popular-sector, labour, and nationalist groups. Pre-existing networks with resources for organizing played a crucial role in developing and sustaining a coherent anti-free trade coalition-building campaign. Moreover, this activity did not occur in a political vacuum. Rather, such efforts were well thought out, strategically implemented, and facilitated by the ongoing and highly unpredictable political drama of the negotiations that were underway. In fact, it was the complementary political opportunities that emerged during these tumultuous and protracted negotiations that gave anti–free trade groups the time necessary to expand their organization and intensify their campaign.

Expanding Political Opportunities: Negotiating Free Trade

Several key events within the Canadian political process enhanced the opportunities for extensive coalition building and for mobilization against the free trade talks.[70] In particular, four instances of conflict and division between political actors during the period of negotiation directly facilitated the coalition-building efforts of the various popular-sector and nationalist groups. The first two cases – tensions over trade policy between the Reagan administration and the U.S. Congress and the conflict in Canada between the federal and provincial governments over provincial participation in the talks – resulted in significant delays to the start of negotiations. Two other cases – the near complete deadlock over substantive issues in the talks between the negotiating teams of the United States and Canada, followed by sharply escalating trade conflicts between the two countries – critically extended the negotiations for an unanticipated eighteen months.

Each of these instances of conflict and division added to the aura of stalemate surrounding the free trade talks. The prolonged standstill served to raise the significance of the free trade issue in the eyes of the Canadian public, heighten public uncertainty, and push the subject into the electoral timetable, and it ultimately set the stage for free trade to become the central issue in the upcoming federal election. At the same time, these divisions provided the anti–free trade forces with the critical time needed to overcome the serious internal roadblocks and doubts involving the implementation of the coalition-building strategy that preceded the creation of the national anti–free trade umbrella network, the Pro-Canada Network.

The conflicts over trade policy that developed between President Reagan and Congress in the spring of 1986 encouraged the anti–free trade mobilization efforts in Canada. By this time, Congress had grown increasingly protectionist in the face of the largest trade deficit in fifty years and what its members perceived as a growing plethora of foreign protectionist policies hurting American industry. At this strikingly inopportune time, Reagan asked for Congressional approval for 'fast track' negotiations to begin with Canada. With Canada on Congress's list of unfair traders, it was a highly unfortunate moment.

The Senate Finance Committee, taking advantage of Reagan's opening, proceeded to use Canada as an example to the rest of the world of its new 'get tough' trade policy on unfair trade restrictions.[71] The committee consequently produced a litany of supposed unfair Canadian trade practices during its hearings on whether to authorize fast-track negotiations. Faced with mounting trade deficits, recession-like conditions in industrial regions, and Congressional elections in November, the committee delayed approval of the fast-track procedure. Only after guarantees from Reagan that his administration would adopt tougher trade policies did the senators approve the procedures. The free trade talks could begin, but unbeknownst to the two negotiating teams a precedent for delay and non-negotiation had been set, one that would cloud the next eighteen months of talks.

A conflict between the Canadian federal and provincial governments also emerged and ran parallel to the other dispute. While the provinces had had little history of involvement in trade policy matters, the proposed free trade agreement threatened to impinge directly on areas of provincial jurisdiction. Concerned about the intrusions, western provinces demanded full provincial participation in talks between Canada and the United States. These demands were bolstered when, following the December 1985 announcement by the Mulroney and Reagan governments to pursue negotiations, Ontario and Quebec also demanded full and equal participation by the provinces.

This dispute remained unsettled throughout the summer of 1986, raising a host of uncertainties and contradictions over the role of the provinces in the talks. In one particularly factious period in the spring of 1986 the chief trade negotiator for Canada, Simon Reisman, ruled out any role for the provinces in the talks. External affairs minister Joe Clark then contradicted Reisman by granting full participation, but then soon contradicted himself by asserting full federal control over the negotiations. These contradictions and missteps by the federal government further weakened its negotiating position and credibility. The effect of the two sides playing a tug-of-war over the issue diverted a significant degree of energy from the Canadian negotiating team at a time when it most needed to shore up its position in the opening volley of talks.[72]

The Mulroney government succeeded in largely containing this conflict in the summer by granting full provincial consultation, but not participation, during the talks. However, a significant side drama continued to play itself out over the course of the talks: Ontario remained steadfastly opposed to the deal. This opposition presented difficulties to the Mulroney government and a boon to the now widely spreading anti–free trade coalitions, given that the opposition of Canada's largest, most economically and politically powerful province attracted a great deal of national publicity. In particular, the Ontario provincial election in September 1987 presaged an unsavory scenario for the Tories. It was fought largely over the issue of free trade, and the trouncing of the Tories by the Liberals seemed to vindicate the staid opposition of Liberal premier Peterson to the talks, further boosting the hopes of the anti–free trade coalitions.

In addition, divisions and differences between Canada and the United States over each other's agendas contributed most directly to the near absence of negotiations that characterized the talks for eighteen months. Canada wanted security of access to the U.S. market, that is, national treatment of Canadian imports into the United States so that Canadian goods would be regarded no differently than U.S. goods. It sought to gain exemption from the trade remedies built into U.S. trade laws, including countervailing and anti-dumping measures. In addition, Canada desired a binational binding dispute mechanism in the form of an arbitration process that would spell out a set of rules to govern Canadian–U.S. trade disputes, and it especially wanted codes for subsidies that would specify the government subsidies that would be illegal under the agreement.

The agenda of the United States directly clashed with the Canadian priorities. In addition to ensuring that it would never again face another Canadian FIRA or NEP, the United States sought to eliminate government subsidies and to secure national treatment on investment, but at the same time have the right to continue to use existing trade remedies. Moreover, the United States baulked at the idea of a binational arbitration panel since it put in question issues of the sovereignty of the United States and of the jurisdiction of Congress over trade policy. Thus, both sides deadlocked and set the pattern of non-negotiation that would characterize the next year of talks. At the same time, support in Canada for free trade fell to 52 per cent, a bare majority, by June 1986.[73]

The first seven months of 1986, which coincided roughly with the inauspicious beginning of the trade talks, witnessed a significant expansion of anti–free trade activities. Environics pollster Donna Dasko argues that 'the low profile given free trade by the government during this critical period after September 1985 allowed opponents of the initiative to seize the moment and to state their objections forcefully to Canadians.'[74] In this period criticism transformed into action, as coalitions and protests sprang to life across the country. The seeds of the anti–free trade strategy were sown at the Dialogue '86 conference in January and bolstered at the successful Massey Hall event that March. The Toronto CAFT also significantly expanded its membership, with larger numbers of anti–free trade workshops and forums held by most of its affiliates, many of which passed resolutions.[75] The CAFT also coordinated protests throughout Ontario on Canada Day, 1 July.[76] In addition to participating in CAFT activities, the labour movement launched its own anti–free trade campaign during this time. The CAW distributed educational and action kits on free trade to its 14,000 members in February, the Ontario Federation of Labour kicked off its anti–free trade campaign that same month, and the CLC began its national campaign in April.

In addition to the favourable climate for anti–free trade activity provided by the lengthy negotiations, trade disputes added greater legitimacy to the protests. A long-simmering softwood lumber dispute between Canada and the United States dramatically worsened just as the second substantive stage of negotiations began in the fall of 1986. By then, Canadian lumber exports were capturing 31 per cent of the U.S. domestic market, and the United States, in the midst of talks designed to prevent such action, placed a 15 per cent duty in October on these exports, claiming that unfair Canadian subsidies of the lumber were damaging the market.

As the free trade talks floundered in the fall and winter of 1986–7, anti–free trade mobilization efforts intensified across many provinces. In Quebec, for the first time in over ten years, the three main labour union centrals, La Fédération des travailleurs et travailleuses du Québec, the Confédération des syndicats nationaux, and the Centrale de l'enseignement du Québec, in cooperation with the main farmers' union, L'Union des producteurs agricoles du Québec, established on 1 October a 'Common Front' to oppose the free trade talks. A Manitoban CAFT also expanded significantly, and an Alberta CAFT held its founding meeting in October. In Newfoundland the Catholic Social Action

Commission initiated a meeting with representatives from the Coalition for Equality to begin cooperating to oppose the talks. In British Columbia the End Legislated Poverty Coalition, a coalition of labour unions and of unemployed, women's, churches, and anti-poverty groups, held a forum on the expected impact of free trade on the province.

The stalemated talks, which bogged down on differences over the dispute settlement process and American trade remedies, failed to produce an agreement in the spring or summer of 1987. Part of the difficulty lay in the different stakes each country had in the talks. Prime Minister Mulroney and the members of his Progressive Conservative Party had by now committed themselves to reaching a deal, while the United States had much less at issue on the outcome of the negotiations. This put the Tories in a difficult position, as the aura of stalled negotiations that had hung over the talks for well over a year increasingly appeared to be part of the strategy of the United States to flush out concessions from the increasingly desperate Canadian government. Thus, with disputes continuing over the issues still up for negotiation even at a late stage of the talks, the United States calculatedly pressed for discussions and concessions over issues that cut close to nationalist concerns, including Canada's energy, cultural, and social programs. This did little to quell the intensifying criticism of the anti–free trade forces or to slow their expanding organizations.

In fact, the anti–free trade movement gained significant momentum from the state of total impasse that characterized the talks during the spring and summer of 1987. A COC activist and the co-chair of the PCN described the atmosphere of stalemate as particularly productive for movement-building:

we charged that things were deadlocked because Canada was being asked to give up things that were going to be dangerous, and that we weren't being told what they were. The time in this country was very nervous, and we were able to ask why there was this deadlock, and what we were giving away. So this was a time of great surge for the movement, a very important time of consolidation for us.[77]

It was during this time that the PCN emerged to become the central national vehicle for opposition to the deal. The ecumenical organization, Gatt-Fly, held a conference on Free Trade, Self-Reliance, and Economic Justice in Ottawa in February, which served as a dress rehearsal for the creation of the PCN at the Canada Summit six weeks later. Over one hundred participants representing all ten provinces and various national groups attended, gave speeches, and developed strategies to coordinate a campaign at the national level against the free trade deal. Participants denounced the 'undemocratic process' of the talks and called for the initiation of 'democratic procedures' – public hearings, a referendum, or an election – should a deal emerge.[78]

Following the creation of the PCN, anti–free trade coalition-building activity continued in the wake of the stalled talks, with PCN affiliates seeking additional groups and coalitions for the network. The Toronto CAFT held a Free Trade Is No Picnic picnic in Toronto in June, while the PCN organized protests at the first ministers conference in July. Anti–free trade literature continued to flourish; the Social Affairs Commission of the Canadian Conference of Catholic Bishops released a booklet, *Free Trade: At What Cost?* which was distributed throughout Canada's Catholic dioceses, while the Working Committee on Social Solidarity prepared for the release of the Declaration on Social and Economic Policy.

By the late summer it appeared unlikely that an agreement on free trade would be reached; the Canadian delegation abruptly broke off the talks on 23 September because of the irreconcilable differences between the two sides. With the original negotiating teams unable to reach an agreement and with a 3 October deadline for an agreement rapidly approaching the drama heightened. After further deadlocks and strategic bluffing failed to produce an agreement, the two sides managed to salvage an accord five minutes before the midnight deadline. It had taken nearly a year and a half to settle the issues that divided the two countries at the start of the exploratory negotiations. In the meantime, the unexpectedly long impasse had provided the anti–free trade forces with crucial time for mobilization, so that by the conclusion of the talks coalitions existed at the national level through the PCN, in nearly every province and territory, and in innumerable localities throughout Canada.

The significance of the opportunities for mobilization and coalition building presented to the anti–free trade forces by these divisions can be evaluated by considering a reversal of events: what effect would a smoothly negotiated, rapidly concluded agreement have had on the mobilization of the anti–free trade movement? Certainly, the diverse groups and coalitions would not have been nearly as organizationally and strategically prepared to oppose the agreement as they were by the fall of 1987. The agreement's delay until October had allowed provincial and national coalitions to be formed and the PCN to hold several assemblies at which parliamentary protest and electoral strategy had been devised.

Moreover, the protracted negotiations significantly raised the Canadian public's awareness of the issue. In particular, the Mulroney government's inept handling of trade disputes between Canada and the United States, as well as the haphazard nature of the negotiations, sensitized the public to exactly those

TABLE 1
Perceptions of how well the government has done informing Canadians on free trade
negotiations (in percentages)

Question: Overall, how good or poor a job would you say the Mulroney government has
done informing Canadians about the free trade negotiations?

	B.C.	Prairies	Ontario	Quebec	Atlantic	Total
Very good job	1	2	5	4	3	3
Fairly good job	28	31	27	35	24	30
Fairly poor job	39	33	34	35	36	35
Very poor job	23	27	29	16	30	24
Unsure	9	7	6	10	8	8

Source: Angus Reid Associates Inc., 'Free Trade: Canadians' Perceptions of the
Implications of the Initiative,' prepared and conducted for the Pro-Canada Network,
August 1987.

controversial aspects of the deal that were being seized upon by the deal's
opponents. As Table 1 indicates, by the summer a majority of Canadians
felt that the government had done a poor job in informing them about the
negotiations.

Furthermore, as pollster Dasko points out, 'the increasing criticism of the
Prime Minister and his government throughout 1987, led to softening support
for what had become in the public's mind at least, the government's major
policy goal.'[79] In fact, the combined effects of intense media scrutiny, the daily
attacks by the opposition in question period, the election of an anti–free trade
Liberal government in Ontario in September, and the anti–free trade activities
of the provincial and national coalitions had by October 1987 reduced support
for the federal Tories to 24 per cent of the decided electorate, a modern-day
low for a governing party in Canada. Perhaps more significant for anti–free
trade forces, support for free trade fell along with that for the Tories to 57 per
cent by that December (see Table 2).

Finally, had it not been for the eighteen months of stalled negotiation it is
likely that the free trade issue would have been settled long before the federal
election campaign came along. The prime minister had at his discretion at least
the traditional four years if not the maximum of five to call the election. Had
the free trade negotiations been satisfactorily concluded in a year by the spring
of 1987 as anticipated the agreement could have been ratified by the legisla-
tures of both countries and become effective without encroaching on the electoral timetable.

TABLE 2
Support for free trade, December 1987 (in percentages)

Question: Please tell me whether you strongly agree, somewhat agree, somewhat disagree or strongly disagree that there should be free trade between Canada and the United States?

	West	Ontario	Quebec	Atlantic	Overall
Strongly agree	30	19	18	20	22
Somewhat agree	36	31	40	37	35
Somewhat disagree	15	16	18	19	16
Strongly disagree	13	21	14	9	16
No opinion	6	13	9	15	10

Source: Donna Dasko, 'The Canadian Public and Free Trade,' in Duncan Cameron, ed., *The Free Trade Deal* (Toronto: Lorimer 1988), 252.

As it happened, however, the agreement in October 1987 was not followed by the completion of the final legal text until 10 December, then there were still another eight months of parliamentary deadlock and wrangling, and so the issue entered the electoral timetable. The deadlock in the negotiations had thus created the most fortunate political opportunity for the anti–free trade forces: the issue was poised to emerge as the key one in the campaign.

The Terms of Debate

By December 1987 the terms of the free trade debate had crystallized, with both sides hardening their positions. On the pro–free trade side stood Prime Minister Mulroney and his Progressive Conservative government, along with most sectors of the Canadian business community, including in particular the Business Council on National Issues (BCNI), and the Canadian Manufacturers' Association (CMA). A notable addition to the pro–free trade side was the Canadian Alliance for Trade and Job Opportunities during the 1986–7 period of negotiations.[80] Founded by leaders of the BCNI and financed by over one hundred Canadian corporations,[81] CATJO sought to bolster the sagging public fortunes of the FTA and to redress what were perceived as the Mulroney government's missteps during the negotiations by a massive media campaign. Ironically, by failing to present a populist pro–free trade perspective, CATJO's founders and its corporate backers instead suggested that support for the free trade concept was limited at best.

The government's communications document that was leaked had made clear its desire to limit the breadth of the debate over the free trade issue. Specifically, the debate, if controlled properly, would centre on the economics of the deal – on the jobs, increased trade, and prosperity that the government argued would flow naturally from the FTA. The government defended its position by referring to the battery of academic economic consultants on its side, whose language of economic modelling seemed to support the government's assertions.[82] As the prime minister himself argued during a House of Commons debate over the issue, 'the motion in this historic debate is designed to create jobs, to generate new wealth, and to create new economic opportunities in all regions of Canada.'[83] To bolster this theme, the government also complemented its huge Trade Negotiations Office with a publicity strategy, which included circulating thousands of its 100-page booklets on free trade, and it sent ministers on speaking tours.[84]

Yet, despite the government's efforts to control and limit the debate, the continuously expanding anti–free trade forces had over the course of the period of negotiations managed to extend its parameters to assert that, fundamentally, the Canadian 'way-of-life' was at stake. According to this view, the deal challenged the generous state subsidies and protectionist measures that had nurtured the arts and a distinctive Canadian culture.[85] In addition, the deal appeared to undermine Canada's system of universal social programs, including those for health care, unemployment, and old-age benefits.[86] Thus, from the standpoint of a critic, while the deal threatened to deindustrialize Canada, and thereby reduce employment opportunities, it also more deeply threatened Canadian culture and social programs, elements that contributed to Canada being distinct from the United States.

Summary

In short, despite the lobbying efforts of the Mulroney government and of CATJO, by December 1987 when negotiations came to an end support for the agreement had fallen dramatically below that for the general idea of free trade (see Table 3). The government had failed to present the agreement credibly. Canadians remained supportive of free trade in theory, not surprising given that Canada's exports drove its economy and that the vast majority went to the United States. However, the free trade agreement as negotiated by the Mulroney government received much lower marks. This gap revealed a striking weakness in the position of the government and of the business lobby, and reflected the degree to which the anti–free trade forces, including the Pro-Canada Network, had sensitized the Canadian public to its criticisms of the deal. The debate had

TABLE 3
Support for the Free Trade Agreement, December 1987 (in percentages)

Question: Do you strongly favour, somewhat favour, somewhat oppose, or strongly oppose the free trade agreement that has been negotiated between Canada and the United States?

	West	Ontario	Quebec	Atlantic	Overall
Strongly favour	11	8	8	10	9
Somewhat favour	31	24	39	35	31
Somewhat oppose	18	21	21	20	20
Strongly oppose	18	25	14	13	19
No opinion	22	23	18	22	21

Source: Donna Dasko, 'The Canadian Public and Free Trade,' in Duncan Cameron, ed., *The Free Trade Deal* (Toronto: Lorimer 1988), 252.

expanded so that the future of Canada's culture and of its social programs and its very sovereignty were now being debated in the media, Parliament, public forums, and academic journals from coast to coast. Ahead lay the parliamentary debate and the free trade election.

4

The Parliamentary Protest Campaign

The previous chapters have shown that a series of shifts and destabilizations in the Canadian political environment from 1981 to the fall of 1987 facilitated the rise of the anti–free trade movement by shaping both the political opportunities for successful collective action and the organizational capacity to exploit those opportunities. At various stages the political instability induced long-term favourable changes in the resources and organization of the anti–free trade group, in political opportunities, and in the consciousness of participants, all of which contributed to the continued expansion of the movement.

This chapter highlights the continuing influence of these variables in the mobilization and the strategic intervention of the movement's parliamentary protest campaign. The twelve months beginning with the signing of the preliminary free trade agreement on 5 October 1987 and ending with the dissolution of Parliament and call for a federal election by Prime Minister Mulroney on 1 October 1988 marked a new stage in the anti–free trade movement's strategic direction and development. The announcement that an accord had been signed ended the tumultuous period of negotiations which had been so favourable to the coalition-building strategy of the anti–free trade forces. Now the nature of the stakes had changed and these forces responded to the transfer of the free trade issue from the negotiating table to Parliament by shifting their strategy towards the development of a national direct political-action campaign.

Changes that were continuing to take place in the three variables of the political-process model – in resources and organization, in political opportunities, and in group consciousness – combined to enable the anti–free trade forces to mount and sustain this national protest campaign against the FTA. First, the political-process model asserts that social movements significantly expand and have their greatest impact during periods marked by a profound increase in the vulnerability of the political establishment to pressure from protest groups. As McAdam argues, it is at such times that 'the power discrepancy between members and challengers is reduced, thus rendering insurgent action more likely, less risky, and potentially more successful.'[1] Such a condition of vulnerability characterized the Canadian political establishment during this period, which significantly enhanced the leverage and bargaining position of the anti–free trade forces vis-à-vis the two federal opposition political parties, the Liberal and New Democratic parties. This unstable political environment also created critical political-opportunity structures which facilitated the movement's strategic intervention in the parliamentary debate on free trade.

The political-process model also focuses on the role played by variations in the strategies, organization, and resources of protest groups for the sustained expansion of social movements. Specifically, a movement must have a high degree of 'organizational readiness' and strength to convert existing favourable political opportunities into an organized, sustained protest campaign.[2] In fact, innovations in group strategies during the protest campaign helped the anti–free trade groups and coalitions consolidate into the Pro-Canada Network, which provided the movement with a nationwide infrastructure to organize and carry out protests more effectively. Moreover, this network aided in the coordination of the resources of the popular-sector anti–free trade forces, which enabled the movement to exploit expanding political-opportunity structures and which sustained the movement's expansion until the fall of 1988.

Finally, new developments in the subjective perceptions of the anti–free trade participants combined with the changing styles of organization and the shifting political opportunities to help sustain the protest efforts of the participants. Specifically, two aspects of the subjective side of the collective action played a role during this stage of the movement's mobilization. First, activists correctly interpreted the unsettled political environment as providing opportunities for strategically pressing their campaign. There was a perception that the conditions for anti–free trade mobilization were favourable. Second, a growing sense of political efficacy emerged after the success of the organizing efforts of the Pro-Canada Network – and from the perception of the participants that their efforts were making a difference in the debate – which bolstered the commitment of the participants to carry their campaign into the parliamentary arena. Simply put, throughout the protest campaign leading up to the election, activists felt strongly that they had the moral upper hand – that their efforts had begun to have tangible effects in turning the Canadian public against the free trade deal. This subjective contribution, working in tandem with the ongoing organizational and political changes, assisted in the mounting and sustaining of the national anti–free trade protest campaign.

Organizational Roots of the Protest Campaign

Social movements are collective phenomena that arise out of previously well-organized parts of a population and that possess the resources necessary to exploit favourable political opportunities. Networks, an autonomous organizational infrastructure, or a so-called social-movement sector can supply a protest movement with the reservoir of resources required for rapid mobilization. Indeed, an agitated population that is lacking such resources, Oberschall argues, has recourse only to 'short-term, localized, ephemeral outbursts and movements of protest such as riots.'[3] Therefore, popular organizations enjoying such a resource base have the capacity to act and sustain an organized campaign of political protest.

At the time of the signing of the free trade accord in October 1987, the anti–free trade movement rested on a formidable country-wide network of over twenty national organizations and associated coalitions in nearly every province and territory. The major national organizations included the Canadian Labour Congress, the Council of Canadians, the National Action Committee on the Status of Women, the Ecumenical Coalition on Economic Justice, or Gatt-Fly, the National Farmers' Union, the Association of Canadian Television and Radio Artists (ACTRA), the National Anti-Poverty Organization, the Assembly of First Nations, the National Federation of Nurses' Unions, the Canadian Peace Pledge Campaign, the One Voice–Canadian Seniors Network, the Canadian Teachers' Federation, Academics Against Free Trade, the Canadian Conference of the Arts, and the Canadian Wildlife Federation.[4] In addition, the movement was bolstered by the activity of provincially and regionally based coalitions, including notably the Ontario-based Coalition Against Free Trade and La Coalition québécoise d'opposition au libre-échange.[5]

The PCN served as the national vehicle for coordination and communication between these various anti–free trade organizations and coalitions. By the fall of 1987 the PCN's organizational structure consisted of four working committees designed to coordinate strategy and action between the affiliated organizations, a research and analysis committee, a media and communications committee, a strategy committee, and a steering committee. The members of the committees represented organizations and coalitions from across Canada, providing the PCN with a broad base.

Over the weekend of 17–18 October, shortly after the signing of the FTA, representatives of the PCN and the provincial organizations that were opposed to the accord met to devise a national campaign strategy. This meeting, as well as the national meetings that would follow, came to be known officially as PCN National Assemblies. National Assemblies came together roughly every two to three months in the next twelve months before Mulroney's call for an election, and each one coincided with a different strategic phase in the PCN's campaign. Each National Assembly developed campaign strategies against the free trade deal, with the PCN's working committees carrying out the more detailed work and putting in place the plans of action that were adopted. In addition, it was often left up to the participating organizations and coalitions to decide about the specific actions that should be given priority in light of the available resources.

The PCN National Assemblies, which consisted of delegates or representatives of constituent organizations (national and provincial) of the PCN, emerged as the key decision-making forums for the PCN. No requirements existed for formal voting on issues at assemblies. Instead, delegates based decision-making on a principle of consensus; they reached decisions with the mutual agreement of the participating organizations and coalitions. Like membership in the PCN, attendance at National Assemblies was based on the organization, not by individual, and organizations participated on an equal basis regardless of their size or of the sector they represented.[6] The non-hierarchical and egalitarian structure and the decision-making process of the National Assemblies helped to ensure a sense of harmonious cooperation throughout the PCN's national anti–free trade campaign.

The first National Assembly that October weekend met to draw up strategies and action plans for the first phase of the campaign. As envisioned by the participants, it would unfold in discussion, ratification, and implementation phases, each one corresponding with a specific stage of the probable political calendar for the FTA. The participants at the first National Assembly had intended hammering out the strategies for phase one of the protest campaign. A general consensus existed regarding two core objectives: to defeat the bilateral Canada–U.S. FTA and to launch a public process for determining alternative directions for economic policy for Canada. Participants crafted three strategies to achieve these objectives: to mobilize public opinion and create a critical awareness of the major issues involved in the accord; to delay or block the legislation implementing free trade, thereby provoking a federal election on free trade and on economic alternatives to it; and to stimulate the provinces into refusing to implement the FTA.[7]

A majority of the activists, staff members, and participants in some of the larger demonstrations related to the anti–free trade movement were at the National Assembly as a result of their prior involvement with or membership in PCN-affiliated organizations and coalitions.[8] This breadth among its representatives was a strong factor in favour of the anti–free trade forces. Activists were apparently being given recognition and they trumpeted the strength of their wide representativeness, asserting in a press statement released during the second PCN National Assembly that

our main strength lies in the links we have organizationally with a diversity of grassroots constituencies that comprise well over ten million people across Canada. In the coming months we will be speaking in a voice that our own constituents understand – on the shop floor, on the farm, in our congregations and conventions. In this way we hope that the vast majority of people in this country will come to know the truth about this deal and decide to reject it through a federal election.[9]

The diverse range of its membership seemed, in fact, to dwarf the relatively narrow support for the deal that was organized within the business community. Moreover, the organizations affiliated to the PCN also supplied the movement with a great deal of its leadership. These leaders brought prestige and organizational skills to the campaign and they would significantly sharpen the impression it would make on the Canadian political establishment.

Popular-sector organizations also supplied the PCN with a communications network that served as an essential resource for the successful unfolding of its national campaign. Social movements often live, thrive, and die on information that is unavailable from 'mainstream' media sources, and the outcome of a struggle for the control of information often makes or breaks a movement. In fact, to the extent that the anti–free trade movement was – at a minimum – a movement for public information and education, the success it achieved would rest on the ability of the PCN to control, influence, and disseminate critical information about the agreement. Lacking the monetary resources to counter the Mulroney government in its own mass media campaign, the PCN concentrated its efforts instead in communicating to the grass-roots through its broad-based constituency.

Groups mounted major campaigns to educate the grass-roots members of the PCN sectorally and within organizations, relying on a variety of alternative vehicles for communication. Thus the PCN became a clearing house for the distribution and exchange of an outpouring of pamphlets, newsletters, fact sheets, books, news clippings, and analyses about free trade. Among some of the more significant publications circulated by PCN organizations were *A Time to Stand Together: A Time for Social Solidarity*, a declaration on alternative social and economic policy directions published by the Working Committee for Social Solidarity; *Responding to Free Trade from a Christian Perspective*, published by a coalition of Canadian churches; and *CUPE: The Facts on Free Trade*. Of particular note was the publication and circulation throughout the network of the *Pro-Canada Dossier*, a monthly newsletter that served as a link between national and regional groups fighting the FTA. The *Dossier* became a major vehicle for communicating within the network, providing information, resources, analyses, and strategies for action to PCN members.

In addition to publishing the *Dossier*, the PCN's research and analysis team played another key role within the network. Its collaborative analysis capability ensured the rapid circulation of sectoral-wide critiques of the FTA. It tapped some of the leading researchers in PCN-affiliated sectors as well as academics in the fields of political science, sociology, and economics. The team rapidly analysed both the 'Elements of the Agreement' released on 5 October and the final text released on 10 December, providing sets of briefing notes and turning out a seventy-five-page critique of the accord that was quickly disseminated to PCN organizations and coalitions across the country. Its analysis contributed significantly to *CUPE: The Facts on Free Trade* and the *Dossier* and it bolstered the presentations of PCN organizations during the fall 1987 parliamentary cross-country hearings on the agreement.

Finally, the PCN discovered that it could also invoke popular symbols to advance the movement's campaign aims. Many dozens of small protest actions conducted throughout the national campaign had an important effect on the media, particularly the electronic media. Demonstrations at the Canada–U.S. border, anti–free trade theatrical reviews, lawn-sign campaigns, marches and parades, Scotch-taping the PCN's manifesto onto the doors of the Parliament Buildings – these actions served to complement the written material distributed by the PCN. They all had an impact on public thinking, combining as they did analysis of the content of the anti–free trade message with actions that projected that message on a symbolic level.

In short, the PCN's infrastructure equipped activists with the resources necessary to mount and sustain a campaign against the FTA. Having this capability is consistent with the expectation of the political-process model that movements depend on a high level of organization in the aggrieved community, in other words, a high degree of organizational readiness, so that they are capable of mounting and sustaining an organized strategic campaign of protest. The critical degree of readiness came about not through infusions of resources or through contributions from groups external to the popular sector. Rather, the coordination of non-partisan, popular-sector resources set the stage for the parliamentary protest campaign. The members and leaders, as well as the communications base provided by the organizations and coalitions affiliated to the PCN, combined to provide the structural potential for collective political action against the FTA.

The resources of the popular sector played an indispensable role in three major national protest actions orchestrated for the PCN's parliamentary campaign. The events – a drive for a national petition, a major response to the legislation implementing free trade legislation, and a National Day of Action – served two purposes, to communicate the central theme of the PCN and to increase public awareness of the PCN as the embodiment of a nationwide movement against the accord.[10] Organizers designed the drive for a national petition to impress upon federal and provincial politicians that a substantial number of Canadians wanted a federal election to be held to decide the free trade issue. In launching it in the summer of 1987, PCN-affiliated organizations and coalitions sent out copies of the petition to their constituents and relied initially on the vast membership base to supply the bulk of signatures. The network structure served a particularly conducive role to a wide-ranging, grass-roots drive, as each organization and coalition was equipped to reach its respective constituency through its own sectoral channels. The PCN facilitated the exchange of information among the various groups undertaking the drive, monitored its status in each region, and promoted publicity on the petition and moved it forward. The PCN's role, as put forth in a document on strategy, was to 'emphasize the national scope of the activity and to provide the sense of solidarity found in a jointly organized campaign.'[11]

In addition to working through its members, the PCN set aside days in the spring for province-wide drives for signatures. Activists garnered signatures through door-to-door canvassing, by setting up tables and booths in malls and shopping centres, and through minor rallies and theatrical revues held across the country. The leaders of the PCN eventually handed the two opposition leaders on 30 May 1988 one of the largest petitions – over 350,000 signatures demanding a federal election – ever presented in Ottawa.[12] The petition ultimately garnered over 400,000 signatures, a large number by the standards of a traditionally politically reticent Canadian population.

By inserting the petition into a larger event, dubbed the National Day of Action against the Mulroney Trade Deal, held on 12 June 1988, the PCN made a response to the legislation implementing free trade that served as a springboard for mobilization both within and outside of Parliament against the agreement. The event's success drew heavily on the resource infrastructure of the network, and it conveyed the PCN's breadth of membership and the prestige of its leadership as well as the credibility of its analysis of the agreement to the parliamentary opposition. Months in the making, the event placed the PCN's research and analysis team on standby, ready to critique immediately the legislation for implementing free trade. PCN leaders and the leaders of the opposition parties also cemented plans to meet and share proposals for preventing the passage of the legislation.

The National Day of Action represented a successful consolidation of the PCN's popular-sector resources and an opportunity for the coalition to voice collectively its opposition to the FTA. The PCN's communication network rapidly distributed the research and analysis team's review of the legislation and released a press statement that included this analysis to organizations and media contacts across the country. Organizations were thereby provided immediately with information to distribute throughout their sectors within forty-eight hours of the tabling of the implementing legislation. Moreover, the event served to awaken the opposition in Parliament to the weight of the PCN's membership and to the prestige of its leadership. A meeting between the leaders and members of the Liberal and New Democratic parties with thirty-two of the most senior leaders and officers of PCN organizations and coalitions (during which the latter leaders stressed that they directed a movement comprising potentially ten million Canadians who were against the agreement) moved the opposition parties to take more seriously the PCN's concerns as well as the electoral potential of its membership. The leaders of the two parties stressed their commitment to 'tear up the deal' if elected, to make every effort to obstruct the legislation in the House of Commons, and to continue to develop working relationships with the PCN.[13] It was at this point, reflected one PCN activist, that 'we realized that the most powerful weapon that we had going for us was the movement that we were building across the country – if the movement became powerful enough, the politicians could not dismiss us.'[14] In fact, the meeting set the stage for the interaction and strategic cooperation of the PCN with the opposition parties throughout the debate on the FTA in Parliament in the spring and summer.

Finally, the PCN coordinated the National Day of Action to build a sense of nationwide solidarity.[15] The events that day conveyed a message that the FTA 'was a bad deal for Canada,' and at the same time allowed for different communities to inject local flavour. Numerous protests and rallies took place across Canada in all ten provinces, including a cavalcade of cars in Vancouver organized by the British Columbia Coalition Against 'Free' Trade; rallies in Alberta where over 2,500 people from twenty-one federal ridings participated and delivered condemnations of the FTA to the offices of their federal MPs; a rally at the federal building in Regina in Saskatchewan where guerrilla theatre performances on Canada's future under free trade were held; protests in Ontario held at border crossings at Queenston, Sarnia, Sault Ste Marie, Fort Frances, Thunder Bay, and Kingston, as well as a 'Free Trade Is No Picnic' picnic held in Sudbury; a protest in Quebec City held at the National Assembly where a sixteen-foot American eagle and a Canadian flag were displayed; and border protests, teach-ins, and rallies held in all four Atlantic provinces, including a 'Carry a Light for Canada Night' in Prince Edward Island where the premier spoke out strongly against the deal.[16] These events demonstrated an opposition across the entire country to the FTA.

The Shifting Structure of Political Opportunities

While the PCN's resources in the popular sector played a central role in its ability to mount a protest campaign, political conditions outside the network also dramatically conditioned its success. As McAdam asserts, 'to generate a social movement, the aggrieved population must be able to "convert" a favorable "structure of political opportunities" into an organized campaign of social protest.'[17] Political-opportunity structures can be viewed as conceptual tools for distinguishing between political conditions that may be either favourable or unfavourable for social movements and their activities.[18] Political factors play a particularly 'crucial role for the successful mobilization of movements which deliberately enter the arena of public and political debates.'[19] This perspective is critical for understanding the role that certain political conditions played in the mobilization of the anti–free trade movement's parliamentary campaign.

Throughout the 1980s the Canadian political environment had become increasingly unstable. It was marked by disruptive political events and conditions which shaped the mobilization of the anti–free trade movement. Because they contributed to a disruption of the political status quo, the destabilizing events included the 1981–2 recession, the landslide election victory of the Tories in 1984, the rise of the free trade issue, and the historically significant shift towards support of free trade by the Tories, in Quebec, and by the business community. Each event put many social and political groups on the defensive against Tory initiatives and created a favourable political context for the emergence of the anti–free trade movement.

These events hit the two opposition parties, the Liberals and New Democrats, particularly hard. The Mulroney election gave the Tories control of the political agenda and they used the opportunity to shake up Canada's social and political environment through neo-conservative policies of privatization, deregulation, and, most importantly, free trade.[20] The latter represented a radical break from the left-of-centre public policy agenda that had been dominant federally since the mid-1960s. The Tory initiatives left the political establishment divided and vulnerable, and they disrupted the power relations of the political status quo that was traditionally dominated by the Liberals and the New Democrats.

The free trade agreement reached by the negotiators of the United States and Canada marked a significant new stage in the period of political instability that characterized the 1980s. It ushered in a heightened period of weakness within the Canadian political establishment, whose vulnerability to anti–free trade pressures and protests was evident when the issue was sent to a bitterly divided Parliament. For, with the initiation of the parliamentary stage of the process, decisive political conditions emerged which would encourage and sustain the collective action and parliamentary protest campaign of the anti–free trade forces.

Party and Parliamentary Divisions

One of the more conceptually relevant political-opportunity structures is the existence (or absence) of divisions among socio-political actors, along with their tolerance (or intolerance) of protest. This variable suggests that divisions, particularly over the policy issues relevant to a movement's cause, can produce periods of stalemate or non-action that provide movements with the opportunity for further mobilization. Such deadlocks can keep issues conducive to mobilizing on the agenda and in the public eye over long periods of time, facilitating attempts to influence opinion. Moreover, movements can exploit the openings created by the fragmentation of political parties and other institutional groups to build alliances with sympathetic political actors as well as to gain greater leverage and stronger bargaining positions for pressing their reforms.

An examination first of the Liberal Party – the traditional 'national' party of Canada – reveals that it had emerged from the 1984 election weak, vulnerable, and badly divided. Table 4 illustrates how anomalous the 1984 election was for the Liberal Party. Its weakness represented a departure from the historical norm for a party that was accustomed to being the dominant force in the majority of Canadian federal elections held between 1896 and 1984. Emerging from the election with a mere forty members in the House of Commons, the party stumbled through the next few years deeply in debt, fearful of losing its tenuous hold as the official opposition, and saddled with a leader, John Turner, who was unpopular with both the Canadian public and many of his colleagues in caucus.

By the summer of 1987 substantive policy issues that went to the heart of the party's traditional agenda had split the caucus. Free trade had been a divisive issue from the minute it surfaced as a potential initiative of the Tories. While most Liberals were cognizant of the need to liberalize global trade, a

TABLE 4
Voting patterns in federal elections, 1965–84 (in percentages)

	1965	1968	1972	1974	1979	1980	1984
Liberal	40	46	39	43	40	44	28
PC	32	31	35	35	36	33	50
NDP	18	17	18	15	18	20	18
Other	10	6	8	7	6	3	4

Source: *Report of the Chief Electoral Officer* (Ottawa: Ministry of Supply and Services 1965–84).

Canada–U.S. free trade agreement represented a potential threat to the mixed-market, interventionist heritage that was cherished by the Liberals and that had marked the preceding decades. As a result, following a national convention in 1986 marked by near disaster, Turner tried to take the middle ground on the issue of free trade between the anti– and pro–free trade wings of the caucus.

The balance of forces in the Liberal caucus began to shift by late summer 1987 in favour of the anti–free traders in the party.[21] When the Canadian and U.S. negotiators finally concluded the agreement in October the pressure on Turner to oppose the deal became overwhelming. Constrained by the now dominant nationalist-left of his caucus, pressured by many anti–free trade groups, and faced with a major Tory initiative Turner announced in the House of Commons that he would 'tear it up' if elected. From than on Turner and especially the left-nationalist trade critic, Lloyd Axworthy, established crucial political leadership for the anti–free trade cause.

The weakness of the Liberal Party and divisions within it meant that it became much more vulnerable – and more receptive to – the protests and concerns of the anti–free trade groups affiliated to the PCN. Throughout the year-long anti–free trade protest campaign, a working relationship evolved between representatives of various groups and some high-profile members of the Liberal Party.[22] Members of the COC and PCN had surprising access to the Liberal caucus, where they frequently presented briefs, exchanged information, provided research and analysis, and co-planned strategy.[23] As one Liberal caucus member recounted,

the PCN was very useful – their representatives could marshall arguments, provide information, and present sectoral analysis on a deal that was so big and so comprehensive that we just did not have the resources to cover. And we could also use the threat of the PCN's electoral base – as a leverage against other members of the caucus – that it might turn on us if we didn't use their information and listen to what they had to say.[24]

In addition to the divisions within the Liberal Party, those within Parliament also created political opportunities for the anti-FTA forces. In particular, the split between the pro–free trade ruling Conservatives and the anti–free trade Liberals and New Democrats created a highly supportive political context for the airing of the concerns of the anti–free trade camp. The entrance of the FTA into this highly charged and divided arena ensured continuous debate and media coverage, which served to keep the issue on the parliamentary agenda and prominently in the public eye throughout the PCN's protest campaign. While the opposition had been hammering away at the free trade stance of the Tories in question period for many months, the conclusion of the agreement in October 1987 heightened the visibility of the issue. Many of the PCN-affiliated groups presented briefs critical of the agreement at parliamentary hearings in the fall of 1987 and the summer of 1988. Widely covered in the national media, these hearings provided national exposure to the anti–free trade position.

Moreover, the tabling of Bill c-130, the free trade implementing legislation, in the spring of 1988 marked the beginning of a strategic, cooperative relationship between the PCN and the Liberal and New Democratic parties. At this juncture, both parties pledged to use every means at their disposal to obstruct passage of the bill. The PCN served as a resource to the parties, neither of which was able to analyse fully the comprehensive deal. A great deal of information and research was exchanged, with the opposition parties utilizing material critical of the deal to justify the variety of procedural delays and obstruction tactics they applied to slow down the passage of the deal. These tactics continued throughout the summer, delaying the first and second readings and prompting the government to organize further hearings; all the while the issue dominated the national media.

In short, the divisions manifested themselves in greater opportunities for access and intervention into the parliamentary process by the PCN. For instance, the anti–free trade forces were provided with more access and influence on the Liberal Party than would otherwise have been the case had it had a stronger leader, been united in caucus with clear goals, and had been higher in the polls. The variety of delaying tactics employed in Parliament by the opposition kept the issue of free trade on the agenda and in the public eye throughout the long summer. The period during which Bill c-130 was being delayed coincided with both a gradual decline in public support for free trade and with an increase in the desire for an election to be held to settle the issue. An

TABLE 5
Regional support for free trade, June 1988 (in percentages)

	B.C.	Alta	Sask.	Man.	Ont.	Que.	Atlantic provinces
Favour	44	53	29	40	31	40	40
Oppose	39	32	49	45	48	33	40
Undecided	17	15	22	15	21	27	20

Source: Poll conducted by Environics Research Group for the *Globe and Mail*, 1 July 1988.

Environics poll in June, for example, showed that the FTA enjoyed majority support only in Alberta, British Columbia, and Quebec (Table 5).[25]

The Growing Salience of the Anti–Free Trade Vote

The highly volatile Canadian electorate complemented the supportive political context for the mobilization of the anti–free trade movement that was created by these divisions. In general terms, a situation where the electorate is unpredictable and volatile has been linked conceptually to one where the political actors are tolerant and receptive in their attitudes; when electoral cleavages are frozen, political actors are less likely to cooperate with insurgents. In the context of a volatile electorate or on the heels of a decisive election, the 'electoral needs' of political parties can lead them to become 'crucial interpreters of groups' preferences.'[26]

The Canadian electorate has been historically an unusually volatile one by the standards of most Western democracies.[27] This instability among voters has in some quarters been linked to the system of 'brokerage parties' in Canada, where parties have mediated between the many diverse and often conflicting regions and interests of the country through the process of coalition building. Scholars have in turn characterized the unpredictable Canadian electorate that flows from this brokering as one consisting of 'flexible partisans,' meaning that voters frequently shift from one party to another as a result of the effects of short-term issues or changing images of leaders.[28] The picture is thus one of a party system that is lacking in followers with principled positions and of an electorate that is frequently swayed by the issues of the day.

Never was this generalization more apt in describing the Canadian electorate than in the years following the 1984 federal election. This period was one of unprecedented electoral instability, when each of the three major federal political parties held the lead in public opinion polls at one time or another. This electoral volatility led many political actors to conclude that an electoral realignment was taking place, a perception potentially just as advantageous to the fortunes of the anti–free trade movement as an actual realignment. This perception was perhaps nowhere more pronounced than in the Liberal camp. Having been crushed in the previous election and hanging on as the official opposition in Parliament with only ten seats more than the NDP, the Liberals viewed the surge of the NDP in 1987 with great concern. The Liberal Party had always harboured the fear that Canada's party system might evolve in the same direction as Britain's, where the parties of the right and the left consolidated, leading to a marginalization of the Liberals. This helps partly to explain the Canadian Liberal Party's expertise at brokerage politics – of coalition building from the left-of-centre – which historically had kept the CCF and then the NDP on the fringe of power. Now, however, with the advance of the NDP it seemed that the Liberal Party's worst fears were about to materialize. Free trade was emerging as a political issue of left versus right, presaging an electoral contest between the NDP and the Tories.

This perception that a realignment was taking place, as well as the desperate electoral needs of the Liberal Party, created a significant political opportunity for the anti–free trade forces. The party's need to at least maintain its position as the official parliamentary opposition, to bolster the unpopular image of its leader, to take the free trade issue away from the NDP, and to distance itself from this major Tory policy initiative pushed it towards adopting a much stronger anti–free trade line. Tacitly, much of the Liberal caucus supported free trade, but in public their electoral needs meant that they could not afford to support this particular agreement.

A bold move in the Senate by Liberal leader John Turner in July 1988 displayed perhaps the most dramatic example of the Liberal Party's strategic articulation of the anti–free trade movement's concerns. With most public opinion polls continuing to fluctuate widely in the first half of 1988 and with Turner garnering the lowest rating of the three leaders, he ordered his colleagues in the Liberal-dominated Senate to hold up the implementing legislation for the FTA. Demanding that the prime minister call an election 'to let the people decide' was a tactic designed to bolster his image as a leader and to elevate free trade as the paramount issue in the upcoming election. Part desperation, part calculation, and part inspiration, Turner's strategy appeared to work. The Gallup poll, for example, reported that 52 per cent of Canadians supported Turner's manoeuvre, compared to only 30 per cent against it.[29] The tactic helped to marginalize the NDP and to heighten the image of the Liberal Party as the main political opponent to the deal.

Turner's strategy, in short, moulded the Liberal Party into the key 'political interpreter' of the anti–free trade movement's concerns. His move capped what had been a surprising degree of receptiveness and cooperation on the part of the Liberals to the PCN groups, and in fact it reaffirmed the Liberal Party's eagerness to embrace its cause. By articulating opposition to the FTA in terms of cultural and social issues, Turner packaged it in the PCN's vocabulary – he touched the cultural and social reservoir of anti–free trade opposition and became a lightning rod for it electorally. A kind of symbiotic relationship emerged: both Turner and the PCN benefited from the Liberal Party's new left-nationalist stance. Indeed, while the PCN gained a greater sense of legitimacy in its major cause and saw its paramount goal of a free trade election realized through the Senate's action, the strategy of the Liberal Party successfully marginalized the NDP from the debate through the election campaign.

The Positioning of Political Allies

In the end the strategic posturing and extensive cooperation that developed between partisan actors and the anti–free trade groups served to legitimize the cause. Tarrow has argued that 'insurgent groups do best when they succeed in gaining support from influential groups within the system.'[30] In some sense this is conceptually intuitive – the existence of sympathetic allies within the political system can help bolster a movement's demands and provide resources and support for the realization of its goals. In fact, the strategic political support provided to the PCN by its allies in the New Democratic and Liberal parties encompassed a wide range of activities, including membership in PCN-affiliated organizations, participation in conference workshops, and speaking out at rallies and assemblies. During its parliamentary campaign, the PCN found allies in prominent frontbenchers of both opposition parties, in the opposition trade critics, in the leaders of the opposition, and among senior Liberal members of the Senate. As a result of these ties, a great deal of strategy development, exchange of research, and consultation occurred between the anti–free trade groups and their political allies. These allies played an essential role in delaying and obstructing the FTA implementing legislation by forcing an election to be called over the issue and in facilitating what was then the paramount goal of the anti–free trade forces.

It was no surprise that the anti–free trade forces considered the NDP as an important political ally, as opposition to the FTA came naturally to its members. The NDP's record of struggling for progressive reform and the leanings of some of its key constituent support groups, most notably the CLC, meant that many anti–free trade groups took its support for granted. What was striking, however, was the level of support given to the movement by members of the Liberal Party. To a great extent this cooperation can be attributed to the general climate of electoral instability and to the party's considerable weakness, and so its trade stance can be equated to its dire electoral needs. Nonetheless, it was the Liberal Party and the actions of its leader, John Turner, that translated best the policy demands of the anti–free trade forces in Parliament. Reflecting the belief held by many activists, John Trent has stated: 'Its safe to say that, once the Liberals and Turner did move against free trade, the Liberal Party became an interpreter of the movement's aims. Once they moved, Turner forced the election by using the Senate to block the deal – and these were things that we just couldn't do.'[31]

The implications of the existence of political allies for the anti–free trade movement are thus profound. While the PCN successfully heightened the Canadian public's awareness about the FTA through its protest campaign, it still ultimately relied on the support of allies within the parliamentary process to force an election. Moreover, these links between the party and the movement gave the latter a greater appearance of legitimacy to a Canadian public unaccustomed and uncomfortable with large-scale protest activities. This is not to suggest that the line between the anti–free trade movement and the party system was blurred. The PCN's national organizational infrastructure, equipped with its own popular-sector resources, propelled an organized, strategic, national protest campaign. Yet the anti–free trade movement and the political process were deeply intertwined and it would be a mistake to overstate the extraparliamentary nature and political marginalization of the movement.

Collectively Conscious of Parliamentary Openings

Structural conditions, while they are undoubtedly crucial to collective action, must also be subjectively viewed as favourable for their full mobilizing potential to be realized. Certainly, developments in the organizational strategy of the popular sector and a string of political opportunities played a highly supportive role in the unfolding national protest campaign against the FTA. Changes in both of these factors facilitated the PCN in grasping collective control over the resources needed for education and protest over the FTA. Yet two aspects of the subjective side to the ongoing anti-FTA collective action played a facilitative role during the parliamentary stage as well: the perceptions of the participants of shifts in the political process (and the awareness that these shifts presented opportunities for action) and the continually growing sense of political efficacy among activists, which provided them with the confidence and solidarity needed to continue the campaign.

Anti–free trade activists, in fact, recognized that opportunities existed in the increasingly unsettled political environment for furthering the movement's goals. For example, the PCN had a strategy for approaching the parliamentary process that implicitly recognized the vulnerability of the political establishment to its protests. At the PCN's first National Assembly in October 1987, when it first drew up the action strategy plans for its national campaign, activists debated how to develop a strategy that would force an election to be held on free trade. An awareness of the potentially supportive role that could be played by the political process was evident in the comments made by a member of the CLC who was also a member of the strategy committee:

the Parliamentary process can assist us, if there is such public outcry that the opposition will create an impasse by obstructing the business of the House. We need to be aware of the complementary role which can be played by an extra-parliamentary movement such as our own. Parliament needs public opinion, needs public actions, if it is going to take the actions we want.[32]

Anti–free trade activists continued to echo sentiments such as these throughout the year-long protest campaign. In addition to its educational and consciousness-raising purposes, the campaign attempted to strengthen the stances of the opposition parties, especially of those Liberal and NDP party members that were sympathetic to the movement's cause. As an incentive to them to join their side, activists framed the vast societal network of opposition to the FTA in terms of a potential pool of votes. As one NAC activist recounted, 'We just went for every single opportunity we saw to intervene in this debate, using the parliamentary process, while maintaining our extraparliamentary presence.'[33]

A strong sense of the political efficacy of their strategy also played a key role in sustaining anti–free trade collective action and protest. In particular, strong solidarity networks helped sustain the cohesion of the movement and the optimism of the participants. Personal networks, cultivated over years of grass-roots activism on the left, provided a level of trust and support conducive to the long struggle against the FTA. The PCN had been built in part on layers of such solidarity networks, where time and experience had given activists the confidence needed to struggle against the FTA at the grass-roots level.

Early in the protest campaign, a PCN strategy document exhibited this confidence at the grass roots when it spelled out how the PCN would 'win for Canada.' Noting that the FTA would be fought at the community level – in the territory of PCN-affiliated groups – the document noted:

the fight has only just begun and it's a fight which will be waged on our ground. Coalitions are springing to life across the country. A national movement is awakening. A movement which will bring this brief and dark chapter of Canadian history to an end in the next federal election by defeating Mulroney's deal and winning for Canada.[34]

The rapid spread of the PCN, as well as the success of the protest-campaign activities, bolstered the sense of the political efficacy of the grass roots. The success of the National Day of Action and of the lobbying campaign, for example, demonstrated to those involved that a real opposition to the FTA existed across Canada. Thus, while these actions presented the public with symbols of nationwide solidarity against the deal, they also reinforced morale within the network. Activists felt more confident that if the struggle for the FTA was to be waged at the community level they had the experience to convince the Canadian public that the FTA was a bad deal for Canada.

Evidence drawn from interviews and strategy documents also strongly suggests that a correlation existed between the growing sense in the political efficacy of the movement and the noticeable shift in public opposition against the FTA. By late summer 1987 polls showing a marked decline in public support for free trade had begun to accumulate. An August 1987 poll prepared by the national polling firm Angus Reid Associates for the PCN revealed that for the first time since January 1986 more Canadians opposed free trade than supported it.[35] With 42 per cent in support and 44 per cent in opposition, this poll showed a 15 per cent drop in support and a 12 per cent rise in opposition over the previous six months. Support for the FTA had declined in every region, with Ontario registering the largest opposition, with only 35 per cent in support and 49 per cent opposed.

This shift in public opinion towards a growing opposition to the FTA and a desire to see an election called before its implementation, greatly raised the sense among activists that their actions were making a difference in turning public opinion against the deal. Reporting on the results of such polls became routine at PCN strategy meetings, with the strategists using them as a means to strengthen the resolve of the participants in the movement. The significance rests not in whether there existed a direct correlation between the coalition-building and protest activities of the PCN and the decline in public support for the free trade initiative, because although no survey directly investigated the Canadian public's views on the PCN and its activities the movement had sensitized the public and political parties through its tactics in its parliamentary campaign. Instead, PCN activists perceived that a connection existed between their protest activities and the decline in public support for the FTA. This sense of political efficacy, strengthened by the perception that the PCN's efforts were making a difference in the struggle for Canadian public opinion, further subjectively contributed towards the anti-FTA mobilization efforts.

Summary

This chapter has demonstrated that three important developments sustained the dynamic for mobilization. First, the consolidation of the many anti–free trade groups into the Pro-Canada Network structure, as well as the meetings of the

PCN National Assemblies, represented crucial organizational developments. The new national infrastructure greatly facilitated the pooling of resources from the various popular-sector groups into an organized campaign of anti-FTA protest. The work of the PCN's strategy, communication, and research and analysis committees aided in the coordination of the major events of national protest during the campaign. This infrastructure represented a critical organizational shift, overcoming a history of sectoral fragmentation in Canadian social movements, and unifying a diverse network of groups and coalitions against the FTA.

Second, as the Canadian political establishment became increasingly vulnerable a series of political opportunities provided the PCN with exceptional access to the parliamentary process. The divisions in Parliament and the electoral instability that marked this vulnerability reduced the discrepancy between the PCN and the two opposition parties as to the amount of power they wielded. At times this levelling even created a reversal of roles, with the opposition parties responding to, and even depending on, the PCN's credible research and analysis capabilities which provided nationwide sectoral critiques of the FTA. The political opportunities enhanced the leverage and bargaining position of the PCN, as was shown by the alliances and cooperative relationships that were forged between the PCN and the opposition parties. As a result, the PCN's mobilization process harnessed the resources of the political establishment, bringing greater credibility and immediacy to its calls for a general election to decide the fate of the agreement.

Finally, important subjective components of the mobilization process played a supportive role in the campaign of protest. Activists perceived that favourable political conditions existed that could facilitate their campaign and they devised strategies around political opportunities to maximize their usefulness. In addition, a strong sense of political efficacy, furnished by an embedded link of interpersonal networks as well as by a positive interpretation of the polls, gave activists the momentum needed to sustain the campaign through the uncertainties of the parliamentary process. The block of Bill c-130 in the Senate and ultimately the election that was forced only heightened this sense of efficacy, which activists then carried with high expectations and momentum into the election campaign.

5

The Constraints of Electoral Politics

Theorists of social movements have been quick to explain the generation of insurgency but they have had less to say about the factors behind the decline and demobilization of movements.[1] Scholars working in the political-process mould have responded to this weakness in the literature by developing a holistic model of the emergence, mobilization, and decline of movements. This chapter continues in this direction by providing an account of the decline and fracturing of the anti–free trade movement during the height of the 1988 federal election campaign.

Initially, favourable political opportunities continued to sustain the movement during the early part of the fall 1988 campaign. The early period of the campaign proceeded in a political environment that continued to be supportive of the activity and mobilization of the movement. In particular, the success of Liberal Party leader John Turner in the leadership debates, the rise in public uncertainty and even opposition over the free trade issue, and the increased intervention in the debate by the public turned the election campaign into a veritable referendum on free trade. The anti–free trade movement successfully exploited this context of political and public vulnerability over the free trade issue by creating and sustaining new opportunities for public mobilization and education while keeping the issue at the top of the agenda.

However, the mobilizing potential of the political-opportunity structure weakened as the campaign progressed. Specifically, three processes within the political environment contributed to the demobilization of the movement and to the overall climate of contracting political opportunity: the successful counter-mobilization of pro–free trade organizations, the introduction of the perennial Canadian 'national question' in the free trade debate and the electoral campaign, and the political constraints of electoralism.

A Proactive Electoral Strategy

By the time of Prime Minister Mulroney's call on 1 October for an election on 21 November the anti–free trade movement had emerged as an organized and increasingly independent force, one able to shape to a great degree its strategy and ongoing organizational development. To be sure, the same key mix of factors – organizational strength, internal resources, and available political opportunities – continued to play an important role in underpinning the movement's activities. Yet, at least during the first month of the election campaign, the movement's development and activities can no longer be analysed simply as the outcome of a single causal chain. Rather, the anti–free trade forces began to influence proactively the political environment; they were no longer simply exploiting available opportunities provided by external political actors but directly creating and influencing them through strategy and action. Consistent with the model of movement development sketched out by the political-process model, therefore, the 'opportunities for insurgency [were] no longer independent of the actions of insurgent groups. Now the structure of political alignments [shifted] in response to movement activity, even as those shifts [shaped] the prospects for future insurgency.'[2]

The anti–free trade movement influenced the broader socio-political environment and subsequently created new opportunities for itself by carrying out a specific set of tactics during the campaign. In fact, the call for an election saw a shift in strategy for the PCN and its affiliated organizations. With its parliamentary goals largely achieved – the Canadian public had generally become sensitized to the PCN's criticisms of the deal, the free trade bill had been successfully delayed in Parliament, and an election had finally been called implicitly to settle the issue – the PCN implemented a new electoral strategy designed to educate further the Canadian public and to mobilize it to vote against the Progressive Conservatives and, in doing so, the free trade deal.

Specifically, the PCN in concert with the provincial and national organizations hammered out a six-point plan of action to attack the FTA and the Tories. Developed during the PCN's National Assembly in Montreal in August 1988, these tactics included the development of a booklet of cartoons about the deal, the distribution of election kits to Liberal and NDP candidates, cross-country briefings on the deal for candidates, visible protest activities such as lawn signs and the distribution of buttons and T-shirts against the deal, and a televised debate between anti–free trade activists and supporters of the deal.

The comic book became the movement's most successful educative piece against the deal. Designed and written by the Canadian playwright, Rick Salutin and the artist Terry Mosher (Aislin), and entitled *What's the Big Deal?*, it contained a series of questions and conversations between two Canadians over the implications of free trade for Canada.[3] Each page featured cartoons and discussions critical of the deal, with the cover depicting Prime Minister Brian Mulroney turning green under a black cloud marked 'Acid Rain' and asking: 'And Why Shouldn't We Trust the Americans on Free Trade?' Beginning on 11 October the PCN distributed over 2.2 million copies to the majority of the metropolitan areas in English Canada.[4] The text and the captions for the cartoons were also translated for distribution in French-language newspapers in Quebec. Costing roughly $700,000 to produce and distribute, the booklet was designed as a popular counterweight to the Progressive Conservative government's $30 million campaign to promote the deal.

In fact, the booklet marked a significant popular educational success for the movement and it was widely cited for its accessibility and common-sense approach to the debate. Canadians reported that its question-and-answer dialogue was much easier to digest than many of the technical pamphlets published for and against the deal.[5] As Salutin remarked at the time, 'the cartoon booklet put out by the coalitions is practically the only item which is accessible to the people below university reading levels – *What's the Big Deal?* tests at grade 7 or 8.'[6] The booklet filled a critical gap in the knowledge many Canadians held about the trade deal, prompting the *Globe and Mail* to write that the 'widely circulated pamphlet against the agreement by the Pro-Canada Network has had a major impact on voter impressions of the deal.'[7] Candidates for the opposition parties largely found the booklet complementary to their campaign themes, while Progressive Conservative candidates grudgingly admitted its effectiveness. 'The pamphlet did affect things,' said Conservative MP Paul McCrossan, who was running in the new Scarborough-Agincourt riding in suburban Toronto. 'I guess it did shake some people.'[8]

The election kits sponsored by the PCN also represented a tactic that, like the booklet, effectively threw the PCN's full weight into the electoral campaign. Organizations affiliated to it, such as the CLC and NAC, had already distributed their own kits to their members across Canada. The PCN election kits also went to Liberal and NDP candidates across the country. The kits contained an extensive collection of pamphlets, booklets, and newspapers on free trade produced by over thirty popular organizations opposed to the deal. Candidates used the kit extensively as a resource to oppose the deal on an issue by issue basis. The kits also provided a list of resource persons (names and telephone numbers of specialists on all aspects of the deal from every region of the country), fact sheets designed to be photocopied and distributed door-to-door by canvassers and at public meetings, and an election primer that discussed basic strategies for effectively highlighting the free trade issue.

The result, and of significance for the effect it would have on the structure of political alignments, was a broad groundswell of uncertainty and opposition that emerged within the Canadian public, complementing the PCN's intervention in the campaign. In fact, by October 1988 the free trade issue had acquired an unusually high profile in the public debate. The socio-political environment became electrified by the heightened discussion, uncertainty, and criticism of the FTA. Beginning with the call for an election, newspapers printed debates every day over the merits of the deal for Canada's future and captured the frenzy that gripped the country at the time. Owing to the sheer numbers of correspondents, the *Globe and Mail*, the self-styled 'national newspaper' of Canada, resorted to reserving space for both pro– and anti–free trade partisans in its letters to the editor section in the weeks leading up to the election.

One particularly noteworthy public intervention in the debate and one that gained national attention was by Marjorie Bowker, a former Alberta Provincial Court judge, who sparked an uproar with her simple but sharp fifty-eight-page critique of the deal.[9] Initially mimeographed from a home-typed essay, it rapidly evolved by late October into a hotly demanded book, *On Guard for Thee*, with over 50,000 copies in print.[10] Picked up by the major news media across the country, her critique was lambasted by politicians, television commentators, and most notably by the minister of international trade. Yet it remained, like the PCN's comic book, one of the more accessible additions to the debate. Roy MacGregor, in the *Ottawa Citizen*, responded to her critique by saying, 'Little did I know when I finished this column [on the essay] that the *Citizen* would receive 1000 calls, 300 of which got through to me. It meant I couldn't even write a column for two days. You have touched a national nerve, Madam Justice.'[11] Marjorie Nichols's column for 6 September in the *Ottawa Citizen* further reiterated the simple appeal of Bowker's critique:

She has taken this complicated document and reduced it to a layman's level with clarity of language to make any ink-stained wretch drool. Bowker, with true judicial impartially declares her personal interest. It is, simply, to spread enlightenment ... I think that Marjorie Bowker is what ordinary Canadians have been looking for: an impartial source who can assist them in making one of the most important decisions of their voting lives.[12]

The reflections of participants in this debate further illustrate the increasingly frenzied context surrounding the free trade debate. A member of the COC recounted: 'In the 1988 election campaign period free trade had become the issue – it's hard to describe – my parents tell me that the war was like that. I mean it was the same kind of gripping atmosphere, where free trade was all that anybody was talking about, and it literally became the single, passionate issue in the election campaign.'[13] A Liberal Party strategist put a particularly political gloss on her description of this environment, remarking that:

traditionally we Canadians have been seen as spectators, not gladiators, with an elitist political culture. But what was extraordinary about the free trade debate was the huge degree to which ordinary Canadians were willing to mobilize. We usually don't have a strong habit of belonging and joining. But the debate demonstrated that there was indeed a reservoir of activism in our social and political culture that was tapped into.[14]

The movement of public opinion against the deal gave further weight to anti–free trade activities. On 1 October a poll pointed to another Progressive Conservative parliamentary majority and a mandate for implementing the free trade deal. Yet, through the month of October, opinion in support for the FTA slowly but consistently declined, even before the leaders' debates at the end of October that would further dampen support for the Tories. Indeed, the results of the 1988 Canadian National Election Study suggest that support for the deal was declining before the debates.[15] For example, Table 6 illustrates the movement of opinion on the FTA by period. It shows that support for free trade among the respondents to the study dropped from 43.2 per cent during the week of 4 to 14 October to 32.7 per cent in the week of 26 October to 6 November while opposition to the free trade agreement rose from 34 per cent to 46.6 per cent in the same period. The Gallup poll of 20–22 October also revealed public opposition to the FTA had risen to 42 per cent, with support dropping to 34 per cent.[16] Further evidence taken from other surveys during this time indicates increasing public uncertainty about the deal.[17]

TABLE 6
Opinion on the Free Trade Agreement (in percentages)

	Support FTA	Neither Support nor Oppose FTA	Oppose FTA
4–14 October	43.2	22.9	34.0
15–25 October	38.8	21.2	40.0
26 October–6 November	32.7	20.7	46.6
7–13 November	37.9	16.4	45.7
14–20 November	38.4	16.5	45.1

Source: Richard Johnston et al., 'Free Trade and the Dynamics of the 1988 Canadian Election,' paper prepared for the American Political Science Association annual meeting, Atlanta, Georgia, 31 August–3 September 1989.

Significantly, by October 1988 the anti–free trade movement had evolved into something more than the sum of its organizations, strategies, and protest activities. In the frenzied atmosphere the movement had become akin to 'a commotion, a stirring among the people, an unrest, a collective attempt to reach a visualized goal.'[18] All activities and discourse – whether inside or outside political institutions, organized and unorganized, in the editorial pages of the Toronto *Globe and Mail*, or in private discussions on subways and buses and over coffee – hinted at the rising tide of opposition to the deal and fell under the broad tide of uncertainty and unrest rising against the free trade deal.

From all appearances, then, a rapidly growing, expanding, and broad-based opposition had formed in Canada against the deal. A shift in public opinion now complemented the PCN-led anti–free trade movement itself and was grabbing the attention of the poll-conscious opposition parties. The actions of the movement were now serving to shape the external political environment and were shifting the existing structure of political alignments. As one PCN activist reflected:

through our actions we were beginning to have an impact on public opinion, changing public opinion, and mobilizing people – through demonstrations and such – and political parties couldn't ignore that. So we began to have an ability to shape public opinion and to some sense add leadership that could be delivered to political parties. This leadership was key, as I don't think that they would have gone out there and taken the strong stand that they did if we hadn't already gone out there. They weren't going to go out there and try and shape public opinion against the deal. It was only after they saw that the tide was beginning to seriously shift because of our work against the deal that they decided, ah!, opposition to free trade would be politically expedient.[19]

A situation of extensive fluidity and interplay had developed, which was characterized also by expanding mutual political opportunity. The dichotomy between extraparliamentary and parliamentary politics had temporarily ended. The movement's relationships with political parties shifted: it was no longer simply pressuring opposition political parties but providing information and resources to them. Its dependence on political parties lifted, the comic book and the election kits having created political opportunities for it. As the coordinator of the booklet recounted, 'the comic book shifted the balance, we no longer had to depend on the political parties, especially the NDP – the comic book and election kits created political opportunities for us.'[20] The movement no longer simply exploited existing opportunities, it created new ones for itself through its impact on the unsteady structure of political alignments.

In fact, the movement's actions and the outcomes of those actions reverberated with considerable impact within the Liberal Party apparatus at both the federal and the provincial levels. Representatives of the PCN briefed the Liberal Party caucus on several occasions[21] and the PCN anti–free trade election kits were made available to every candidate. Reflecting on this fluid relationship, the PCN's political action coordinator, Peter Bleyer, remarked that 'the Liberals maintained a very positive relationship with the PCN – they showed their sophistication and their strong sense and ability in dealing with the myriad of oppositional groups.'[22] A leading Liberal Party MP reciprocated, saying that 'electorally, the PCN were good people to have a relationship with, especially with the public movement against free trade during the election campaign.'[23] Another Liberal campaign strategist captured this context of shared political opportunity: 'the extent to which we could broaden our base made sense, so we cooperated with the PCN as much as possible. What they offered us was a vehicle for reaching people we couldn't have reached otherwise – they were pushing our position, we were pushing theirs.'[24]

This context of mutually reinforcing political opportunity arose out of the Liberal Party's electoral and resource needs. The activities and growing influence of the anti–free trade movement directly affected the Liberals – the movement's overarching aims fit the party's 'electoral needs' – and the party's decision to make opposition to the free trade deal the centrepiece of its electoral campaign emerged from the impact that the movement was having on the broader political environment. The movement was in fact creating political opportunities for the Liberal Party; the anti–free trade protest activities, the dramatically heightened and ubiquitous public debate, and the growing movement in public opinion against the deal provided the Liberal Party with the ammunition for mounting a full-fledged electoral drive against free trade. At the same time, the 'payoff' for the movement – where the Liberal Party most dramatically threw its weight behind the anti–free trade cause – occurred during the now famous nationally televised leaders' debates.

The debates and their impact on public opinion polls have been analysed and debated in great detail.[25] One key theme that emerges from these studies is the performance of Liberal Party leader John Turner in the debates as the crucial factor behind the unprecedented swing in the public opinion polls, in this case at the expense of the Progressive Conservative Party and of the free trade deal. It can certainly be argued as well that the PCN, its affiliated national and provincial organizations, and the movement in public opinion against the deal constituted a much more complex set of causal mechanisms behind the declining fortunes of the FTA in the period leading up to the debates.[26]

The debates took place in late October. Free trade was not a major issue during the first debate, conducted in French, and it did little to change the fortunes of the still sagging Liberal Party. The debate in English held on 25 October, however, provided Turner with an opportunity to make his case on the free trade issue. In this nationally televised debate, Turner, in the midst of a heated, finger-pointing argument with the prime minister, articulated in only a few moments the message that the anti–free trade forces had been popularizing for at least the preceding three years:

I happen to believe you've sold us out ... we have built a country, East and West and North, on an infrastructure that resisted the continental pressure of the United States. For 120 years we've done it, and with one stroke of the pen you've reversed that, thrown us into the north-south pull of the United States. And that will reduce us, I'm sure, to an economic colony of the United States, because when the economic levers go, the political independence is sure to follow.'

The analysis by electoral behaviour specialist Lawrence LeDuc of the impact of Turner's performance merits citation:

Turner's success in the debates had several immediate effects. It eclipsed the possibility that the NDP might supplant the Liberals as the principal opposition party, and effectively restored the campaign to a Liberal-Conservative contest. It threw the smooth-running Conservative campaign off stride, and created a new atmosphere of political uncertainty. But most importantly, it turned the remaining four weeks of the campaign into a debate on free trade.[27]

The analysis by Blais and Boyer of the impact of the televised debates also indicates that they 'had a substantial and enduring impact on the vote,' particularly 'in the contest for second place between the Liberals and the NDP.'[28]
    The debates, in fact, did help mould the last few weeks of the election campaign into a referendum on free trade. Every opinion poll taken in the week following the debates revealed that Turner's outburst had tapped into all of the concerns and uncertainty that had been building up over the preceding years over the free trade deal. The Gallup poll results of 7 November revealed the largest single shift ever recorded by Gallup in Canada.[29] Moreover, the decline in support for the FTA in the wake of the debate was just as striking. Another Gallup poll, released on 8 November, shows that in Canada as a whole opposition to the deal stood at 50 per cent of those polled, with support having plummeted to 26 per cent.[30] Still another sampling of the country by province

or region carried out from 3 to 8 November by the polling firm Environics for the *Globe and Mail* revealed broad opposition to the accord. Table 7 shows that in the Atlantic provinces and in four of the other six provinces the opposition held sway, with only the provinces of Alberta and Quebec remaining in support of the accord.

Thus, the Liberal Party's strident anti–free trade stance that was dramatically articulated in the English-language debate represented a crucial political opportunity for the movement. It also seemed to vindicate the efforts undertaken by the movement over the past several years to highlight the perceived dangers of the FTA. As one anti–free trade activist argued:

The fact that the free trade issue became the pivotal issue of the debate was proof that we had done our job – that debate would never have taken the turn it did if it wasn't for us, and free trade wouldn't have been the issue if we hadn't made it public. We tilled the ground, we made the issue.[31]

The Liberal Party and its leader, John Turner, had become the critical political party that interpreted the anti–free trade movement's efforts, thereby injecting valuable legitimacy and prestige into the movement's ongoing mobilization efforts. By the first week of November, with the polls showing a dramatic gain in support for the Liberal Party at the expense of the Progressive Conservative Party and a further decline in support for the FTA, the survival of the deal actually seemed to be in doubt. In fact, it is reasonable to assume that if an election had been held a week after the English-language debate, the Liberals very well might have won, with the Tories at most remaining as a minority government, which would have doomed the free trade deal.

TABLE 7
Regional support for the Free Trade Agreement, 3–8 November 1988 (in percentages)

	National	Atlantic provinces	Que.	Ont.	Man.	Sask.	Alta	B.C.
Favour	39	38	47	32	38	39	56	31
Oppose	51	45	42	60	48	58	32	59
Undecided	11	17	11	8	14	13	12	10

Source: Poll conducted by Environics Research Group for the *Globe and Mail*, 3–8 Nov. 1988.

Yet, despite the evident success of the movement, the remarkable activities of October 1988 represented the high water mark in terms of the efforts of the anti–free trade movement and of its impact. Just when the movement had been most effective in the political arena on public opinion and party alignments and had encouraged the Liberal Party and its leader to adopt with confidence a firm anti–free trade electoral stance, the movement's impact would soon have, paradoxically, a negative effect on the prospects for continued insurgency in the period remaining before the election. Although expanding political opportunities and cross-sectoral organizational consensus and strength had, according to polls, propelled the movement tantalizingly close to a defeat of the Conservatives and free trade in the election, a rapid and complex interplay of organizational division, counter-mobilization, and closing political opportunities rebuffed the movement and its goals in the final four weeks of the campaign.

A Reactive Counter-Mobilization

What would turn out to be a long, gradual decline and demobilization of the anti–free trade movement began as a result of significant instances of counter-mobilization on the part of pro–free trade forces. Whether viewed from the perspective of McAdam's 'social control response' to insurgency or from Klandermans's interpretation of 'constraint systems' of the multi-organizational fields of movements, the conceptual significance behind such counter-mobilization remains consistent. Social movements face serious barriers to continued insurgency when the actors whose interests are threatened by the goals and activities of a movement respond by significantly constraining the availability of resources and political opportunities.

The decline of insurgency is influenced by a complex interplay of factors. These include the significant contraction of political opportunities, the decline of organizational strength within a movement, the weakening in group solidarity and consciousness needed for continued mobilization, and the increased repression by opponents of a movement.[32] According to McAdam the key to the extent such factors come into play to disrupt insurgent momentum is the degree to which a movement represents a threat to the realization of the interests of other actors in the external political environment.[33] Meyer and Staggenborg concur, adding that a movement can expect a strong counter-mobilization from affected interests, which in turn may significantly constrain the former's ability to take advantage of favourable political opportunities.[34]

Specifically, if interests consider themselves as threatened by a movement's goals, then a countermovement may emerge to constrain the resources and political opportunities previously fuelling the mobilization of a movement. Such countermovements, Klandermans adds,

try to deprive a social movement organization of resources and political opportunities by increasing the costs of participation in the social movement, by undermining its organizational strength, declaring specific tactics illegal, abolishing specific opportunities, criminalizing the organization, offering symbolic concessions, and campaigning to turn the public against the social movement.[35]

A reaction occurred with dramatic speed against the anti–free trade movement in the middle of the federal election campaign.

The Pro–Free Trade Response

The bulk of the analysis has so far supported the political-process contention that most movements confront a political establishment that is divided in its reaction to the challenge posed by the insurgency.[36] Certainly, divisions at the level of the political parties, of Parliament, and of free trade negotiating teams strongly contributed to the sustained mobilization of the anti–free trade movement. During this time, however, one part of the political establishment remained firmly committed to the passage of a free trade agreement between Canada and the United States, Canada's business community.[37] Yet it did not interpret the efforts and results of the anti–free trade movement as serious enough to warrant a major counter-mobilization to halt the movement's goals until midway through the election campaign.[38] To be sure, the business community and its allies federally and provincially in the Progressive Conservative Party had engineered a substantive pro–free trade media campaign that was spearheaded by the emergence of the pro–free trade lobby group, the Canadian Alliance for Trade and Job Opportunities.[39] Yet, at least until the aftermath of the leaders' debates, when the political fortunes of both the Tories and the FTA took a considerable turn for the worse, the business community had not felt its interests so threatened as to warrant a direct and open intervention in the election campaign.

This concerned but restrained stance dramatically changed in the aftermath of the PCN's comic book and the leaders' debates. With every poll forecasting the defeat of the Tories and the deal in four weeks, the business community mobilized a major counter-response designed to turn back the efforts of the anti–free trade forces and to ensure the election of the Tories. Their response was immediate after the debates. On 3 November, as polls continued to return the news about the declining support for the Tories and the agreement, CATJO, backed principally by the BCNI, began an unprecedented public campaign to support the free trade stand of the Tories. Included among the business community's tactics was CATJO's own four-page cartoon booklet entitled 'Straight Talk on Free Trade,' five million copies of which were placed in forty-two daily newspapers, two weeklies, and one major national magazine across Canada beginning on 3 November.[40] An obvious counter-response to the PCN's booklet, CATJO's was distributed twice during the last three weeks of the campaign. Again, the pro–free trade counter-response is consistent with the proposition of Meyer and Staggenborg, which argues that movements may encourage counter-mobilizations by interests that are threatened when the movements are effective in creating or exploiting events.[41] Certainly, the anti-FTA forces had successfully exploited the Canadian public's uncertainty over free trade with the United States for some time.

In addition to the advertising campaign, the business community began to lobby companies and their employees to support the deal. The American business daily, the *Wall Street Journal*, reported on the remarkable events north of the border and described the 'aggressiveness' of Canadian businessmen, who by 'taking politics to the shop floor' risked 'alienating unions or being accused of meddling in the democratic process.'[42] Other business activities included a request by the CMA in letters to its 3,000 member companies to lobby its workers about the merits of the deal, and letters to its 170,000 member businesses urging them to 'go out there and shake the trees for free trade.'[43]

Some supporters of the pact argued that the intervention by business merely levelled the playing field and evened the odds in the free trade debate. President Roger Howel of the Canadian Chamber of Commerce, for example, argued in letters to his members that in the absence of an intervention, 'our silence is their greatest strength.'[44] Yet, in addition to the impressions of those involved in both sides of the debate and the struggle for public opinion, studies of this third-party advertising and of its impact on the election campaign and its outcome strongly suggest that the business community's countermovement seriously constrained the resources and structure of political opportunities for the anti–free trade movement.

A post-election study that was commissioned by the research program of the Royal Commission on Electoral Reform and Party Financing and that was prompted in part to review the impact of the unprecedented monetary and advertising intervention by third parties during the 1988 federal election, reveals that the business community and its pro–free trade provincial and political allies heavily outspent the anti–free trade forces on advertising (see Table 8).[45]

TABLE 8
Election advertising expenditures by third parties during the election period, 1988

Canadian Alliance for Trade and Job Opportunities	$2,307,650
National Citizens' Coalition	150,000
Alberta Government	727,000
Pro-Canada Network	752,247
Campaign Life	75,000
Other (pro–free trade, anti–free trade, and unrelated issues)	717,187
Total	4,729,104

Source: Janet Hiebert, 'Interest Groups and the Canadian Federal Elections,' in F. Leslie Seidle, ed., *Interest Groups and Elections in Canada* (Ottawa: Ministry of Supply and Services Canada 1991), 20.

More dramatic for the impact it had on curtailing the influence of the anti–free trade movement was the relationship between third-party advertising and the spending of the three main political parties at the national level. Table 9 shows that pro–free trade groups spent 77 cents for every dollar of the Conservative Party advertising budget, while anti–free trade forces spent only 13 cents for every dollar spent by the opposition Liberals and NDP. The royal commission study concluded that this discrepancy in spending 'undermined principles of fairness and equity'[46] in the 1988 election to the benefit of the Progressive Conservative Party and its pro–free trade allies.

TABLE 9
Free trade advertising expenditures as a proportion of party advertising during the 1988 election

Amount of pro–free trade advertising for every $1.00 of Progressive Conservative Party advertising	0.77
Amount of anti–free trade advertising for every $1.00 of Liberal Party advertising	0.23
Amount of anti–free trade advertising for every $1.00 of NDP advertising	0.28
Amount of anti–free trade advertising for every $1.00 of Liberal and NDP advertising	0.13

Source: Hiebert, 'Interest Groups and the Canadian Federal Elections,' 23.

The conclusions of the study clearly suggest that the structure of political opportunities shifted drastically for the worse for the anti–free trade movement during the latter half of the election campaign. On one level, the political opportunities for anti–free trade advertising were severely constrained and diluted by the overwhelming advertising blitz of the pro–free trade groups. Moreover, the wide discrepancy in expenditures as a proportion of national party advertising strongly aided, as the study for the royal commission concluded, the Conservative Party at the expense of the Liberals and the NDP. Subsequent studies suggest that the impact on voters intentions may, in fact, have been much higher.[47] For the anti–free trade movement, then, the discrepancy in spending had the effect of severely curtailing its opportunities for spreading its message, especially where the movement had previously exploited its cooperative relationships with the Liberal Party and the NDP to further its cause. The pro–free trade advertising message dramatically limited the effectiveness of the Liberals and the NDP, both of which had served so usefully as the prominent political interpreters of the movement's goals.

This climate of constraining political opportunity convinced many anti–free trade activists that the movement may have reached the peak of its effectiveness by the end of October. In fact, while the comic book by Rick Salutin and Terry Mosher represented a peak, it was, in conjunction with the effects of the leaders' debates, also the high point of the campaign. As one church activist reflected, 'the comic book represented our crowning glory, but it was also our furthest point of advance.'[48] The movement, and specifically the PCN, lacked the funds to respond to the effective pro–free trade advertising campaign. With its resources exhausted, the movement was severely constrained in its ability to match the media and propaganda campaign of the pro–free trade forces.[49] The comic book represented 'the last major event for the coalition,' concurred another activist; 'when the business community reacted so vigorously, we just didn't have any counterpunch left after that.'[50]

The context of constrained resources contributed towards a gradual breakdown in those shared cognitions that had supported the mobilization of the anti–free trade movement in the election campaign. The movement's longstanding sense of political efficacy quickly evaporated in the face of the contracting structure of political opportunities. Both the weakening of the Liberal and NDP campaigns and the new shift in public opinion in favour of the Progressive Conservative Party contributed to the declining optimism and a growing feeling of impotence. The sense of political efficacy that had bolstered and sustained the movement throughout its coalition-building period, during its parliamentary protest campaign, and well into the election campaign thus gradually weakened in the unsupportive political environment. This dynamic contributed in a reciprocally negative way to a further weakening and demobilization of the movement.

Electoralism and Movement Decline

In addition to the impact of the business counter-response, another factor that severely hampered the anti–free trade movement during the election campaign was the emergence of rifts and conflicts between groups affiliated to the movement and around relationships between the movement and political parties. Specifically, the pressures and demands of electoral politics drove a wedge between the PCN and both its affiliated groups and the federal NDP. While the PCN remained firmly committed to defeating the agreement in the 1988 election, the NDP distanced itself from the free trade issue during the crucial final weeks of the campaign. As a result, the relationship between the PCN and the NDP became estranged, and in the process the organizational solidarity of the anti–free trade movement was significantly weakened, further reducing the political opportunities for activity and mobilization.

Three factors exacerbated conditions leading to the estrangement. The first revolved around the normal tensions between political parties jockeying for advantage during any electoral campaign. While the PCN attempted to maintain a non-partisan stance, the strong and surprisingly cooperative relationship that had built up between the PCN and the Liberal Party infuriated many within the NDP who felt not just confused but more frequently betrayed. Members of the NDP were taken aback by the relationship between the PCN and the Liberal Party, and somewhat suspicious as to how it would evolve during the campaign period. As a result, the federal NDP became much less responsive to the overtures of the PCN during the later part of the campaign, and it was hesitant to rely on the same strategic materials and advice that the PCN provided to the Liberal Party. As the political action coordinator of the PCN recounted, 'there were some astounding developments with the NDP during the election campaign. Their federal campaign strategy team was much less responsive to our overtures than the Liberals.'[51]

The sentiments of a member of the Prince Edward Island PCN captured the flavour of the country-wide experiences shared by PCN activists and the federal NDP:

we took seriously the Pro-Canada Network's national mandate to brief the political parties ... and in fact, the four Liberal candidates who were briefed were very aggressive; they were on the offensive against free trade all during their campaign. The Liberal Party also bought 'No, eh' buttons from us. They bought a number of cartoon booklets for their rallies and pushed very hard to have the cartoon booklet in the *Summerside Journal Pioneer*. So there's a lot of activity there and commitment by the Liberals, which unfortunately, we are not getting in a similar way from the NDP.[52]

The second factor that contributed to the rift between the movement and the NDP was the sense of rivalry that was perceived to be developing between the two camps.[53] From its emergence as a radical agrarian force in the 1930s to its modern appearance in the 1960s as a champion of the labour movement, the NDP has viewed itself as a leading social movement struggling for progressive change in Canada. However, the arrival of the PCN-directed movement against free trade threatened the NDP's historical position. On one hand, the newly mobilized popular-sector movement could be viewed as competing for the leadership of the powerless, disenfranchised sectors of Canadian society. On another and even more threatening scale, the tight links that were evolving between organized labour and the popular sector and the deep involvement of organized labour in the leadership and financing of the movement's cause represented a potentially devastating loss to the NDP, dependent as it was on the same organizational and resource support of labour. 'The NDP was simply uncomfortable with the whole extraparliamentary movement and activities,' reflected one labour activist; 'it was bought into the electoral process.'[54]

In fact, the root of the NDP-PCN rift, as well as the third factor behind the damaged relationship, lay in the nearly inescapable trap of electoralism. For the NDP it meant the lure presented by potential electoral success; the commitment to the electoral process took the upper hand over extraparliamentary gain at the crucial moment of elections. The NDP marginalized the free trade issue in its campaign and sought instead to broaden the issues at the base of its electoral appeal.

To be sure, the NDP had decided quite early in the anti–free trade campaign that it would stand alongside the labour movement in opposition to any agreement.[55] In fact, the NDP was seen as the natural and obvious political and institutional ally to the anti–free trade movement during its early stages of mobilization and protest. Furthermore, the NDP was a key political interpreter of the movement's goals during the coalition-building and parliamentary protest campaigns. Yet, when the critical moment arrived for the NDP to make opposition to the agreement the crux of its electoral platform, it shrank from the cause, and its leader, Ed Broadbent, even failed to mention the issue in his opening campaign speech. Thus, had the NDP remained firmly committed to the anti–free trade cause and built it into its campaign platform, the charge of electoralism would have carried much less weight, both for the party and for the movement that it abandoned. The party's reluctance to carry the issue through the campaign, however, cost the movement a key political ally and voice during the already difficult and contracting stage of its mobilization. The NDP's detachment from the free trade issue resulted in the marginalization of what had previously been a key political ally for the movement. Moreover, with a great many activists being themselves life-long New Democrats, the impact proved to be especially demoralizing. Instead of sustaining the anti–free trade mobilization through the electoral campaign with social democratic allies that were taken for granted, the relationship between the movement and the NDP deteriorated into a defused, tension-filled, and uncertain alliance between NDP-holdouts such as labour and other groups that were more thoroughly resentful of the NDP's tactics.[56] A post-election introspection by ardent anti–free traders and PCN members revealed their deep frustration and confusion over the NDP's approach. The PCN's communications director lamented that

the preoccupation with electoral and parliamentary politics has made the [NDP] party unable or unwilling to engage effectively in the battle for social change on other fronts. Had the NDP used its party organization to mobilize its membership in support of the coalitions' actions in the struggle against free trade it could have made a significant difference.[57]

A prominent activist in the women's movement remarked:

The anti–free trade forces simply could not convince the NDP that this was precisely an election issue when considerations of leadership should focus on an issue. The NDP did not exactly ignore free trade, but it certainly was reluctant every step of the way and let the Liberals take the lead on the issue.[58]

Another PCN activist was less diplomatic in his critique of the NDP's election strategy:

The NDP is deservedly doubly damned. With a social movement in place the likes of which this country had never seen, with a central role being played therein by that very labour movement with which the NDP is allied, the NDP pretended none of this had happened and it was in no way beholden. The arrogance, the disdain for a people's movement by a party that claims to speak for 'ordinary Canadians' was stunning and unforgivable.[59]

Essentially, the problems in the relationship between the PCN and the NDP highlighted the PCN's larger problem of maintaining a non-partisan stance during a highly politically charged election period. The many competing and overlapping lines of political commitment and membership between individual activists and the Liberal and New Democratic parties increasingly threatened to split the movement apart during the last stages of the election campaign. A demobilizing climate of suspicion developed not just between various groups and individuals within the movement but also between the movement and the two opposition parties. Both parties resented the non-partisan stance of the movement, with each one arguing that the most strategically advantageous stand would be to support it.

At the same time, the reluctance of the NDP, on the one hand, and the opportunistic anti–free trade commitment of the Liberals, on the other, produced acute tensions within the movement: some activists leaned towards supporting the NDP at all costs, while others, despite their long-standing roots in the NDP, saw traditional party lines as less important than defeating the Tories and free trade – through the Liberals if necessary.

The unwillingness of both parties, moreover, to work together – having incumbent members of one party run unopposed by the other, for example – aroused the anger of many within the movement who felt that defeating the FTA should be placed ahead of partisan politics. The COC and PCN had toyed with election strategies, but dissention in the movement and between the two opposition parties prevented any sort of strategic implementation. One observer who wrote after the election under the sub-heading 'the unindicted co-conspirators,' captured the sense of many within the movement that an historic opportunity for cross-party collaboration had been lost: 'the two parties must share a major part of the blame for the disaster of the election. When grandchildren of today's Liberals and NDPers ask them what they did when the nation's fate was on the line, they will have to answer "we fought each other."'[60]

The most debilitating conflict lay within the complex relationships between the anti–free trade movement, labour, and the NDP. The close link between the CLC hierarchy and the federal NDP created strains and counter-tendencies within the movement, with many labour affiliates revealing towards the end of the election campaign that their allegiance, both organizationally and financially, lay primarily to the NDP. The setting was certainly not reminiscent of the Social Solidarity fiasco in British Columbia. The PCN relied much less dangerously on labour leaders, having built instead a structure broadly representative of the popular sector. Moreover, significant anti–free trade opposition groups existed in such CLC affiliates as the CAW and CUPE. Nonetheless, the anti–free trade movement, like Social Solidarity, was unable to escape the fault line of electoralism built into the volatile political environment. Again, while the labour affiliates did not all abandon the anti–free trade movement, the constraints of electoral politics were enough to seriously weaken the organizational strength and morale of the movement at precisely the moment of the strong counter-response by the business community.

In sum, the estrangement of the PCN from the NDP, combined with the intra-movement tensions that resulted from it, further constrained the structure of political opportunities during the election campaign. A key political ally of the movement had detached itself from the central mobilizing issue, thereby removing a key institutional voice in opposition to the FTA, splitting the movement into several uncertain camps, and further reducing the necessary sense of political efficacy in sustaining mobilization. The political environment had become increasingly less exposed to pressure from the movement, with the NDP affixing its campaign away from the free trade issue. The defection of the NDP, in combination with the business community's highly effective counter-response that succeeded in shifting media and public attention to its pro–free trade position, meant that the movement had lost a great deal of the political weight it needed to continue to advance its goals. Simply put, the movement lost much of its bargaining position within the political arena. This failure of the movement to maintain leverage in political and public opinion resulted in its increasing ineffectiveness and demobilization, and eventually the defeat of its hopes on election day.

The Unresolved Question of Quebec

While the business counter-mobilization and various electoral constraints seriously curtailed the anti–free trade movement's election campaign momentum, long-standing internal Canadian political realities finally sealed the fate of its cause on election day. The movement's inability to overcome historical Canadian regional and national cleavages throughout the entire lifespan of the campaign must be viewed as one of its more fundamental and debilitating weaknesses, especially during the fateful election period. The province of Alberta, while standing firmly behind the FTA, nevertheless remained the single anglophone province strongly supportive of the deal. Quebec, on the other hand, saturated as it was with all the history of French-English conflict and misunderstanding, posed a far greater problem for the anti–free trade forces. The movement lacked political opportunities and was organizationally weak in the province – too feeble to bind the anti–free trade sentiment that did exist to the movement's pan-Canadian cause. In fact, here lay the crux of the dilemma: a predominantly anglophone movement simply could not convince a majority of French-speaking Quebeckers to identify with and support the strongly Canadian nationalist anti–free trade cause.

In Quebec the movement failed, to its great cost, to overcome the political, social, and cultural divides of nationalism. True, the PCN made minor attempts to bridge the barrier: the PCN, COC, and other affiliated groups made an effort to have bilingual people available during press conferences and lobbying sessions and the PCN staffed its national office with an anglophone Quebecker, held the key August 1988 National Assembly in Montreal, and translated the *What's the Big Deal?* comic book into French for distribution throughout Quebec. Yet these overtures remained the exception to the rule. Reflecting on the limitations of the movement's links to Quebec nearly a year following the federal election, a PCN researcher succinctly concluded: 'I can remember saying to various people at various times that we should be paying more attention to Quebec, we had work to do with Quebec – and that never really happened ... within the anti–free trade movement, it was basically an Anglophone movement.'[61]

The anti–free trade movement failed to bridge the Quebec barrier for two fundamental reasons, one symbolic and the other political. For all of the movement's success in grasping and articulating the symbolic dimensions of the debate – the manner in which the issue deeply touched shared cultural and national sentiments of Canadians – these appealed almost exclusively to anglophones. In fact, one of the movement's first mistakes in its attempt to reach a Québécois audience lay in the name 'Pro-Canada.' In 1980 Prime Minister Pierre Trudeau had adopted the slogan 'Pro-Canada' to describe his Liberal government campaign to defeat Quebec nationalists and separatists in the 1980 referendum. In Quebec the lasting bitter memories of this 'Pro-Canada' campaign plagued the PCN and made its name an ineffective slogan for building a truly pan-Canadian coalition that included Quebec. An activist from Quebec bluntly told a 1989 conference on free trade that 'the concept of the Pro-Canada Network was simply not acceptable to the popular organizations in Quebec.'[62]

Unacceptable symbolism extended beyond this slogan to include the actions and goals of the movement as well. Many in Quebec perceived the movement as reflecting primarily Anglo-Canadian nationalism, which simply carried little emotional appeal. Such concerns as protecting Canadian cultural identity, strengthening Canadian sovereignty, and preserving the powers of the central government over the provinces failed to mobilize the francophone majority in Quebec. Even as late as the August 1988 PCN National Assembly, one of the few Quebec representatives within the PCN pleaded with the movement to focus on jobs, the environment, or some other less sensitive cause in Quebec. 'Nationalism isn't working in Quebec,' he argued,[63] but little time remained for the PCN to alter its message to an already suspicious Quebec population.

Daniel Latouche's reply to Philip Resnick's 1990 *Letters to a Québécois Friend* nicely captures the sentiments held by many Québécois when faced with the question of supporting the FTA. In his book Resnick, a political scientist from the University of British Columbia, decries Quebec's lack of support for the anti–free trade cause and its unsympathetic view of Canadian nationalism. Latouche, in response, explains that the Pro-Canada Network failed to reach out and make room for Quebec in it's 'save Canada' movement and failed to convince the Québécois that they should fear the FTA or the prospect of further decentralization, which in fact appealed to many Québécois desirous of a scaled-back role for the federal government.

There was simply no room for us in the 'Save Canada' movement of the Anti–Free Trade Coalition ... [T]he more we listened to some of the arguments of the coalition, the more we felt a sudden urge to join the Mulroney campaign ... [N]ot once did I hear a 'dump free trade' advocate point out that free trade was dangerous because it posed a special menace to the originality, dynamism, and distinctiveness of Quebec.[64]

While the symbolic features of the anti–free trade movement certainly handicapped its attempts to reach Quebeckers, the nearly complete lack of political opportunities or organizational allies within the province especially curtailed the movement's room for manoeuvring. Organizationally the movement failed to develop cooperative links with those social groups that did oppose the agreement within Quebec. This failure can be attributed to the strong Québécois nationalist sentiment within the province's unions and the unwillingness on the part of many Québécois activists to work outside their own provincial organizational structures. Even those social groups that fell within the descriptive category of 'popular sector' remained either uninterested or suspicious of the intentions of what they perceived to be an Anglo-Canadian movement.

Finally, Quebec's political environment remained totally unconducive to anti–free trade mobilization and intervention. The leaders of the two major provincial parties, Liberal premier Robert Bourassa and Jacques Parizeau of the separatist Parti Québécois, stood firmly in support of the agreement. Bourassa's pro–free trade leadership and his high level of support in the polls left him nearly invulnerable to critiques of the policy, while the support of the Quebec business establishment created an inhospitable atmosphere for delivering the anti–free trade message.

In short, no substantive political or organizational openings existed within Quebec for the anti–free trade movement. No political leverage existed for the movement to begin to advance its interests in the province. In effect, the free trade debate proved to be susceptible to the perennial conflict between the

English- and French-speaking communities that has plagued the Canadian polity for over two centuries. Recognizing this fact, nearly a year after the election the chair of the PCN reflected that 'the challenge of the election and everything that came out of it posed a fundamental question of how two nations worked together within the coalition.'[65] The defeat of the movement at the polls – due in no small part to Quebec's pro–free trade stance – revealed that the working relationship had been a feeble one at best.[66]

The Election and Its Outcome

The outcome of the 21 November election represented an anticlimax for the anti–free trade movement. The contracting political opportunities and weakening organizational strength in the several weeks preceding the vote had presaged a Tory victory. On the surface, the official results (Table 10) appeared to vindicate the claim of Prime Minister Mulroney that voters had provided the Tories with a mandate on free trade.

The Progressive Conservative Party received 169 of the 295 seats in Parliament, with the Liberal Party winning 83 and the NDP 43. However, the Tories gained their considerable margin of victory by virtue of Canada's single-member riding, first-past-the-post electoral system, which generously translated 43 per cent of the vote into 169 seats, while the Liberal's 32 per cent share resulted in only 83 seats and the NDP's 20 per cent in 43 seats. Thus, in fact, 52 per cent of the vote had supported the two parties opposed to the FTA.

In light of the discrepancy between popular vote and seats received, there was a considerable outcry from the anti–free trade community, which claimed that the Tories lacked the mandate to implement the agreement.[67] The opinions

TABLE 10
Federal election results in 1988

	Vote (in percentages)	Seats
Liberal	32	83
PC	43	169
NDP	20	43
Other	5	0
Total		295

Source: *Report of the Chief Electoral Officer* (Ottawa: Ministry of Supply and Services 1988).

in the scholarly community, however, remain mixed. A number of studies suggest that while the free trade issue dominated the 1988 election the 52 per cent of the popular vote garnered by the opposition parties did not in fact necessarily translate into a majority anti–free trade vote.[68] This unresolved debate aside, one revealing aspect of the electoral outcome, as far as its impact on the fate of the anti–free trade movement was concerned, lies in the division of the opposition vote between the Liberal and New Democratic parties. The outcome signalled a critical contraction of political opportunity for the movement; that is, while divisions between political actors had provided critical political-opportunity structures for sustaining the movement throughout the lifespan of its emergence and mobilization, a final and devastating division between its two key political allies climaxed its decline on election day.

The election thus marked the end of the mobilization and protest campaign of the anti–free trade movement. Rebuffed, demoralized, organizationally fractured, and facing a considerably circumscribed post-election political opportunity structure, many activists considered the difficult road ahead under a pro–free trade, Progressive Conservative government. True to conceptual expectations, the movement had achieved significant success in the first half of the election campaign by strategically exploiting a still favourable political opportunity structure and by relying on its continued strong sense of efficacy and organizational strength. Yet the movement's eventual demise resulted from the final set of factors that constrained and curtailed the anti–free trade insurgency.

First, the movement's organizational strength was depleted by the combined effects of the counter-response from the business community, by the constraints imposed by electoral politics, and by the movement's inability to pierce the barrier erected by Quebec nationalism. The business countermovement especially drained what remained of the movement's resource base, leaving it unable to respond effectively to the pro–free trade message during the final weeks of the campaign. Second, the structure of political opportunities closed drastically during the last half of the election campaign, leaving the movement with few political openings and little institutional leverage to lobby for its cause. The business response closed many opportunities for reaching the Canadian public, the NDP's intransigence on the free trade issue essentially removed an institutional ally that had previously been key to the cause, and Quebec simply represented an inaccessible fortress, where the movement made little headway. Finally, the valuable sense of political efficacy, which had propelled and sustained the movement through the struggles of the previous year, dissipated in the face of the emerging divisions within the movement and of the increasingly inhospitable environment of the election campaign. In the face of these organizational and political constraints, then, and without the collective sense of political efficacy that had served the movement so well in the past, those committed to sustaining the PCN and the popular coalitions were forced to look beyond the lost free trade election for other themes that might again mobilize the population.

Summary

In addition to giving further support to the significance of political opportunities for the sustained activity of movements, this chapter highlighted a final factor that initiated the gradual decline and demobilization of the anti–free trade insurgency. The second half of the election campaign witnessed a dramatic shift in the structure of political opportunities and the level of organizational strength, which served to demobilize and significantly curtail the movement. Specifically, the pro–free trade counter-response by the business community, combined with the erosion of the sense of political efficacy, served to deflate the anti–free trade efforts following the leaders' debates. In short, this chapter introduced an important piece to the overall political-process argument developed in the study. It linked the pattern of expanding and contracting political opportunities and organizational strength to the success and eventual decline in the activity and impact of a movement, a decline temporarily reversed in this case with the advent of negotiations for a North American Free Trade Agreement, as described in the next chapter.

6

NAFTA and the Structuring of Domestic and Transnational Protest

In the aftermath of the 1988 free trade election, the ability of activists to sustain popular mobilizations and protests came under severe strain. The collective will persisted: individuals and groups affiliated with the broad anti-FTA mobilization decided soon after the election to remain committed to a network-structured and coalition-building style of politics as a means of countering both continental free trade and the neo-conservative agenda of the Mulroney government. The core organizations and coalitions remained; aside from a retooling of their image and strategy, both the PCN and the COC remained viable and active in the popular contestations that were waged against the government's agenda, particularly in regards to the negotiations over a North American Free Trade Agreement. What the popular mobilizations would lack, however, was a supportive political context similar to the one that existed during the years prior to the federal election of 1988: in the years between this election and that of 1993 the mobilizing potential of the Canadian political-opportunity structure greatly weakened.

Yet, as domestic opportunities for protest and political leverage became increasingly constrained, new, transnational political opportunities arose within the context of the NAFTA negotiations. Thus, the possibilities for political protest and popular-sector coalition building expanded: Canadian groups no longer limited their attention to the domestic political context but expanded the scope of political exchange and mobilization to the United States and Mexico. The negotiation process of NAFTA would highlight several important developments in the evolving popular mobilization: the diffusion of the Canadian experience with coalition-building tactics and with structuring networks throughout the United States and Mexico; ways that the structure of both domestic and transnational protest activities could be affected by the

international negotiations; and the emergence of sustained institutions of popular-sector exchange and cooperation across the North American community.

Resiliency: Fighting Back against the 'Corporate Agenda'

Despite the setback of the election, the PCN, its member organizations, and
related popular-sector coalitions remained committed to building a broad progressive social movement for political change in Canada.[1] Thus, while the
'movement' against the FTA came unglued with the Progressive Conservative
victory, popular-sector education and coalition building remained a high priority. The defensive, reactionary posture of the past had to be replaced by a more
positive, proactive response to future Tory plans. Activists from the various
PCN-related organizations decided shortly after the election defeat to remain
together as a network in order to expand the scope of their activity beyond a
single-issue focus.

In fact, the PCN, or Action Canada Network, as it renamed itself in 1991 in
an effort to construct a broader country-wide coalition that would include
Quebec,[2] did, in fact, actively intervene in a number of high-profile campaigns
against Tory policy initiatives. The manner in which these campaigns were
carried out demonstrates the continued variability of political-opportunity structures and the utility and viability of the loose structure of the network as a
critical extraparliamentary voice. Various member organizations would initiate
'fight back' campaigns, drawing on the knowledge and cooperation of member
groups and utilizing the network with its research and communications capabilities to facilitate regional mobilizations across the country.

The PCN and later the ACN served as a key vehicle for communications in
raising national protests against proposed government cuts to various social
and cultural programs including the CBC, unemployment insurance, and medicare. Through the *ACN Dossier* it reached dozens of organizations and their
members with articles and news stories drawn from its research arm. The
bimonthly publication continued to critique the FTA by keeping track of job
losses linked to the pact, by reporting on protests and related news of members
of the network, and by providing critical contacts and resources for upcoming
campaigns. A piece in the 'network watch' that appeared in *Dossier* soon after
the election was indicative of the positive role the publication played in boosting the flagging sense of collective efficacy in the PCN: 'At times when it is
easy to become discouraged at the enormity of the task facing us in fighting a
federal government that scoffs at democracy, it is important to look at our
victories and accomplishments. There is a lot of activity out there, and a lot of
reason for optimism.'[3] Such coverage served to prop up the morale of member

groups still reeling from the re-election of the Mulroney government and the implementation of the FTA.

Other useful vehicles for supporting the PCN's early 'fight back' campaigns against Tory economics in 1990–1 included *CLC Today*, as well as editorial support and favourable journalistic coverage in the *Canadian Forum* and *Canadian Dimension* magazines. The Canadian Centre for Policy Alternatives also proved valuable, with its staff and consulting researchers producing a string of timely research studies and monographs sharply critical of the effects of the FTA.[4] A video package, produced by Repeal the Deal Productions, a committee of the Action Canada Network (British Columbia), also served as an educational tool and was designed to mobilize Canadians in a campaign to abrogate the FTA. Its two features, 'We Can Say No!' and 'Fighting Back,' featured PCN and COC members analysing the effects of the FTA on Canada's economy, society, and culture.

More specifically, in the two years up to 1990 PCN member organizations mobilized several notable campaigns against the so-called Tory 'corporate agenda.' One action revolved around the 1989 Tory budget, dubbed by the PCN as the 'first free trade budget,' in which it helped organize an Alternative Budget Popular Planning Process to challenge the government's budget-cutting priorities.[5] The Tory budget helped reactivate many members of the PCN coalition whose protests sought to highlight the budget cuts to social services, education, and crown corporations.[6] NAC spearheaded the campaign, organizing anti-budget strategy meetings at its annual meetings and encouraging a 'riding the rails' cross-country Via Rail protest.

A second action, the so-called Campaign for Fair Taxes, developed in conjunction with the CLC and the Quebec Coalition against the GST as a response to the government's proposed Goods and Services Tax. It targeted the aspects of the government's tax that it perceived as regressive, and sought to disseminate information and encourage popular and parliamentary discussion of fair-tax alternatives. The CLC in October 1990 held regional coalition-building workshops designed to support extraparliamentary protest activities and to create or strengthen established coalitions at the grass-roots level.[7]

The PCN and its regional affiliates also organized a National Day of Action on 10 November that was built around the 'national recall and sign-up day' planned by the CLC. This broad campaign involved popular discussion and articulation of alternative proposals for generating revenue as well as garnering over 2.3 million signatures on ballots placed in communities and workplaces across the country to protest the GST. PCN organizations also funded the production and circulation of another popularly accessible comic book, *The GST in the Big Tax Picture*, as part of the overall Campaign for Fair Taxes.

The PCN's continuing loose working relationship with the Liberal Party also played a key role in the GST drama. PCN activists met with members of the Liberal caucus, providing them with copies of briefs, and advised Liberals on the scope and context of the Campaign for Fair Taxes.[8] Liberal and independent senators, in a move reminiscent of John Turner's tactics during the debate in 1987 over the FTA, stalled the GST legislation with a variety of procedural obstacles.[9] Claiming that the Tories did not have a mandate to implement the new tax, opposition Liberal senators stonewalled Tory attempts to pass the legislation by receiving briefs and information from PCN-member groups.[10] The cross-country protests that spiralled out of the National Day of Action provided the Liberals with visible evidence of public opposition to the legislation and gave a measure of legitimacy to their actions in the Senate.[11]

Moreover, the PCN ran full-page advertisements in major Canadian newspapers that backed a Liberal plan to override the House of Commons on the GST. Encouraging Canadians to phone the Senate to register their support for the plans of the Liberals to block the GST, a full-page ad in Toronto's *Globe and Mail* read:

Brian Mulroney says there's an impasse between the House of Commons and the Senate. He's wrong. There's an impasse between Brian Mulroney and the Canadian people. There is a fair tax alternative: tax according to ability to pay. That's why we support the action by the Opposition in the Senate to kill the GST. No government should be allowed to sidestep the will of the people.[12]

The loose association with the federal Liberals two years after the FTA debate demonstrates the continued utility of the divisions in Parliament to the coalition. The PCN retained a vocal ally in the Liberal Party through its attempts to block the GST and it enjoyed news coverage in the mainstream media as a result of its relationship with the federal party.[13] The Liberals could point to the protests inspired by the PCN across the country as evidence of public support for their actions. The situation of mutual political opportunity helped breathe life into the PCN and later the ACN as it sought to expand its *raison d'être* beyond opposition to the FTA.

The winter of 1992 witnessed the ACN's grass-roots intervention in the debate over the Charlottetown Constitutional Accord. With a membership that by that time included over fifty national groups, considerably more than during the free trade election, the ACN encouraged constitutional discussion and presented an array of alternatives to government policies from a broader spectrum of the public than had previously been possible. Feeding on the popular disdain of many Canadians concerning the process of the earlier Meech Lake Accord,

ACN activists participated in five so-called 'people's conferences' across the country that were designed to extract views and proposals for constitutional renewal differing from those in the federal government's recommendations.[14] Significantly different values did arise from these conferences; activists staked out a 'three nations' asymmetrical approach to restructuring the constitution.[15] While it was not ultimately integrated into the Charlottetown deal that was soon to fail, the 'nations centred' approach nevertheless did reflect a popular penchant for prioritizing social and cultural goals and for re-evaluating the historical origins and paths of Canada's founding peoples.[16]

Opposition to NAFTA

The results of the 1988 federal election proved sobering to nationalist and social activist groups across Canada, but, as noted earlier, most of them remained committed to the PCN coalition as the best means to continue the fight against continental free trade.[17] Moreover, a significant shift occurred in both the mindset and the strategy of these groups, which had witnessed their left-nationalist campaign falter against the determined efforts of a well-organized and well-financed pro–free trade transnational business community. Groups began to explore the possibility of developing tri-national cooperative educational and strategic links across the North American community. To be sure, the COC and PCN did not abandon efforts to pressure the federal government into abrogating or renegotiating the FTA.[18] COC chapters, coalitions linked to the PCN, and other grass-roots organizations fought against the proposed NAFTA pact through education campaigns, provincial lobbying, and pan-Canadian coalition building.[19] Yet an important lesson learned from the results in 1988 led to a greater willingness to reach across borders and to cultivate alliances with U.S. and Mexican groups similarly opposed to NAFTA.[20]

This strategic shift reflected in part the significantly constrained Canadian political-opportunity structure following the federal election. Although the federal NDP gave itself a new leader and adopted an uncompromising stance against continental free trade, it was a weak and uncertain ally in the opinion of many people in the PCN. The NDP's attitude during the anti-FTA campaign had alienated many activists, necessitating a process of healing that would occur over the first few years following the election.[21]

The Liberals, on the other hand, presented a different problem. While Liberal senators had fought the good fight with PCN groups against the GST, old fissures in the Liberal caucus concerning continental free trade quickly resurfaced following the election. Liberal leader and ardent anti–free trade campaigner John Turner quickly and quietly faded off the political stage following the election. Desperate to position themselves favourably with a pro–free trade business community and in need of financial support to prepare for the next federal election, the Liberal signalled a shift in their party's position during their leadership race in the spring of 1990. As trade critic for the Liberals, Lloyd Axworthy had strongly placed himself in the left-nationalist bloc of the caucus prior to the election, but he withdrew from the race in January because of his 'want of resources.' 'I sensed a deep desire for a progressive agenda and a need to address the concerns of many Canadians who feel excluded from today's political system. However, there is another political reality in this country and in this party and that is the dominant factor of big money.'[22]

Axworthy's withdrawal helped smooth the way for Jean Chrétien to be chosen as the new Liberal leader, which raised concerns among anti-FTA activists who began to question the commitment of the Liberals to end the deal. In fact, Chrétien would, over the next year and a half, carefully position the Liberals along the political fence on the issue of free trade. From a strongly abrogationist stance prior to the 1988 election, Chrétien shepherded the party towards a policy of 'renegotiation' by the summer of 1990.[23] Moreover, Chrétien seemed to signal in November 1991 his acceptance of the FTA at the party's biennial conference in Aylmer, Quebec, where he embraced globalization as 'a fact of life.'[24] With talks on NAFTA under way, Liberal leaders closed ranks around an increasingly continentalist trade position.

The weakness of the federal NDP and the uncertainty of the federal Liberals presented the member organizations of the ACN with considerably less political leverage on the free trade issue than in 1988. The two key political allies that had articulated its anti–free trade concerns during the FTA deliberations were now much less reliable. Polls also demonstrated less volatility among the electorate – the weak or even fearful Liberal partisans of the mid to late 1980s had been replaced by people who were still cautious but nonetheless more confident – which reflected the public's growing antipathy towards the federal Tories. The Liberals did not need the PCN, its message, or its resources as they had in the pre-election period in 1988, and with the negotiations over NAFTA progressing the ACN found its efforts constrained by a much less supportive national political-opportunity structure.

In fact, its weakened and reduced mobilizing potential can be attributed to what Liberal leader Jean Chrétien called the 'fact of life' of economic globalization. This process of ongoing international economic and communications interdependence reduces the mobilizing potential of national political-opportunity structures.[25] Canadians in the early 1990s were witnessing the effects of globalization in the FTA. While not immediately fulfilling the doom-laden, if not conspiratorial, scenarios painted by some in the anti-FTA camp, the agreement certainly imposed limits on the options traditionally available to the Canadian government, which was accustomed to being able to intervene in the national economy and to manage and distribute resources for the collective good.[26] The increased mobility of capital, finance, and even culture, spurred on by the FTA, helped to blur national boundaries, constraining the traditional capabilities of the Canadian state.[27]

In turn, as the 1990s progressed Canadian national political-opportunity structures that had previously provided the ACN with leverage for making and airing claims directly to the state weakened – the state became increasingly either indifferent to the demands of the member organizations of the ACN or unable to respond to them. Thus, as the locus in the state for domestic protest receded, the member organizations of the ACN sought to establish new, cross-border alliances and to exploit emerging transnational opportunities for mounting and sustaining an anti-NAFTA campaign of protest.

Thus, no longer would activists from ACN groups limit their protests to Canadian soil. Opportunities for transnational collective action about the discussions on NAFTA could arise across the political environments of Canada, the United States, and Mexico. To be sure, the emergence of transnational political-opportunity structures did not relegate the significance of protest in individual sovereign states to the dustbin, but the transnational contention emerging out of the NAFTA deliberations of the early 1990s demonstrated that the state no longer represented the sole constraint or supporter of movements.[28]

As early as mid-1990, barely a year after the FTA had been in place, representatives of the PCN began meeting with Mexican labour, church, and human rights organizations in anticipation of the NAFTA negotiations. The Toronto-based Common Frontiers, a working group on North American economic integration that had emerged out of a visit in September 1988 by representatives of various social groups to the border of the United States and Mexico to investigate the implications of the Maquiladoras area for Canada under the FTA, had begun assisting the PCN. Common Frontiers brought together labour, church, human rights, environmental and economic justice organizations in a multi-sectoral network to carry out research on and to mobilize around the economic and social justice issues of the increasingly integrated continental economy.[29] Building on the experience of the PCN coalition against the FTA, Canadian groups shared, through Common Frontiers, the still-fresh memories and lessons from the 1988 campaign with their Mexican counterparts.[30]

The cross-border diffusion of movement strategy through Common Frontiers played a crucial role in stimulating the development of formal working relationships between Canadian, Mexican, and U.S. coalitions. Common Frontiers organized regularly scheduled strategy meetings that developed tri-national analyses of the NAFTA texts.[31] One key early meeting in October 1990 in Mexico City brought dozens of Mexican and Canadian organizations together for a 'Canada-Mexico Encuentro,' where Canadian groups discussed the potential implications of NAFTA for Mexican sovereignty and democracy.[32] The conference also helped spawn the Mexican Action Network on Free Trade, which, by the time of the completion of the NAFTA negotiations, had developed into a coalition representing over one hundred women's, environmental, community, independent labour, and other groups. Its emergence, moreover, highlighted the diffusion of the strategy of coalition building to Mexico.

The cross-border construction of strategies continued to build up steam parallel to the start of the formal tri-national NAFTA negotiations on 12 June 1991. Activists from all three countries staged a media event in January against free trade in Washington, D.C., while PCN activists in February attended a forum on strategies to combat free trade with dozens of Mexican environmental, religious, women's, and labour organizations.[33] A working group on continental free trade, comprising a number of groups connected with the ACN, held a news conference in Toronto on 23 May, the day both houses of the U.S. Congress authorized 'fast track' NAFTA negotiations, to publicize the existence of the cross-border opposition to free trade. A Common Frontiers representative noted how the internationalization of the trade talks through NAFTA had created broader, transnational opportunities for collaborative protest and opposition: 'Our work with our U.S. and Mexican counterparts has expanded the debate on continental free trade beyond our borders. There is significant opposition in all three countries. This makes it a lot easier to monitor the negotiations and keep a public spotlight on them.'[34]

The 1st of June marked the beginning of cross-Canada protest actions and information campaigns coordinated by the ACN that were designed to put pressure on the Canadian government to abrogate the FTA and to pull out of the NAFTA talks. The coalition members of the ACN in cities across the country passed out thousands of leaflets on tri-national free trade and cards to mail to the prime minister calling on him to pull Canada out of the talks.[35]

The participation of regional coalitions was widespread. The Action Canada Network (B.C.) held an Impact, Alternatives, and Action Conference in Vancouver from 31 May 31 to 1 June, which included the launching of a new video by ACN titled 'We Can Say No,' and a demonstration that drew 300 people out to sign and post a proclamation against free trade on the door of the Vancouver Trade and Convention Centre. The Action Canada Network (Alberta) protested the FTA by posting proclamations calling for the resignation of the prime minister, and from 8 to 15 June Edmonton's Catalyst Theatre hosted the Bread and Water: The Canadian Popular Theatre Alliance Festival, with workshops addressing how theatre can bring about economic change. The Saskatoon Social Justice Network passed out thousands of anti-FTA leaflets at the city's farmers' market. The Winnipeg-based Choices: A Coalition for Social Justice held a piñata party, where activists broke Brian Mulroney's piggybank, which was full of caramels and also contained a one-way ticket to Mexico for a worker to visit his or her job. In Toronto, Common Frontiers held a news conference, and the Quebec Coalition on the Trilateral Negotiations[36] did the same in Montreal. The Pro-Canada Network of Prince Edward Island passed out leaflets and mail-back cards.[37]

The slow pace and closed nature of the early NAFTA negotiations also provided activists with valuable time to consolidate cross-border ties and strategies. The trade representatives of the United States pressed the Canadian and Mexican delegations on such issues as intellectual property rights and investments, which hampered talks over the detailed legal issues that were required. Little progress was achieved during the August 1991 Seattle ministerial meeting, raising hopes among activists that NAFTA would fail to be ratified prior to the 1992 U.S. presidential elections.[38] Moreover, pressures on President George Bush from a wavering, if not overtly protectionist, Democratic Congress forced an expansion of the NAFTA negotiations to include separate, albeit parallel, bilateral U.S.–Mexican negotiations over labour and environmental standards. These delays and complications increasingly focused the attention of activists on the political process in the United States and were viewed as providing valuable opportunities for lobbying and protest. Moreover, the delays created the potential for expanding the debate in Canada over free trade, perhaps even spilling the NAFTA debate over into the campaign of the next federal election, expected in 1993.[39]

A critical event in the tri-national coalition-building process took place in Zacatecas, Mexico, in October 1991. Coinciding with the third formal meeting of the trade ministers for negotiating NAFTA, an International Citizen's Forum, comprising more than three hundred popular-sector representatives from Canada, the United States, and Mexico, came together. Billed as a 'counter-conference,' the meeting solidified a relationship of trust and mutual direction among the tri-national representatives and it endorsed a declaration that proposed an alternative to NAFTA for continental development.[40] In addition to trade, the proposal emphasized development, democracy, self-determination, and the elevation of living standards; it represented a significant response to those who had criticized the Canadian anti-FTA campaign for its lack of a clear alternative.[41] The International Citizen's Forum also provided an important opportunity for activists to publicize the cross-national opposition to the accord. The chair of the ACN personally presented the Alternative Declaration to the Canadian minister of finance, a move that ultimately persuaded the U.S. and Mexican trade ministers to agree to meet with opposition delegations from their own countries.[42]

The Citizen's Forum demonstrated how the pace of the negotiations over NAFTA had served to structure increased opportunities for transnational collaboration and protest. In particular, this event, as well as the ministers' meeting in Zacatecas, served several important purposes for activists. The negotiations pressed Canadian activists to seek other solutions to counter the 'corporate agenda' beyond the Canadian border. It demonstrated that, in collaboration with the Mexican Action Network and the Mobilization for Development, Trade, Labor, and Environment in the United States, the ACN could articulate broad alternatives to the economic agenda of neo-liberalism and free trade. This new confidence in itself reflected a significant maturation for the ACN from the period of its anti-FTA struggle, when its predecessor, the PCN, fell prey to criticism that it lacked an alternative to the Tory government's free trade agenda. Finally, in a political environment hostile to democratic protest and mobilization, the transnational coalition building spawned by NAFTA helped legitimize a fledgling Mexican grass-roots opposition movement. The presence of Canadian and American representatives undoubtedly served as a deterrent to an otherwise repressive Mexican police force, one not unaccustomed to routinely harassing and imprisoning activists.

The year 1992 witnessed more extensive tri-national collaborative efforts, both sectorally and inter-sectorally, in opposition to the NAFTA negotiations. Two important resources for tri-national organizing became available, mirroring the spread of the ACN's scope of protest activity from Canada to the rest of the continent. *Cross Border Links*, published by the Inter-Hemispheric Education Resource Center in Albuquerque, New Mexico, listed over five hundred organizations, their contacts, addresses, telephone numbers, and publications, along with information on their interests in relations between Canada, the United States, and Mexico. Also available was *Trading Freedom*, jointly published by the Institute for Food and Development Policy and the Institute for Policy Studies. It presented critiques of NAFTA, as well as broad alternative proposals, from the perspectives of various opposition movements and coalitions in the three countries that had mobilized against the accord.[43] Meanwhile, environmental groups from all three countries mobilized protests in March 1992 against the dumping of toxic wastes in the Maquiladoras areas.

In February 1992 Mujer a Mujer (Woman to Woman) and Mujeres en Acción Sindical (Women in Union Action) brought women's groups together from across North America in the First Trinational Working Women's Conference on Free Trade and Continental Integration, held in Valle de Bravo, Mexico. Attended by over one hundred women representing unions, community, church, social justice, and research and policy institutes, the conference consisted of workshops and presentations that analysed the experiences of women's lives under accelerating continental integration. The coalition-building experience of both the NAC and the ACN provided important models for organizing and providing coherence in research, strategy, and action against continental integration. Participants highlighted the especially difficult conditions facing working women across the tri-national communities, and released a unanimous joint statement and plan of action designed to explore the possibility of forging stronger links among women's organizations to exchange information, experiences, and materials.[44]

The agreement between the trade ministers of the three countries on the NAFTA texts in Mexico City in January 1993 brought renewed tri-national inter-sectoral social collaboration, which focused specifically on mobilizing opposition to the proposed accord in the United States.[45] In early March, activists from all three countries lobbied members of Congress against NAFTA, by sharing with them the experience of the PCN during the anti-FTA campaign, the economic conditions in Canada following the implementation of the accord, and the conditions in the Maquiladoras in an effort to convince them to vote against the accord.

The NAFTA process thus opened new political opportunities for groups from all three countries whose own domestic settings proved less hospitable, either temporarily, or more permanently, to effective protest. Groups linked to the ACN, recognizing the structural impediments to influencing the NAFTA process that were inherent in the parliamentary process as well as the relative decline of national political opportunities in the post-1988 context, found new openings for opposing NAFTA outside the domestic setting. The lobbying in March 1993 of members of the United States Congress marked an excellent example of a cross-border political opportunity for those Canadian groups seeking added leverage and time for drumming up broader opposition to the accord. Reflecting on the lobbying effort in the United States, the chair of the ACN noted that

the feeling of our American counterparts is that they can't be too radical. But they can open the space for us. It may be too much to expect opposition organizations to stop NAFTA. But perhaps things can be delayed long enough that a good, close look at what NAFTA does mean will be taken. And then anything might happen.[46]

Certainly, the opening up of cross-border political opportunities also aided Mexican groups, whose own nation-centred protests collided with the nearly impenetrable and undemocratic political system under the control of the long-ruling Institutional Revolutionary Party.[47] NAFTA's successful passage through the Mexican political system was a foregone conclusion. But the diffusion of Canadian movement activity, which helped to consolidate the emergence of the Mexican Action Network, and the openings for political protest, especially in the United States, served to highlight the doubt, uncertainty, and opposition to NAFTA that existed within Mexican society.

Finally, protests in each national setting demonstrated that the possibilities for collective action were now being significantly influenced by international processes. Opposition to NAFTA, in particular the closed negotiation process and the potentially broad-ranging impact of the accord, stimulated a wide array of protest focused in the domestic arena. Both the Mexican Action Network and the U.S. Citizen's Trade Campaign borrowed noticeably from the PCN's coalition-building tactics against the FTA when they launched broad-based protests against NAFTA.[48]

In addition to this ongoing and expanding tri-national networking, Canadian groups maintained a parallel commitment to defend Canadian national sovereignty by lobbying the federal government to abrogate or renegotiate NAFTA. A mass demonstration in May 1993 on Parliament Hill to 'Reclaim Our Future,' drew an estimated sixty to one hundred thousand protestors from various Canadian groups to oppose economic policies of the Tories, including free trade.[49] Solidarity events also took place across Canada to represent those groups and individuals unable to attend the mass rally, with a caravan taking the anti-NAFTA message to communities from British Columbia to Newfoundland before arriving on Parliament Hill to coincide with the mass action rally.

The 1993 Federal Election: A Dramatic Closure of National Political Opportunity

Riding the momentum of the earlier cross-border coalition building, the Campaign for Canada in the fall of 1993 also knitted together various groups through the COC and ACN in an effort to elect candidates opposed to NAFTA in order to prevent its implementation before the 1 January 1994 deadline. Groups targeted specific ridings across Canada for mass action and education campaigns in an attempt to elect anti-FTA and anti-NAFTA candidates from either the NDP or Liberal parties. The election strategy hinged centrally upon an improbable outcome: the defeat for the Progressive Conservatives and the election of a minority government with the Liberals dependent upon the staunchly anti-FTA and anti-NAFTA NDP for support in a coalition government.[50] However, compared to the political environment of 1988, that of 1993 presented to Canadian protest groups a dramatically constrained, if not closed, national political opportunity structure.

Because political opportunities are unstable – external political openings can close quickly for movements when the field of contention shifts – the influence of movements can be fleeting at best. 'Opportunity structures are fickle friends to movements,' notes Tarrow, a fact clearly in evidence in Canada by 1993.[51] By this time the political environment had grown increasingly less hospitable to popular-sector concerns. The major political openings that had helped sustain such initiatives as the anti–free trade, anti-GST, and various budget campaigns, had dramatically narrowed. By the early fall of 1993 the Tories were clearly headed for defeat, and the electoral needs of the Liberal Party were disengaged from the concerns of the popular sector. The split within the Liberal Party that had proved so opportune in 1988 had been papered over. The popular sector's two principal parliamentary allies had essentially evaporated as far as it was concerned – the Liberal party by virtue of its probable electoral victory and evident shift towards supporting the FTA and NAFTA, and the NDP by virtue of its near political extinction at the federal level and loss of credibility in several provinces.

The differences between the Liberal Party of 1988 and the Liberal Party of 1993 were stark. Under the leadership of Jean Chrétien, the party in 1993 continued to pay lip service to such popular-sector concerns as the GST and NAFTA during the lead up to the election campaign.[52] Yet Chrétien had already signalled the direction he intended to take his party at the crucial policy conference in Aylmer, Quebec, in November 1991. While not intent on burying social welfare concerns, Chrétien made clear the party's commitment to free trade and the global economy. Moreover, in 1993 the party interacted with popular-sector groups from a position of much greater overall strength and unity compared to 1988, when weakness and division had characterized its condition. The divisions between the left-leaning, anti–free trade nationalists and the right-leaning free traders had been papered over. The party dominated the symbiotic relationship that had developed between the ACN and party members since the 1988 election, and it is clear that it successfully co-opted a number of dissatisfied NDP supporters and other activists linked to the ACN under its decisive plank to 'renegotiate' FTA and NAFTA.

Moreover, the popular sector simply failed to fulfil the electoral needs of the Liberal Party. Flush with resources – contributions from the business community, new candidates, ideology, and leadership – the Liberals found popular-sector pressures annoying at worst. Despite a campaign led by the ACN and

COC that was designed to force the Liberals into a pre-election commitment to nullify NAFTA, a vague promise to renegotiate was all that resulted.[53] The popular sector had simply lost the leverage and bargaining power it once had with the Liberal Party. With that loss, its influence in the political arena was significantly diminished.

The Liberal Party could afford to be forceful and independent in the period leading into the campaign because it had successfully positioned itself as the strongest and most viable opposition to the increasingly despised Progressive Conservatives. In contrast, the NDP in this election period did not pose a significant threat. To be sure, the federal NDP represented the most vocal opponent to continental free trade and it was the only viable public and parliamentary articulator of popular-sector concerns. Its leader, Audrey McLaughlin, and her federal caucus publicly and in Parliament in question period consistently opposed NAFTA, argued for the abrogation of the FTA, and stood firmly against various cut-back measures in social policies introduced by the Tories. Yet its support, according to public opinion polls, by that fall hovered in the single digits, and McLaughlin did little to inspire the confidence of the Canadian public, or indeed undermine the confidence of the Liberals. Described variously as rudderless and incapable of articulating an attractive alternative program to an increasingly disaffected Canadian public, the federal NDP found its credibility wanting with groups linked to the ACN and with the broader Canadian public in several respects.

First, the federal NDP in 1993 carried the baggage of its ineffective and, to many, alienating 1988 campaign. The party's decision to play up the personality of its leader, Ed Broadbent, and to play down opposition to the FTA had alienated many within the coalitions linked to the ACN, a disaffection that continued into 1993. Moreover, the NDP entered the 1993 federal campaign on the heels of a series of constitutional crises, a severe recession, and the rise of the populist, albeit right-wing, Reform Party.[54] The Reform Party would lure traditional supporters of the NDP in the upcoming election, in part through its message but also as the recipient of protest votes, against a backdrop of popular disgust at the manoeuvrings of provincial NDP governments.

In fact, the federal NDP suffered perhaps most dramatically in 1993 from a harsh, popular-sector backlash against unpopular actions taken in the preceding years by the three provincial NDP governments in British Columbia, Saskatchewan, and Ontario.[55] Under pressure from declining revenues, rising unemployment, and burgeoning debt NDP provincial governments had slashed budgets, affecting especially social programs that were dear to the hearts of social democrats and the broader popular-sector community. Perhaps the strongest anger was reserved for the Ontario government of Premier Bob Rae.

What began as high hopes for many within the popular sector with Rae's unexpected victory in 1990 in the industrial and financial heartland of Canada, ended with disillusionment for many traditional supporters of the NDP. The early, glowing reports of Rae's electoral victory, and of the supportive role played by many groups and individuals in the popular-sector community in this win, contrasted sharply with the commentaries and actions of the same constituency towards the mid to latter part of Rae's tenure.[56] Rae's decision to impose a 'social contract' inspired by deficit-cutting on the government's employees enraged and alienated many groups and strategists in both the ACN and Ontario's popular-sector and social democratic coalition.[57] Labour's dissatisfaction with the Rae government was such that it threatened to spill over and damage the broader and long-standing relationship that existed between the federal NDP and the Canadian trade union movement.[58] Moreover, the issue encouraged and ultimately revealed the deep fissures in the relationship between the federal and provincial NDP parties.[59]

In the end, the federal NDP failed to distinguish itself adequately from its provincial counterparts, encouraging apathy or protest voting by its traditional political constituency. With support in the low teens, a message at odds with the deficit-cutting that was sweeping the country, and an uninspiring leader, the NDP was reduced to a mere rump of its former self. When the results were in the party would lose its official status in Parliament, its broad, cross-country roots, and its position as a vocal public articulator of popular-sector concerns.

The rightward tilt of the federal Liberals under Chrétien and the near disappearance of the hapless NDP created a political vacuum for groups affiliated to the ACN that had sought political leverage during the election campaign. Moreover, two new parties inhospitable to the goals of the ACN and the COC filled this vacuum: the Western-based Reform Party and the separatist Bloc Québécois. Both parties clearly threatened the base of support for the Tories rather than that of the Liberals, providing the Liberals with further room for manoeuvre on the issues of the FTA and NAFTA. Finally, a political environment including the new, albeit short-lived, National Party, which competed with the NDP for the anti-FTA and anti-NAFTA votes, helped to fracture grass-roots opposition to these policies and spoiled any opportunity for strategic voting for specific anti-FTA candidates.

Ultimately, the results of the 1993 election closed dramatically those political openings that had nurtured and sustained popular-sector influence on the Canadian party and parliamentary system (see Table 11). The Tories earned

TABLE 11
Federal election results in 1993

	Vote (in percentages)	Seats
Liberal	41	177
PC	16	2
NDP	7	9
BQ	14	54
Reform	19	52
Other	3	0

Source: *Report of the Chief Electoral Officer* (Ottawa: Ministry of Supply and Services 1993).

the worst defeat in the history of the major political parties in Canada, reduced to near political oblivion; the Liberals were handed a significant victory. The Liberal Party emerged with a strong parliamentary majority, and it would essentially be immune to further popular-sector critique for the foreseeable future. The NDP, the party with the strongest continuing links to the popular sector and the one that had campaigned on popular-sector social-welfare and anti-NAFTA themes, meanwhile potentially faced political oblivion and a hard struggle to win back traditional but alienated supporters.

In retrospect, despite its record of ongoing mobilization and of active intervention and protest in the early 1990s, the ACN did not enjoy anything like the influence that the PCN had acquired during the period leading up to the 1988 election. The public fervour that had surrounded and supported the movement led by the PCN against the free trade agreement had all but evaporated. The movement's symbolic glue, the historical concerns of the Canadian public over American hegemonic interests, had been dissipated by less dramatic issues on taxing and spending and diluted by the lack of a historical relationship between Canada and Mexico.

To be sure, the majority of the most significant partners of the coalition remained, and the ACN's breadth in representation had in fact grown. Yet Tory budgets continued to be adopted, the GST was implemented, and the government's proposed Charlottetown Accord failed to reflect any of the visions or positions put forth by the ACN's grass-roots unity campaign. In short, what was especially missing was a favourable structure of political opportunity, one similar to the supportive environment that was exploited by the PCN during the anti–free trade campaign. The ACN's bargaining position and leverage had severely contracted, leaving it with little room to influence the political process.

The results of the election of 1993 represented therefore a decisive closure of political opportunity for the popular sector. In fact, such results strongly validate the central underlying argument of the political-process model, that politics matter crucially to the fate of social movements. The core popular-sector organizations waged a high-profile anti-NAFTA campaign during the election period. Their internal resources remained intact – the communications and research network structure, the publications including the *Dossier*, and popular-sector leadership – and they all combined in a focused anti-NAFTA campaign. In short, the popular sector still retained the internal organizational capacity to mobilize a protest campaign. But, critically absent were the political-opportunity structures, and it was an absence that undermined the potential strengths of the popular sector. By late October 1993 the Canadian state and the party system proved themselves to be much less vulnerable to popular-sector collective action than they had been five years earlier.

The electoral victory of the Liberals and the party's subsequent implementation of NAFTA despite promises to renegotiate the accord would force groups in Canada to re-evaluate their nearly decade-old commitment to oppose free trade. Questions would arise concerning the direction and goals of popular-sector groups: were the national campaigns that characterized the anti-FTA and anti-NAFTA mobilizations now obsolete in the face of an increasingly integrated continental economy? When would it become necessary to stop pressuring a federal government on free trade and to focus energies instead on improving human rights, social welfare, and democracy across the tri-national communities in the face of the continental economy?

Summary

Domestic political conditions outside the internal resources and organizational capacity of the Canadian popular sector proved increasingly unfavourable to sustaining popular protest campaigns in the years between the 1988 and 1993 federal elections. The popular sector lacked the critical 'conversion potential' to transform the organizational network structure into a influential political force even though it was still viable. By 1993 the Canadian political-opportunity structure had demonstrated its variable, ephemeral nature.[60]

However, the emergence of sustained and ongoing incidents of tri-national protest and coalition building highlighted the critical degree to which the NAFTA negotiation process had structured both transnational and domestic opportunities for collective action. This economic and political arrangement had created new tri-national opportunities for activists from the three countries to identify common concerns and to collaborate on common strategies. New transnational networks for issues had arisen, notably through Common Frontiers, spurring political exchange between Mexican, U.S., and Canadian groups. While still rooted in separate national settings and hardly exemplary of a unified transnational social movement, the rise of such political exchanges demonstrated the degree to which the continental integration inspired by NAFTA had blurred the traditional boundaries and foci of the strategy and mobilization of movements. Thus, while the domestic political context in Canada appeared increasingly constrained to popular-sector mobilization by the fall of 1993, increased opportunities for transnational mobilization would significantly shape movement strategy in the years to come.

7

From National Sovereignty towards Popular Sovereignty?

Within the context of the North American continental economy, a subtle shift has been taking place in the protest strategies and tactics adopted by various popular-sector groups across Canada. Previously rooted primarily in state-centred campaigns that mobilized around the concepts of the 'nation' and 'national sovereignty,' increasingly groups have begun to mount broader collective campaigns that transcend both national sovereignty and national borders to focus on transnational democracy and popular sovereignty. The broad impetus behind this evolving shift in strategy and focus is the globalization of the world's economy. Globalization, by constraining the powers and capacities of the state to intervene in traditional areas of social, political, economic, and cultural concern, has in turn reduced somewhat the attractiveness of the state as the sole locus for protest. This by no means heralds the end of traditional national social movements in Canada, but it does point to an era of greater transnational activity and protest by movements within a context of growing North American continental integration.[1]

This chapter takes a brief look at the recent evolution of strategies – from national to transnational – of protest in Canada resulting from the decline in the power of the state and in the concomitant national political-opportunity structures. It extends the more specific concern of this book – the rise and pattern of anti–free trade, popular-sector coalition-building activity – by analysing the shift in some activities and strategies from nation-centred to transnational. As this book has documented, each stage of the process of the economic integration of North America marked discernible shifts in both strategy and consciousness for the groups that mobilized across Canada to oppose such agreements. From the highly nationalist anti-FTA campaign and the transnationalist anti-NAFTA mobilization to the post-NAFTA reality of community-based resistance and anti-corporate campaigns, social groups across Canada have had to rethink traditional methods of protest in an era of shrinking governmental power and resources.

Globalization and the Canadian State

Historically the state has represented the pivot around which various social movements have arisen, mobilized, and protested on behalf of social constituencies. More specifically, the rise of labour, women's, civil rights, environmental, and peace movements, to name a few, can frequently be traced to the emergence of favourable political-opportunity structures in a state. This book's analysis of the Canadian political-opportunity structures has revealed how political institutions, actors, and rules helped to facilitate and shape the mobilization of popular-sector campaigns across Canada over the past fifteen years.

Globalization has begun to change the historical pattern. Globalization – the ongoing process of international economic and communication interdependence – has reduced the mobilizing potential of Canadian political-opportunity structures. Magnusson, in a well-formulated argument, suggests that the constraints imposed by globalization have 'de-centred' the state, providing new avenues for critical social movements outside the traditionally conceived boundaries of the Westphalian state system.[2] The traditional state system, as well as its actors – the state, parliament, national political parties – is giving way to the 'global city' and to critical social movements that represent a pluralism of identities and transnational causes.[3] Sovereignty, then, is breaking down, with the destabilization of authority and the devolution of governance from different centres that is characteristic of states in an age of the global economy.[4] Similarly, Elkins envisions a twenty-first century where technological developments, aided by the dynamic of globalization, have altered the balance between the citizen and the state towards possibilities of governance greatly influenced by non-territorial identities and organizations.[5]

A related approach is the globalization of social movement thesis, which contends that governments are witnessing a dramatic decline in their ability to manage the polity and its resources.[6] The flexibility of capital, labour, finance, and culture have blurred the boundaries of sovereign states, constraining the ability of the state to act on behalf of its citizens, to distribute resources, and to plan confidently for the future. Social welfare programs have come under intense pressure through various neo-liberal policies across the Western world, while programs of social reform are prohibitively expensive in developing states, which are also being pressured into austerity programs by agencies such as the International Monetary Fund and the World Bank.[7] In turn, national political-opportunity structures that had earlier supported the rise of national social movements may be giving way to international political-opportunity structures that support the growth of transnational social movements. Canada is particularly vulnerable to the constraints posed by globalization on the efficacy of the national government. Canada is dominated by its relationship to the United States, increasingly decentralized and strained by ever bolder provinces, marked by high levels of foreign ownership, and bombarded daily by the popular culture of the United States. Moreover, the Canadian government has been especially constrained by its membership in both the FTA and NAFTA. These continental agreements have left the Canadian government of the late 1990s with few of the options that were once available to it for intervening in the national economy and for managing and distributing resources for the collective public good. Gone for the foreseeable future are such types of interventionist devices as the Foreign Investment Review Agency or the National Energy Policy; even apparently mild postal subsidies for Canadian media have been challenged by the United States through the World Trade Organization as unfair practices.

That the national government as a locus for Canadian national identity should be weakening is nothing new. Academics and laypersons alike have been variously worried over the demise of the Canadian nation-state for years or declaring that it has already happened.[8] The historically binational (albeit increasingly multicultural) character of the Canadian state has always limited the support for the pan-Canadian national view. The reality of Quebec has certainly limited the appeal and strategy of the ACN and the COC over the past fifteen years. Moreover, the past years of multinational politics and continentalism have only served to weaken the strength of the one-nation view of Canada.[9] The recent emergence of an increasingly vocal English Canada, combined with growing efforts to counter Quebec nationalism through a Canadian 'Plan B,' are notable additions to this pattern.[10]

Certainly the political context in Canada of the mid to late 1990s has become much less favourable to sustained, pan-Canadian, national campaigns and mobilizations. Removed from the political arena are viable political allies to collaborate in significant parliamentary interventions. To be sure, in the 1997 federal election the NDP regained official party status in Parliament under the leadership of Alexa McDonough after finding particular success in the Atlantic provinces. Yet the federal NDP remains a weak image of its former self in the House of Commons, chastened by a rank and file that was not amused by the neo-conservative record of provincial NDP governments, particularly that of former premier Bob Rae in Ontario. The Liberal Party, on the other hand, has picked up where the Progressive Conservative Party left off after its decisive defeat in the 1993 federal election by implementing NAFTA and deficit-inspired cutbacks to Canada's social welfare system. Particularly harmful was the Liberal's pre-election NAFTA renegotiation strategy, which enabled it to co-opt many disaffected NDP supporters and gave it a massive electoral victory. Re-elected by a slim parliamentary majority in 1997, the Liberals promise little change on the issue of NAFTA and hemispheric free trade.[11]

Thus, as the Canadian state and its national government have retreated, popular-sector groups across Canada have had to rethink traditional means of protest and mobilization. Past Canadian political-opportunity structures have either weakened or become altogether non-existent. This is by no means indicative of a permanent erosion of supportive opportunity structures; one of the major thrusts of this book has been the documentation of the variability of the structure of political opportunities in a given country. However, at the edge of the millennium, groups that are lacking a viable sympathetic opposition and are faced with a national government politically committed to continentalism and globalization have begun to explore transnational opportunities for mobilization that have arisen alongside the FTA and NAFTA.

Post-NAFTA Strategies

The constrained political context has especially affected the activities and roles of the ACN, which has witnessed a significant shift in its operations since the heady days of the anti-FTA and anti-NAFTA campaigns. No longer the central coordinator of national campaigns, it now serves primarily as a facilitator for communications by providing assistance to groups seeking to build an activist base.[12] Few groups seek to set up, as many did in the past, a pan-Canadian locus of leadership. As a result, the campaigns carried out by networking and alliance structures that characterized the anti–free trade period have been replaced by more ad hoc resistance at the sectoral, regional, and provincial levels; protests have flared in British Columbia, in Quebec, and especially in Ontario against the deficit-driven cutbacks in social programs of the Harris government. The CAW strike against General Motors in the fall of 1996 also typifies the prevailing sectoral as opposed to national campaigns reminiscent of the earlier era.

The retreat from national campaign mobilizations reflects in part the lack of an overriding issue in the current post-NAFTA political context. The free trade 'glue' that united nationalist and other social groups in sustained mobilizations has been replaced by more disparate challenges in the social, economic, and cultural realms. A preoccupation with provincial struggles against cutbacks in social services has left social groups across Canada with little energy or resources for joint pan-Canadian mobilizations.[13] As the former chair of the ACN reflected amidst the post-NAFTA constraints, 'the siege mentality generated by the corporate agenda has shut down debate about viable alternatives,' leaving 'little energy' for work on 'alternative policies and strategies.'[14] Sectoral struggles to fight against cutbacks have severely weakened the collective will and broad-based popular-sector solidarity that helped sustain the anti-FTA and anti-NAFTA campaigns.[15]

Moreover, the ongoing regionalization, if not balkanization, that is encouraged by the continental free trade agreements and by the retreat of the federal government from the social, political, and cultural realm has severely retarded the appeal of pan-Canadian campaigns. The lack of a political alternative further contributes to the regionalization; the disappearance of viable, pan-Canadian national parties apart from the Liberals has further constrained the political opportunity context for mobilization. The NDP and Liberal political allies that sustained and collaborated with the ACN and the COC during the anti-FTA and anti-NAFTA campaigns have either been temporarily discredited among the traditional rank-and-file base or, for Liberals, been severed from the record because of the refusal of the government to renegotiate NAFTA.

In contrast to the ACN, the COC continues to experience a vitality and a growth in membership commensurate with its status as one of the few alternative, pan-Canadian political vehicles left after the political vacuum of the 1993 federal election.[16] The COC has applied lessons learned from the anti-FTA and anti-NAFTA campaigns in making a significant shift in strategy and political consciousness that addresses the challenges facing groups in an increasingly integrated continental economy. It has moved beyond its often-criticized early position as mildly centre-left and now endorses a much more radical critique of the prevailing forces of globalization and of governmental straitjacketing because of the unregulated power of transnational corporations. The re-election of the Liberals, moreover, has done little to alter the theme of the COC's call for a new era of citizen politics in Canada.[17]

The growth in the COC's membership is a testament to its ability to evolve as much as to the appeal of its message. It has grown from 16,000 members during the 1988 anti-FTA campaign to over 100,000 in spring 1998. The centrepiece of the COC's rethinking is its new Citizen's Agenda for Canada,[18] which emerged out of the 1994 annual general meeting as part of its re-evaluation of the decade-long struggle against free trade. The Citizen's Agenda reflects a major shift in mindset and strategy, from solely promoting Canadian national sovereignty and pressuring governments on free trade to challenging transnational corporations and cultivating links with similar organizations in other countries. The anti-NAFTA tri-national campaigns laid the foundation, but the reality of streamlined governments and mobile corporations has led the COC to question the notion of sovereignty and the ability of Canada's national political system to protect democracy and sovereign rights.[19] This rethinking is reflected in the thoughts of one former prominent anti–free trade organizer who argues now that 'with the passage of NAFTA, the struggle for national sovereignty is lost.'[20]

The refocusing does not mean, however, that the COC has completely abandoned its efforts to pressure the federal government and to critique the ongoing effects of the continental free trade agreements.[21] What it does signal is an attempt to reinstall a sense of civic responsibility and action – popular sovereignty on the domestic stage – as a natural precursor to executing national sovereignty on the international stage. In this context, then, challenging the federal government has become less relevant, at least temporarily, and new targets and activities involving monitoring corporations have been developed within the rubric of the COC's Citizen's Agenda for Canada. Through recent *Action Link* bulletins, the COC has targeted the efforts of the transnational giant Monsanto to introduce rBGH into Canada's milk supply, the new block-funding arrangement put in place by the federal Liberals for Canada's medicare system, and the entry of Wal-Mart, the giant U.S. retailer, into the Canadian retail market.[22]

In addition to these campaigns that are still centred on the nation and that focus on transnational corporations and community-based resistance, the Citizen's Agenda calls for the strengthening of tri-national and hemispheric alliances.[23] Building on the experiences of the tri-national anti-NAFTA coalitions, groups in July 1994 expanded into Chile, Columbia, Brazil, and Guatemala in anticipation of attempts by their governments to enter NAFTA. An international conference in Mexico City in July 1994 on 'Integration, Development and Democracy: Toward a Continental Social Agenda' drew 150 activists from across North and South America to develop a communications network among hemispheric organizations.[24] The participants at the conference also developed a final declaration calling for the creation of a hemispheric social charter and of network mechanisms to monitor the ongoing social and economic effects of NAFTA.

Common Frontiers has also continued to play a key role in encouraging groups to coalesce across national borders around social and economic issues relevant to the global economy. In response to President George Bush's Enterprise for the America's Initiative, designed to promote hemispheric free trade, Common Frontiers has networked with groups across Latin America.[25] One project, 'Challenging Free Trade in the Americas,' draws from the resources of the Canada–Chile Coalition for Fair Trade and encourages developmental alternatives to the NAFTA and export-oriented growth models that are favoured by the two governments.[26] Other efforts at hemispheric and global popular education and resistance have included the formation of the International Forum on Globalization, a progressive think-tank of intellectuals and public figures from around the world dedicated to forging democratic alternatives to corporate and economic globalization,[27] and joint work by dozens of social groups in Chile, Mexico, the United States, and Canada in drafting and sending a letter to the leaders of each country protesting the expansion of NAFTA across the hemisphere.

Towards a Transnational Social Movement?

Although it was an unsuccessful bid to defeat the FTA in the 1988 federal election, the anti-FTA campaign in Canada provided valuable lessons to networking groups across the North American continent. Previously rooted in a left-nationalist mindset that limited their interventionist potential in the face of an already mobilized transnational business community, these groups rebounded in the anti-NAFTA campaign by reaching across borders to coalesce with groups in the United States and in Mexico. The post-NAFTA reality of imminent hemispheric free trade has suggested a further lesson for the North American social groups: national governments may be increasingly less willing or less able to exercise the same degree of political sovereignty in the face of constraints imposed by continental trade agreements.

This new reality does not suggest, however, that a new era of transnational North American social movements has arrived. Clearly, globalization has encouraged the rise of transnational political opportunities and expanded resources for continental mobilization. Transnational political exchange has accelerated, with new networks on specific issues sprouting up across North and South America. The Internet has become an important resource and an example of the globalization strategy: Canadian, U.S., and Mexican groups have developed detailed sites for the transfer and sharing of tactics and information to challenge the spread of NAFTA across the hemisphere.[28] However, this pattern represents a continuation of the diffusion of the tactics and strategy of Canadian national movements south through the United States and into Mexico. The era of national political and social movements has not been transcended, merely significantly constrained.

Will popular sovereignty replace national sovereignty as a major theme around which people will organize and mobilize across North America? By their actions and goals, increasing numbers of people in labour, church, academic, environmental, and other hemispheric organizations have been drawn in that direction. However, despite the strides made in expanding both international consciousness and tri-national strategic coalition building over the past years, the effects of the ongoing activity have not been broadly noticed by the wider public in the nations of this vast region. The experience suggests that while organizational networking across North America marks a significant transnational leap forward in cross-border cooperation at the level of civil society, the general public of Canada, the United States, and Mexico remains rooted in the familiar confines of the nation state.[29] That people remain rooted in the collective images of the sovereign nation state in the face of dramatic and ongoing integration at the financial, trade, and policy levels underscores the dilemmas facing those groups that are still seeking to debate the implications of economic integration for democracy and social welfare in the North American region.

8

Political and Theoretical Implications

As presented in this book, the popular contention that was directed against continental free trade through coalition building, mobilization, and protest challenged long-standing expectations regarding Canadian politics. Rather than defer to the neo-conservative and continentalist policies of the Progressive Conservative government and of the Liberal government that followed it, Canadians from all walks of life defied the expectations of the elite and mobilized into various domestic and transnational coalitions and networks. The development of such wide-scale, national, inter-sectoral coalitions defied historical precedents for popular-sector groups to remain split along sectoral lines. The intervention by these coalitions in parliamentary debates and procedures and the spirited challenges they threw down to the party system also defied patterns of the past whereby popular-sector groups were co-opted by ruling elites and their parties. Finally, these groups challenged as well what appeared to be the established orthodoxies of the liberal-economic world-view with such statements and actions as Social Solidarity, Ethical Reflections, mobilizations against the FTA and NAFTA, and the more recent experience of transnational networking.

However, despite this record, by the mid to late 1990s the energy, organization, and efficacy that had sustained such popular contention within Canada seems to have waned. Many of the central organizations remain; the CLC continues to represent the vast majority of unionized workers in Canada, the NAC is an instrument for women's issues, the ACN remains a vehicle of popular-sector communication, and the COC warily critiques Liberal government initiatives. Yet the contentious politics – the protests, the cross-sectoral coalition building, the interventions in parliamentary debate – these activities have lost momentum. Has the popular-sector experience been only an interesting blip on the Canadian political landscape? Are there lessons to be learned by the experience? This final chapter briefly addresses these questions and assesses the interaction of theory and empirical data and implications for future research.

Political Riddles

Certainly a first lesson points to the essential role played by political processes in the various mobilization campaigns of the popular sector. Whether the issue was electoral instability, divided elites, dramatic elections, weak parties, or parties open to popular-sector initiatives, the argument remains the same, that politics shaped mobilization. Notwithstanding the obvious contributions of such variables as organizational strength and resources, political efficacy and solidarity, collective consciousness, and even sympathetic public opinion, ACN-related groups and coalitions could not and – it can reasonably be argued – cannot shy away from negotiating with the state and the party system.[1] Thus, regardless of how much activists might have considered themselves apolitical, non-partisan, or extraparliamentary, what counted and still counts in regards to the success and failure of popular movements is the extent to which popular campaigns can directly challenge, influence, or otherwise reform the state and existing institutional arrangements. Over the past fifteen years the state, the party system, and the electoral process in Canada have survived, albeit in different forms, and often they have proved quite impervious to the concerns and critiques of the popular sector.

Yet, as Tarrow has correctly pointed out, the shifting and transitory nature of political-opportunity structures does not mean that movements, such as those spawned by popular-sector activity, are irrelevant.[2] The actions and repertoires chosen by various popular-sector groups have unquestionably expanded the scope of legitimate Canadian political discourse and action. The cross-sectoral coalition-building style of politics left its mark on the free trade and constitutional debates; at the very least the precedent has been set for extraparliamentary actors to take the initiative away from elites on issues of crucial concern to the public. Certainly the continued growth and visibility of the COC reflects today the Canadian public's disenchantment with political elites and with traditional political institutions and actors.

In fact, while the current opportunity structure in Canada remains unfavourable to large-scale popular mobilization, there is reason to suggest that a large spectrum of the Canadian public remains restive, anxious, and potentially receptive to further challenges to established orthodoxy should the political opportunities arise.[3] A great vacuum exists in the political party system in Canada today, feeding public cynicism and uncertainty. While the media and academic professions still tend to gravitate towards familiar images of party and Parliament, the politics acted out by the popular sector succeeded in turning attention during this period to those challenges at the boundaries of the political spectrum, in terms of both minds and institutions.

This study also reminds observers that the perennial realities of regionalism and nationalism have not exited the Canadian political stage but continue to exert a large degree of influence over the Canadian political agenda. The political designs of English-speaking Canadians, whatever their political stripe, have always been affected by the distinctly different society in Quebec. Yet history continues to repeat itself, with the free trade and constitutional sagas clearly stumbling over the Quebec question. Prime Minister Trudeau failed to resolve the Quebec issue with the proclamation of the 1982 Constitution. The anti–free trade movement failed to come to grips with it in 1988. Prime Minister Mulroney failed soon thereafter with the twin debacles of the Meech Lake and Charlottetown accords. And popular-sector groups continue to struggle to bridge the divide between different national visions held in Quebec and in the rest of Canada.

Thus, the popular sector's political missteps in Quebec seem in this light to be less the exception than the rule. Until the political, social, and cultural place of Quebec in the Canadian polity is resolved, the very place of Canada, both continentally and globally, will remain uncertain. The inability or refusal of many popular-sector activists to recognize the separate ethno-nationalist reality of Quebec politics thus mirrors what will continue to be the central political dilemma threatening the viability of the Canadian state.

It should be noted again that, despite the constraints imposed by continental free trade, the mobilizing potential of the Canadian state persists, though it is now dormant. The Canadian state remains a key locus for identity, loyalty, and action. The pendulum will inevitably swing back towards centre and centre-left politics. A great potential exists for the resurfacing of a viable political party on the left – the potential is greater with globalization, where persistent social justice and welfare concerns clash with the excesses of the global market. The return to the political stage of Parliament of such a political party would once again create important domestic political opportunities for sustained and influential popular contention.

Nonetheless, it is clear that a pan-Canadian nationalism is at a particularly low ebb.[4] This era of divisive constitutional politics and continental free trade has furthered both the structural and the mental balkanization of Canada.[5] The Western Canada–based Reform Party and the separatist Bloc Québécois epitomize this regionalization. Moreover, although the public remains afflicted with a deep sense of constitutional fatigue, a variety of processes inherent to continentalism encourage Quebec separatists that a third referendum is theirs to win. This context is clearly unreceptive to the revival of a pan-Canadian, left-nationalist popular movement.

Implications of the Research

The interaction of empirical data and theory contained in this book presents a clear case of political processes driving popular contention. Specifically, four factors integral to the political-process approach explain this pattern of contentious politics. First, and most significantly, a shifting and gradually supportive structure of political opportunity from the period 1981–8 created the critical space within the Canadian political environment for the emergence and sustained mobilization of the popular-sector coalition-building and anti–free trade campaigns. The initial anti–free trade mobilization resulted from the shifting, unsettled Canadian political environment of the early and mid-1980s that was brought about especially by a deep recession, a shift by government to economic liberalization, and the results of the 1984 federal election. This weakened, vulnerable political environment then sparked increased activism on the part of excluded, popular-sector groups who secured greater negotiating power with the political elites as a result of a string of expanding political opportunities. Such favourable opportunities included divisions within and between party and parliamentary elites, electoral volatility and political realignments, and the emergence of political allies both inside and outside the political system.

In short, it is important to recognize that shifting political conditions and expanding political opportunities represented crucial determining factors in the emergence and sustained mobilization of the anti–free trade movement. Resources, organization, and skilled leadership helped, of course, to determine the rise of the popular movement. Yet major organizations and resources abounded prior to the rise of the movement; in fact, many of the groups that would become part of the anti–free trade movement had for some time received government funding. What was missing prior to the movement's emergence were the political opportunities for collective action: groups remained excluded from the polity, the political system was stable, and the bargaining position of these excluded groups was insignificant. The difference in the outcome of the popular-sector mobilization at this stage, then, was located in the political realm.

While political opportunities played a central determining role in the development of the popular-sector coalitions and mobilization campaigns, the secondary influence of internal organization and resources obviously played a strong role in the unfolding mobilization. The PCN, in particular, drew strength from a pre-existing internal organization and from the adoption of a strategy of coalition building between various popular-sector groups. The PCN's high degree of organizational readiness and strength, especially as seen in its communication, research, and analysis capabilities, helped it greatly in converting existing political opportunities into a sustained, organized protest campaign.

The third factor conducive to the sustained anti–free trade mobilization was the development of a strong sense of political efficacy and collective consciousness among the participants in the anti–free trade movement. The shifting, unsettled Canadian political environment, sparked initially by the recession and the election of a Progressive Conservative government and followed by the intense uncertainty surrounding the free trade debate, directly affected the collective outlook in the movement. Activists experienced a transformation in collective consciousness during the early stages of organizational mobilization, when a strong sense of internal solidarity and a growing sense that the debate could be shaped by collective protest and activity helped to sustain the movement into the period of the 1988 federal election campaign.

Yet, fourth and finally, this political approach has framed the current state of decline for popular-sector mobilization through the concepts of societal countermobilization and contracting political opportunity. When the survival of the FTA appeared to be in doubt, the social and political groups with interests at stake struck back. The resulting mix of the business community's countermobilization, the loosening of alliances between parties and movements, and the pro–free trade stand of the province of Quebec all severely curtailed anti–free trade efforts and activity in the latter half of the election campaign. Thus, the loss of key social and political allies, the draining away of resources, the weakening of internal organization, resolve, and efficacy, and the severely constrained structure of political opportunity all combined to demobilize effectively the anti–free trade movement by election day. The campaigns that were sandwiched between the 1993 and 1997 federal elections exhibited the same weaknesses, which were linked to the gradually contracting structure of domestic political opportunity, because the political environment no longer became destabilized in the face of popular-sector pressure.

This study also suggests that the political-process approach that was adopted could benefit from theoretical expansion and development. Specifically, as the narrative unfolded this perspective failed to capture the mutual political opportunity dynamic from which both the movement and especially the political parties that were its allies benefited. This dynamic appeared during the parliamentary protest campaign, the 1988 federal election campaign, and the anti-GST protest. An example was when the resource-depleted Liberal and New

Democratic parties benefited from the PCN's sectoral-wide research of the free trade agreement; at the same time the PCN and the broader movement gained valuable legitimacy and support from the anti–free trade delaying and debate tactics of the opposition parties in Parliament. Similarly, a case of mutually gained opportunity arose during the election campaign when the Liberal Party exploited the public's uncertainties over the deal – stoked primarily by the activities of the anti–free trade forces – while the movement's goals inched closer to reality with the Liberal leader's performance during the debates.

What this suggests, then, is how artificial the boundaries between the polity and the non-polity frequently became during some of the more frenzied moments in the campaign. The flow of resources and the structure of political opportunities were not always on a one-way street. Rather, resources and opportunities were frequently shared between what became at times a quite amorphous movement against the Free Trade Agreement, the boundaries of which overlapped what are conventionally viewed as the parliamentary and extra-parliamentary realms. Thus, room exists for building a constructive theory around the concept of mutual political opportunity.

In short, bringing the political framework into the study of movements through some variant of the political-process approach remains valuable. Recent work on cross-national issues continues to demonstrate the persistence of the interplay of political opportunity, organization, and collective consciousness and solidarity in sustaining contentious politics.[6] Moreover, the incorporation into the political-process approach of international processes represents an important area for theory-building. Movements are not 'prisoners of their states,'[7] as the experience of the 1990s transnational activities of the COC, ACN, and Common Frontiers can attest. Free trade agreements, trading blocs, monetary regimes, and international agencies have increasingly both encouraged and structured new possibilities for domestic and transnational collective action. International processes often create new transnational opportunities for protest at the very time that these processes are constraining the mobilizing potential of the state. The phenomenon of the social movement has, in fact, been given new life in the global age.

The evolving transnational mobilization linked to NAFTA invites further contributions towards building a research agenda on the North Americanization of protest. Not nearly enough has been said on this burgeoning topic, in contrast to the work on the so-called Europeanization of protest.[8] The cross-continental popular contention that spun around NAFTA presents fertile ground for research into how the agreement and its probable extension across the Western hemisphere is potentially encouraging new forms of transnational contention and collaboration.

Researchers might take a lesson from those who are engaged in this cross-national enterprise. Rigid adherence to anachronistic disciplinary or sub-disciplinary boundaries seems self-defeating in an era of growing global interdependence. The bridging of not only the division between political science and sociology but also that in the sub-disciplines of political science between the study of international relations and of comparative politics springs quickly to mind. Sovereign states have failed to contain popular collaboration; why should sovereign disciplines try to contain interdisciplinary and collaborative research?

Appendix:

Methods

This study has relied on qualitative methods to unearth rich data on the phenomenon of popular-sector activity in Canada. Interviews, primary and documentary sources, and secondary research generated the detail and in-depth analysis needed for accounting for this collective activity. The personal reflections of activists, politicians, and academics, the interactions between popular organizations and political parties, the records of the countless meetings that were held, all these contributed towards the recounting of the political process that was involved in the mobilization of the various popular-sector campaigns.

Both documentary and primary sources provided crucial first-hand information about organizations and the individuals involved in them for the years of popular-sector coalition-building and protest activity contained in this study. Available documentation included secondary sources, reports on the mass media, opinions expressed in editorials, speeches, and public opinion polls, and pamphlets and other related literature produced and distributed by the various popular-sector groups. Information was also gleaned from parliamentary debates and committee hearings and from National Archives of Canada publications.

The data retrieved from the files and archives of some of the central popular-sector organizations in Canada proved valuable. The files and archives of the following organizations were especially useful: the Council of Canadians, the Action Canada Network, and the Canadian Centre for Policy Alternatives, all in Ottawa; and the Ecumenical Coalition for Economic Justice and Common Frontiers in Toronto. The knowledge gained from these sources – and from the conceptual expectations of the political-process model – helped identify relevant individuals for interviews.

Interviews with key participants and observers of the past fifteen years of popular-sector mobilization constituted a critical source of data (see List of

Persons Interviewed on page 197). Over forty semi-structured interviews were conducted with activists, members of Parliament, civil servants, strategists for political parties, and academics. Depending on their position, most interviewees were asked a set of prepared questions structured frequently around concepts useful to an exploration of the role of core political-process variables in the popular mobilizations. Interviews lasted on average about two hours, with some persons contacted again for one or two follow-up interviews that were often conducted by telephone. Nearly all the initial interviews were conducted in person, using a tape recorder and notes for data collection.

Interviewees were encouraged to reflect on their behaviour and on their contacts with the movement and with political groups and institutions. Interviews were crucial for the study because the events of the anti–free trade struggle were still very fresh in the minds of the activists and politicians, many of whom remained actively involved in opposing the free trade agreement and other government initiatives at the time of their interviews. Many of the interviews were with key informants who suggested corroboratory evidence and frequently led to research in other sources.

Aside from the obvious empirical aims of this study, it has sought to assess the conceptual applicability of a political-process model to the Canadian case. Such analytic generalization, as opposed to statistical generalization, is one of the major justifications for and benefits of the case study. The core theoretical variables from the political-process model helped in determining which data required attention and in reducing the number of relevant events to be studied to manageable proportions. As such, this study provides more than just a narrative of Canadian political idiosyncrasies, it reveals findings that can be generalized beyond the immediate case study, and, it is hoped, further strengthen the political-process analysis of social movement mobilization in other cross-national settings.

The use of multiple sources of evidence has served to strengthen the validity and reliability of this study. Multiple sources of data have helped to validate the applicability of a political-process approach to the study, with one source of evidence being compared against others in an attempt to ascertain the value of the available political-process concepts. In short, this study is built upon an array of various corroborating sources, providing a comprehensive analysis of major popular-sector mobilizations in Canada over the past fifteen years.

Notes

Introduction

1 Duncan Cameron and Daniel Drache, eds., *The Other Macdonald Report: The Consensus on Canada's Future that the Macdonald Commission Left Out* (Toronto: James Lorimer and Co. 1985).

2 Grinspun and Kreklewich argue that the FTA and NAFTA represented corporate and elite-driven 'conditioning frameworks' that promoted and consolidated neo-liberal restructuring across North America not unlike that imposed in Latin America and elsewhere in the name of economic competitiveness. Rarely, note the authors, is such neo-liberal restructuring encouraged through 'popular free choice.' Richardo Grinspun and Robert Kreklewich, 'Consolidating Neoliberal Reforms: Free Trade as a Conditioning Framework,' *Studies in Political Economy* 43 (Spring 1994), 33.

3 Tony Clarke, 'Coalition-Building: Towards a Social Movement for Economic Justice,' *Policy Alternatives*, Spring–Summer 1983, 29.

4 Douglas McAdam, Sidney Tarrow, and Charles Tilly, 'To Map Contentious Politics,' *Mobilization*, no. 1 (1996), 17. See also Sidney Tarrow's review essay on social movements and contentious politics for another excellent overview of this direction in research: 'Social Movements in Contentious Politics: A Review Article,' *American Political Science Review* 90, no. 4 (1996).

5 Of course, I am drawing on an extensive and impressive array of studies that have contributed towards a political-process approach to studying movements. For some of the more recent and excellent overviews of such works, see Douglas McAdam, John D. McCarthy, and Mayer N. Zald, *Comparative Perspectives on Social Movements: Political Opportunities, Mobilizing Structures, and Cultural Framings* (Cambridge: Cambridge University Press 1996), especially chapters one and two; Sidney Tarrow, *Power in Movement: Social Movements, Collective Action, and*

Politics (Cambridge: Cambridge University Press 1994); and Marc Traugott, ed., *Repertoires and Cycles of Collective Action* (Durham, N.C.: Duke University Press 1995).

6 See for example Friedhelm Neidhardt and Dieter Rucht, 'The Analysis of Social Movements: The State of the Art and Some Perspectives for Further Research,' in Dieter Rucht, eds., *Research on Social Movements: The State of the Art in Western Europe and the United States* (Boulder, Colo.: Westview Press 1991); William K. Carroll, ed., *Organizing Dissent: Contemporary Social Movements in Theory and Practice* (Toronto: Garamond Press 1992); and Aldon Morris and Cedric Herring, 'Theory and Research in Social Movements: A Critical Review,' in S. Long, ed., *Annual Review of Political Science* 2 (1987).

7 See Douglas McAdam, *Political Process and the Development of Mass Insurgency, 1930–1970* (Chicago: University of Chicago Press 1982), for the earliest formulation that utilized these three concepts.

8 A systematic analysis of popular-sector mobilization of the past years has yet to appear in the scholarly literature. What little has been written is largely confined to journalistic accounts in popular magazines or represented by impressionistic polemics by activists in the struggle over free trade. Accounts of this sort can be found liberally sprinkled over the past ten years in such magazines as *Canadian Forum, Canadian Dimension*, and *This Magazine*.

9 See the Appendix for a detailed discussion of the methods employed in this study.

1: Studying Movements Politically

1 Peter Eisinger, 'The Conditions of Protest Behavior in American Cities,' *American Political Science Review* 67 (1973); Frances Fox Piven and Richard Cloward, *Regulating the Poor: The Functions of Public Welfare* (New York: Pantheon 1971); and Piven and Cloward, *Poor People's Movements* (New York: Vintage Books 1977); and William A. Gamson, *The Strategy of Social Protest* (Homewood, Ill.: Dorsey 1975).

2 McAdam, *Political Process*, 127.

3 Martti Siisiainen, 'Social Movements, Voluntary Associations and Cycles of Protest in Finland, 1905–91,' *Scandinavian Political Studies* 15 (1992).

4 Sidney Tarrow, 'The Phantom at the Opera: Political Parties and Social Movements of the 1960s and 1970s in Italy,' in Russell Dalton and Manfred Kuechler, eds., *Challenging the Political Order: New Social and Political Movements in Western Democracies* (New York: Oxford University Press 1990).

5 Hanspeter Kriesi, 'The Political Opportunity Structures of the Dutch Peace Movement,' *West European Politics* 12 (1989), 295–312; Bert Klandermans, 'Linking the Old and the New: Movement Networks in the Netherlands,' in Dalton and Kuechler, eds., *Challenging the Political Order*, 122–36; and Ben Schennk,

'From Peace Week to Peace Work: Dynamics of the Peace Movement in the Netherlands,' *International Social Movement Research* 1 (1988), 247–79.

6 Herbert Kitschelt, 'Political Opportunity Structures and Political Protest: Anti-Nuclear Movements in Four Democracies,' *British Journal of Political Science* 16 (1986), 57–85; Mary Katzenstein and Carol Mueller, *The Women's Movements of the United States and Western Europe: Consciousness, Political Opportunity, and Public Policy* (Philadelphia: Temple University Press 1987); Hanspeter Kriesi et al., 'New Social Movements and Political Opportunities in Western Europe,' *European Journal of Political Research* 22 (1992); and Thomas Rochon, *Mobilizing for Peace: The Antinuclear Movements in Western Europe* (Princeton, N.J.: Princeton University Press 1988).

7 J. Craig Jenkins and Charles Perrow, 'Insurgency of the Powerless: Farm Worker Movements (1946–1972),' *American Sociological Review* 42 (1977), 249–68; J. Craig Jenkins, *The Politics of Insurgency: The Farmer Worker Movement in the 1960s* (New York: Columbia University Press 1985); R.W. Griffin, 'Political Opportunity, Resource Mobilization, and Social Movements: The Case of the South Texas Farm Workers,' *Social Science Journal* 29 (1992).

8 Edwin Amenta and Yvonne Zylan, 'It Happened Here: Political Opportunity, the New Institutionalism, and the Townsend Movement,' *American Sociological Review* 56 (1991).

9 Harold R. Kerbo and Richard A. Shaffer, 'Lower Class Insurgency and the Political Process: The Response of the U.S. Unemployed, 1890–1940,' *Social Problems* 39 (May 1992).

10 McAdam, *Political Process*.

11 Jeffrey M. Ayres and Robert Geyer, 'Rethinking Conventional Wisdom: Political Opposition towards Integration in Canada and Denmark,' *Journal of Commonwealth and Comparative Politics* 31, no. 3 (1995); Jane Jenson, 'Naming Nations: Making Nationalist Claims in Canadian Public Discourse,' *Canadian Review of Sociology and Anthropology* 30 (1993); and Carroll, ed., *Organizing Dissent*.

12 Charles Brockett, 'The Structure of Political Opportunities and Peasant Mobilization in Central America,' *Comparative Politics* 23 (1991), 253–74; Alfred G. Cuzan, 'Resource Mobilization and Political Opportunity in the Nicaraguan Revolution: The Theory,' *American Journal of Economics and Sociology* 49 (October 1990).

13 Theda Skocpol, 'What Makes Peasants Revolutionary?' *Comparative Politics* 14 (April 1982).

14 Cynthia McClintock, 'Why Peasants Rebel: The Case of Peru's Sendero Luminoso,' *World Politics* 37 (October 1984).

15 Manus Midlarsky and Kenneth Roberts, 'Class, State, and Revolution in Central America: Nicaragua and El Salvador Compared,' *Journal of Conflict Resolution* 29 (June 1985).

16   Thomas Rochon, 'Political Movements and State Authority in Liberal Democracies,' *World Politics* 23 (1989), 299-313; and Sidney Tarrow, 'National Politics and Collective Action: Recent Theory and Research in Western Europe and the United States,' *Annual Review of Sociology* 14 (1988), 421-40.

17   Tarrow, 'National Politics,' 438.

18   John McCarthy and M. Zald, 'Resource Mobilization and Social Movements,' *American Journal of Sociology* 82 (1977), 1212-41. Others in agreement with this assertion include Anthony Oberschall, *Social Conflict and Social Movements* (Englewood Cliffs, N.J.: Prentice-Hall 1973), and M. Useem, *Protest Movements in America* (Indianapolis: Bobbs-Merrill 1975).

19   McCarthy and Zald, 'Resource Mobilization,' 1216.

20   Ibid., 1222.

21   Morris and Herring, 'Theory and Research in Social Movements,' 163.

22   Jenkins, 'Resource Mobilization Theory and the Study of Social Movements,' *American Review of Sociology* 9 (1983), 527; Jenkins, *The Politics of Insurgency*.

23   See Eduardo Canel, 'New Social Movement Theory and Resource Mobilization: The Need for Integration,' in Carroll, ed., *Organizing Dissent*; Neidhardt and Rucht, 'The Analysis of Social Movements'; Morris and Herring, 'Theory and Research in Social Movements'; and Margit Mayer, 'Social Movement Research and Social Movement Practice: the U.S. Pattern,' in *Research on Social Movements: The State of the Art in Western Europe and the USA*, ed. Dieter Rucht (Boulder, Colo.: Westview Press 1991).

24   Sidney Tarrow, *Struggle, Politics, and Reform: Collective Action, Social Movements, and Cycles of Protest* (Western Societies Program Occasional Paper, no. 21, Center for International Studies, Cornell University, Ithaca, N.Y. 1989), 57.

25   Mayer, 'Social Movement Research and Social Movement Practice,' 69.

26   Ibid.

27   Russell Dalton and Manfred Kuechler, 'New Social Movements and the Political Order: Inducing Change for Long-Term Stability?' in Dalton and Kuechler, eds., *Challenging the Political Order*, 10.

28   See for example Klaus Eder, 'The "New Social Movements": Moral Crusades, Political Pressure Groups, or Social Movements,' *Social Research* 52 (1985), 869-90; Alberto Melucci, 'The New Social Movements: A Theoretical Approach,' *Social Science Information* 19 (1980), 199-226; Klaus Offe, 'New Social Movements: Challenging the Boundaries of Institutional Politics,' *Social Research* (1985), 817-68; and Alain Touraine, *Anti-Nuclear Protest* (Cambridge: Cambridge University Press 1983).

29   Ronald Inglehart, *The Silent Revolution: Changing Values and Political Styles Among Western Publics* (Princeton, N.J.: Princeton University Press 1977), and *Culture Shift in Advanced Industrial Society* (Princeton, N.J.: Princeton University Press 1990).

30 Dalton and Kuechler, eds., *Challenging the Political Order.*

31 Touraine, *Anti-Nuclear Protest.*

32 Alan Scott, *Ideology and the New Social Movements* (London: Unwin Human 1990).

33 Katzenstein and Mueller, *The Women's Movements*; Thomas Rochon, 'The West European Peace Movement and the Theory of New Social Movements,' in Dalton and Kueschler, eds., *Challenging the Political Order*; McAdam, *Political Process*; and Kitschelt, 'Political Opportunity Structures.'

34 Klandermans, 'Linking the Old and the New,' 135.

35 Bert Klandermans and Sidney Tarrow, 'Mobilization into Social Movements: Synthesizing European and American Approaches,' in Bert Klandermans et al., eds., *From Structure to Action: Comparing Social Movement Research Across Cultures* (Greenwich, Conn.: JAI Press 1988), 23.

36 Charles Tilly, *From Mobilization to Revolution* (Reading, Mass.: Addison-Wesley 1978).

37 McAdam, *Political Process*, 36.

38 Jenkins, 'Resource Mobilization Theory,' 532.

39 Neidhardt and Rucht, 'The Analysis of Social Movements,' 444.

40 Tarrow, *Struggle, Politics, and Reform*, 83.

41 Jenkins, 'Resource Mobilization Theory,' 547.

42 Tilly, *From Mobilization to Revolution*, 213.

43 Cuzan, 'Resource Mobilization'; Jenkins and Perrow, 'Insurgency of the Powerless'; Siisiainen, 'Social Movements'; Schennk, 'From Peace Week'; and Kriesi, 'The Political Opportunity Structures.'

44 Piven and Cloward, *Poor People's Movements.*

45 Cuzan, 'Resource Mobilization.'

46 Siisiainen, 'Social Movements.'

47 Tilly, *From Mobilization to Revolution.*

48 Jenkins, 'Resource Mobilization Theory,' 546.

49 Klandermans, 'Linking the Old and the New,' 123.

50 Brockett, 'The Structure of Political Opportunities'; Jenkins and Perrow, 'Insurgency of the Powerless'; and McAdam, *Political Process.*

51 McAdam, *Political Process*, 43.

52 Aldon Morris, *The Origins of the Civil Rights Movement* (New York: The Free Press 1984); Jenkins, *The Politics of Insurgency.*

53 Mayer, 'Social Movement Research,' 68.

54 Carol Mueller, 'Building Social Movement Theory,' in Aldon Morris and Carol Mueller, eds., *Frontiers in Social Movement Theory* (New Haven, Conn.: Yale University Press 1992), 10.

55 McAdam, *Political Process*, 48.

56 Jenkins, 'Resource Mobilization Theory,' 538.

57 Klandermans, 'Linking the Old and the New.'
58 Rick Fantasia, *Cultures of Solidarity: Consciousness, Action, and Contemporary American Workers* (Berkeley: University of California Press 1988).
59 David Snow et al., 'Frame Alignment Processes, Micromobilization, and Movement Participation,' *American Sociology Review* 51 (1986).
60 Quoted in Morris and Herring, 'Theory and Research in Social Movements,' 165.
61 The volume edited by Morris and Mueller, *Frontiers in Social Movement Theory*, is entirely dedicated to exploring – and possibly remedying – this lack of a sociopsychological feature in the resource-mobilization school.

2: The Origins of a Movement

1 This short section on the politics of free trade has been drawn in part from an earlier piece, Ayres and Geyer, 'Rethinking Conventional Wisdom,' 387–8.
2 Randall White's historical account of the politics of free trade between Canada and the United States provides greater detail on this long-standing issue in dispute between the two countries. See Randall White, *Fur Trade to Free Trade: Putting the Canada–U.S. Trade Agreement in Historical Perspective* (Toronto: Dundurn Press 1988).
3 For a simple elaboration of this perspective, see Philip Resnick, *Letters to a Québécois Friend* (Montreal, Kingston: McGill-Queen's University Press 1990), chapter 1–10.
4 Christopher D. Merrett's analysis of the free trade agreement echoes the doubts expressed by opponents of the accord in Canada. See Merrett, *Free Trade: Neither Free Nor about Trade* (Montreal: Black Rose Books 1996).
5 Representative views can be found in Laurier LaPierre, ed., *If You Love This Country* (Toronto: McClelland & Stewart 1987).
6 For a few select samples of these arguments, see John Crispo, ed., *Free Trade: The Real Story* (Toronto: Gage Publishing 1988); and Marc Gold and David Leyton-Brown, eds., *Trade-Offs on Free Trade: The Canada–U.S. Free Trade Agreement* (Toronto: Carswell 1988).
7 *Canadian Trade Policy for the 1980s: A Discussion Paper* (Ottawa: Department of External Affairs 1983).
8 For an extended description of the changes initiated by the Progressive Conservative Party, see Sylvia Bashevkin, *True Patriot Love: The Politics of Canadian Nationalism* (Toronto: Oxford University Press 1991); Cameron and Drache, eds., *The Other Macdonald Report;* Bruce Doern and Brian Tomlin, *Faith and Fear: The Free Trade Story* (Toronto: Stoddart 1991), chapters 1 and 2; and Brooke Jeffrey, *Breaking Faith: The Mulroney Legacy of Deceit, Destruction, and Disunity* (Toronto: Key Porter Books 1992).

9 *Globe and Mail*, 23 June 1983.

10 Thomas d'Aquino, president of the Business Council on National Issues, notes that past efforts to achieve free trade with the United States had been opposed by the business community in Canada because 'it did not have the confidence that it could compete internationally.' Quoted from House of Commons, *Committee on External Affairs and International Trade* (33rd Parliament, 2nd session, issue no. 35, 1987), 73.

11 House of Commons, *Committee on Labour, Employment, and Immigration* (33rd Parliament, 2nd session, issue no. 2, 1987), 22–3.

12 While business interests, both large and small, voiced their support for some form of freer trade between Canada and the United States, the principal push came from the BCNI, an interest group representing over 150 of the largest corporations in the Canadian market, many of them multinational American corporations and many with an interest in free trade that extended beyond the Canadian national interest. For accounts of the BCNI's role in the government's decision to pursue a free trade accord, see Linda McQuaig, *The Quick and the Dead: Brian Mulroney, Big Business, and the Seduction of Canada* (Toronto: Viking 1991); and David Languille, 'The Business Council on National Issues and the Canadian State,' *Studies in Political Economy* 24 (1988).

Other influential Canadian business organizations jumped on the pro–free trade bandwagon including the Canadian Federation of Independent Businesses, the vast majority of trade associations, the Canadian Chamber of Commerce, and perhaps most critically the Canadian Manufacturers' Association, which had been the leading opponent of free trade with the United States since the 1911 election.

13 *How to Secure and Enhance Access to Export Markets* (Ottawa: Department of External Affairs 1985).

14 *Globe and Mail*, 19 March 1985.

15 *Competitiveness and Security: Directions for Canada's International Relations* (Ottawa: Department of External Affairs 1985).

16 Information from the Special Joint Committee on Canada's International Relations, *Report*, no. 1 (July 1985).

17 Representatives from the Canadian Labour Congress and the Council of Canadians, two of the most effective anti–free trade organizations, appeared before the special committee.

18 *Minutes of Proceedings and Evidence of the Special Joint Committee of the Senate and of the House of Commons on Canada's International Relations* (Ottawa: Queen's Printer 1985), 41.

19 See journalist and columnist David Crane's defence of the 'crusading role' played by the *Toronto Star* during the free trade debate in James P. Winter, ed., *The Silent*

Revolution: Media, Democracy, and the Free Trade Debate (Ottawa: University of Ottawa Press 1990).

20 *Toronto Star*, 13 June 1985.

21 *Minutes of Proceedings and Evidence of the Special Joint Committee of the Senate and of the House of Commons on Canada's International Relations.*

22 Royal Commission on the Economic Union and Development Prospects for Canada, *Report* (Ottawa: Minister of Supply and Services 1985).

23 *Globe and Mail*, 27 September 1985.

24 Duncan Cameron, ed., *The Free Trade Papers* (Toronto: James Lorimer 1986), 3.

25 Ibid., 8.

26 *Globe and Mail*, 1 October 1985.

27 *Globe and Mail*, 4 October 1985.

28 *Globe and Mail*, 23 December 1985.

29 John Trent interview Ottawa, 13 February 1992.

30 The importance of the CIC as an inspiration for the COC was confirmed by a score of interviews I conducted, in particular Rose Potvin, Ottawa, 22 April 1992, and Maude Barlow, Ottawa, 21 April 1992.

31 Privy Council Office, *Foreign Ownership and the Structure of Canadian Industry: Report of the Task Force on the Structure of Canadian Industry* (Ottawa: Queen's Printer 1968). From the tabling of the report, known as the Watkins Report, in 1968 to the creation of the Canadian Development Corporation in 1971, the tabling of the Report on Foreign Direct Investment (Gray Report) in 1972, and the passage of Bill c-132, the Foreign Investment Review Agency, in 1973 the Liberal government played an active, interventionist role in Canada's economy to the delight of Canadian nationalists.

32 Most notably, again, FIRA and NEP.

33 'New Climate for Investment in Canada,' Speech by the Right Honourable Brian Mulroney, prime minister, to members of the Economic Club of New York, 10 December 1984.

34 Confirmed in several interviews: John Trent, 13 February 1992, Maude Barlow, 21 April 1992, Rose Potvin, 22 April 1992, and Kenneth Wardroper, interview Ottawa, 2 June 1992.

35 John Trent interview, Ottawa, 2 April 1992.

36 From letters in the files of the national headquarters of the Council of Canadians, Ottawa.

37 Council of Canadians, press release, 11 March 1985, Ottawa, Ontario.

38 Council of Canadians, 'Statement of Purpose' (1985), national headquarters files, Council of Canadians, Ottawa.

39 Peter Brimelow strongly criticizes the CIC for its claim to represent 'Canadian' nationalism, which to him is belied by the group's overwhelmingly anglophone

roots. See Peter Brimelow, *The Patriot Game: National Dreams and Political Realities* (Toronto: Key Porter Books 1986).

40 Debbie Dunville interview, Ottawa, 11 June 1992.

41 *The Council of Canadians*, newsletter, 1986, national headquarters files, Council of Canadians, Ottawa.

42 A letter by COC organizer Debbie Dunville in March 1985 to Hurtig refers to several 'mobilization points,' including the release of Joe Clark's green paper and the decision of the government to set up a special parliamentary committee to study it. Dunville viewed these as 'heaven-sent opportunities for the Council to make itself known on a national basis.'

43 Special Joint Committee of the Senate and of the House of Commons on Canada's International Relations, *Minutes of Proceedings and Evidence* (1st session of the 33rd Parliament, 1984–5, 10 July 1985). COC national chairperson Mel Hurtig was among those who made a presentation to the committee.

44 'Success' in this case can be measured both in terms of the increase in membership attributed to the action (approximately 1,000) and of the effect it may have had on the government's decision to create straight baselines or boundaries around the Canadian Arctic islands to make it clear that all the waters inside those boundaries are subject to Canadian sovereignty.

45 'Use the Arctic or Lose it, Panel on U.S. Voyage Told,' *Globe and Mail*, 30 July 1985.

46 Dan Smith, 'Inuit Leaders Attack Ottawa's Arctic Stand,' *Toronto Star*, 8 August 1985; 'Mulroney's Arctic Silence,' editorial, *Toronto Star*, 8 August 1985.

47 'Arctic "Incursion" Protest Planned,' *Globe and Mail*, 6 August 1985.

48 'Nationalists Claim Arctic Protest Success,' *Toronto Star*, 9 August 1985.

49 Matthew Fisher, 'Polar Sea Gets the Message as Plane Drops Flags on Deck,' *Globe and Mail*, 9 August 1985.

50 Supportive and sympathetic opposition party members included Liberals Sheila Copps and Herb Gray and New Democrats Pauline Jewett, Lorne Nystrom, and Nelson Riis.

51 Lloyd Axworthy interview by telephone, Ottawa, 10 June 1992; Herb Gray interview, Ottawa, 11 May 1992; and Steven Langdon interview, Ottawa, 19 May 1992.

52 A look at the participants at the inaugural conference of the Council of Canadians reveals a number of MPs, including Steven Langdon, Herb Gray, Lloyd Axworthy, Sheila Copps, and Lynn MacDonald.

53 Maude Barlow interview, 21 April 1992, and Rose Potvin interview, 20 April 1992.

54 Confirmed through interviews with both Rose Potvin and Maude Barlow.

55 Duncan Cameron, 'Political Discourse in the Eighties,' in Alain-G. Gagnon and Brian Tanguay, eds., *Canadian Parties in Transition: Discourse, Organization, and Representation* (Scarborough, Ont.: Nelson Canada 1989), 75.

56 Canadian Conference on Catholic Bishops, *Ethical Reflections on the Economic Crisis* (Ottawa: Concacan Inc. 1983).

57 Tony Clarke interview, Ottawa, 23 June 1992, and Dennis Howlett interview, Toronto, 30 April 1992.

58 The CCPA, a left-wing think-tank based in Ottawa, emerged in the early 1980s to provide a counterweight to the dominant conservative think-tanks such as the Fraser Institute. It would ultimately play a key role in disseminating research to popular-sector leaders during the anti–free trade campaign. Sandra Sorenson interview, Ottawa, 6 May 1992.

59 Bishop Remi De Roo, bishop of Victoria and Chairman of the Episcopal Commission for Social Affairs of the Canadian Conference of Catholic Bishops, in 'What's Wrong with Canada? Facing Up to the Crisis,' Canadian Centre for Policy Alternatives, 18 March 1983.

60 Miriam Smith, 'The Canadian Labour Congress: From Continentalism to Economic Nationalism,' *Studies in Political Economy* 38 (1992).

61 Sylvia Bashevkin, 'Free Trade and Canadian Feminism: The Case of the National Action Committee on the Status of Women,' *Canadian Public Policy* 15 (1989), 364.

62 Dennis Howlett interview, 30 April 1992, and Laurell Ritchie interview, Toronto, 18 June 1992.

63 See Special Joint Committee on Canada's International Relations, *Minutes of Proceedings and Evidence*, issue no. 5, 6–20, for the reaction of the Canadian Labour Congress to early Progressive Conservative initiatives.

64 Smith, 'The Canadian Labour Congress.'

65 Sylvia Bashevkin, 'Free Trade and Canadian Feminism,' 367.

66 Several people interviewed suggested that popular-sector groups were less suspicious of women and the women's movement in general than they were of other opponents of the Tories. That there was something to the conventional wisdom that women are conciliatory and can be trusted, see Laurell Ritchie interview, 18 June 1992, and John Foster interview, 8 June 1992.

67 Marjorie Cohen, 'The Anatomy of the Decision: The Efforts of Coalitions,' in Jane Jenson, ed., *The Free Trade Agreement of 1988: Implications for the Future of Canadian–American Relations* (Harvard University: The Center for International Affairs 1989).

68 National Action Committee on the Status of Women, 'Free Trade Could be Costly for Women Workers,' *Feminist Action* (October 1985), 2.

69 Cameron and Drache, eds., *The Other Macdonald Report*, taps into the popular sector's counter-discourse on Canada's political economy with a compilation of

many of the briefs to the commission by its member groups. Dennis Howlett, activist with the ECEJ argued that 'some of the analysis in the *Other Macdonald Report* moved away from the more reformist, liberal orientation of many social and economic welfare groups to the more radical position – you could see that from many of the different sectors.' Interview, 30 April 1992.

70 Peter Bleyer, 'Coalitions of Social Movements as Agencies for Social Change: The Action Canada Network,' in Carroll, ed., *Organizing Dissent*, 105.

71 Marjorie Cohen, 'The Macdonald Report and Its Implications for Women,' paper for the National Action Committee on the Status of Women (November 1985).

72 Laurell Ritchie, 'The Potential Impact of Free Trade and the Macdonald Commission on Women in Canada,' presentation to the meeting of the COC, 14 November 1985.

73 Ibid.

74 Laurell Ritchie and Rick Salutin recounted the events of the meeting in separate interviews. Ritchie interview, 18 June 1992, and Rick Salutin interview, Toronto, 13 May 1992. A similar, albeit less detailed account, can be found in Rick Salutin, *Waiting for Democracy: A Citizen's Journal* (Markham, Ont.: Penguin 1989).

75 Laurell Ritchie interview, 18 June 1992.

76 Tilly, *From Mobilization to Revolution*.

77 John W. Warnock, *Free Trade and the New Right Agenda* (Vancouver: New Star Books 1988), 298.

78 McAdam, *Political Process*.

3: The Politics of Coalition Building

1 Jenkins, *The Politics of Insurgency*, 13.

2 McAdam, *Political Process*, 43.

3 Jenkins, *The Politics of Insurgency*, 7.

4 As indicated in ibid., 13.

5 Tilly, *From Mobilization to Revolution*, 145.

6 Minutes of the meeting of the Coalition Against Free Trade, Toronto, 13 February 1986.

7 With the release of this strategy memo, one activist at the meeting exclaimed that 'this is a declaration to the government that the organization that you feared has arrived.' Laurell Ritchie interview, 18 June 1992.

8 See Smith, 'The Canadian Labour Congress,' for details on the politics and strategies behind Canadian labour's delayed adoption of the intersectoral coalition-building strategy.

9 Gatt-Fly, *Ah-Hah! A New Approach to Popular Education* (Toronto: Between the Lines 1983).

10 The Ecumenical Coalition for Economic Justice, also known as Gatt-Fly, has since its inception in 1973 been a national project of five Canadian churches (Anglican,

Roman Catholic, Lutheran, Presbyterian, and United) and is mandated to assist popular groups struggling for economic justice in Canada and in the Third World.

11 See Dennis Howlett, 'Social Movement Coalitions: New Possibilities for Social Change,' *Canadian Dimension*, November–December 1989, 41.

12 The events of the summer and fall of 1983 have been described in much greater detail, and with differing analyses, elsewhere. For broader reflections on this experience and the effects of the provincial government's 'restraint' policies, see Bryan D. Palmer, *Solidarity: The Rise and Fall of an Opposition in British Columbia* (Vancouver: New Star Books 1987); Bruce Magnusson et al., eds., *The New Reality: The Politics of Restraint in British Columbia* (Vancouver: New Star Books 1984); and William K. Carroll and R.S. Ratner, 'Social Democracy, Neo-Conservatism, and Hegemonic Crisis in British Columbia,' *Critical Sociology* 16, no. 1 (1989). Several observers and popular-sector activists in the Solidarity Coalition have provided valuable insights, in particular Art Kube, who in 1983 was head of the British Columbia Federation of Labour and at the time of interview director of special projects of the CLC. Art Kube interview, Ottawa, 30 June 1992.

13 Warnock, *Free Trade and the New Right Agenda*, 301.

14 This coalition drew upon various local labour organizations, including the Canadian Union of Public Employees, the Canadian Union of Postal Workers, the Canadian Association of Industrial, Mechanical and Allied Workers, the Independent Canadian Transit Union, and the United Brotherhood of Carpenters and Joiners of America. These labour locals joined with other popular-sector groups including organizations representing members of professions and small business owners, senior citizens, the unemployed, educators and students, ethnic minorities, human rights and anti-poverty organizers, churches, and environmental and peace movements. See Carroll and Ratner, 'Social Democracy,' 39.

15 Ibid.

16 Carroll, 'The Solidarity Coalition,' 98.

17 In compiling these five flaws I have synthesized the analysis of Palmer, *Solidarity*, and Warnock, *Free Trade and the New Right Agenda*.

18 Palmer, *Solidarity*, 89.

19 Warnock, *Free Trade and the New Right Agenda*, 301.

20 Palmer, *Solidarity*, 91.

21 Ibid., 89.

22 Warnock, *Free Trade and the New Right Agenda*, 301.

23 Palmer, *Solidarity*, 92.

24 Warnock, *Free Trade and the New Right Agenda*, 301.

25 For greater detail on the Socred restraint legislation in the period after the Solidarity Coalition, see Carroll and Ratner, 'Social Democracy.'

26 These reflections were conveyed to me by numerous activists, including Laurell
     Ritchie interview, 18 June 1992; Dennis Howlett interview, 30 April 1992; and
     Art Kube interview, 30 June 1992.
27 Howlett, 'Social Movement Coalitions,' 41.
28 Ibid.
29 Canadian Conference of Catholic Bishops, *Ethical Reflections*. A sense of just how
     important the bishops' statement was as a morale booster and as a spark for
     coalition building to popular-sector groups became evident by the number of times
     it was mentioned in an unsolicited manner by the activists interviewed. When
     asked which events in particular stuck out in their minds as being particularly
     conducive to the start of the anti–free trade movement, the vast majority mentioned
     the bishops' statement as a key to sparking coalition building and to boosting the
     sagging morale of popular-sector groups that were still reeling from the recession.
     In particular, Laurell Ritchie interview, 18 June 1992; Tony Clarke interview, 23
     June 1992; Michael McBane interview, 27 May 1992; Duncan Cameron interview,
     Ottawa, 6 May 1992; Dennis Howlett interview, 30 April 1992; and John Foster
     interview, 8 June 1992.
30 Tony Clarke interview, 23 June 1992.
31 See Ed Finn, 'Church, Labour Agree on Need for "New Social Movement,"'
     Policy Alternatives, Spring–Summer 1983.
32 See Clarke, 'Coalition-Building.'
33 Tilly, *From Mobilization to Revolution*, 62–3.
34 Jenkins, *The Politics of Insurgency*, 9.
35 Dennis Howlett interview, 30 April 1992. A cross-sample of church, women's, and
     labour media reveals that each group gave comparable attention to the anti–free
     trade message during the spring of 1986. See for example Gatt-Fly, 'Churches
     Urged to Oppose Free Trade with the U.S.,' *Gatt-Fly Report* 7 no. 1 (March 1986),
     Marjorie Cohen, 'Undressing Macho-Economics: the Macdonald Report's
     Implications for Women,' *Our Times*, June 1986; and 'Dialogue '86,' *Canadian
     Labour*, February 1986.
36 Jenkins, *The Politics of Insurgency*, 9.
37 Dennis Howlett interview, 30 April 1992. Subsequent interviews with John Foster,
     Tony Clarke, and Laurell Ritchie confirmed the importance of the less formal
     dynamic of personal, solidarity friendships.
38 James Q. Wilson, *Political Organizations* (New York: Basic Books 1973).
39 Klandermans, 'Linking the Old and the New,' 125.
40 Department of Industry, Trade, and Commerce, *Major Canadian Projects, Major
     Canadian Opportunities: A Report by the Major Projects Task Force on Major
     Capital Projects in Canada to the Year 2000* (Ottawa 1981). Smith, 'The Canadian

Labour Congress' also suggests that the CLC took steps to build alliances with other popular-sector groups opposed to the Tory government 'even before the anti–free trade campaign got under way.' Yet the CLC was quite hesitant to commit itself fully to the coalition-building approach in case it should jeopardize opportunities for compromise with the government for securing policy gains. The Dialogue '86 conference highlighted the CLC's intrasigence on the coalition-building issue.

41 Characterizations given as such in interviews with John Foster, Laurell Ritchie, and Dennis Howlett.

42 Canadian Labour Congress, brief submitted to Dialogue '86, Conference 'Outline of Conference Themes' (Ottawa, 12–14 January 1986).

43 Quoted from, Tony Clarke, 'A Report and Recommendations to the Canadian Council of Churches Concerning Sponsorship and Participation in the Follow-Up to the National Economic Conference, Called Dialogue '86' (Canadian Conference of Catholic Bishops, Social Affairs Office, October 1985), 2.

44 Marjorie Cohen, brief submitted to Dialogue '86 Conference on behalf of the National Action Committee on the Status of Women (January 1986), 3.

45 Bishop Adolphe Proulx, on behalf of the Canadian Council of Churches, 'Notes for Initial Commentary at Dialogue '86, National Economic Conference' (Ottawa, 12–14 January 1986), 3.

46 Smith, 'The Canadian Labour Congress,' 40.

47 Letter, Dick Martin, executive vice-president, Canadian Labour Congress, to Laurell Ritchie, Confederation of Canadian Unions, 19 February 1986.

48 Marjorie Cohen, 'Discussions about Coalition-Building,' in Ronnie Leah, ed., *Taking a Stand: Strategy and Tactics of Organizing the Popular Movement in Canada* (Ottawa: Canadian Centre for Policy Alternatives, 1992), 33.

49 Insights drawn from interviews with Dennis Howlett, Laurell Ritchie, Tony Clarke, and Nancy Riche, Ottawa, 25 June 1992.

50 Tony Clarke interview, 23 June 1992.

51 This program later appeared in the book by John Calvert, CUPE's research director, *Government Limited: The Corporate Takeover of the Public Sector in Canada* (Ottawa: Canadian Centre for Policy Alternatives 1984).

52 For an elaboration of this move, see Sam Ginden, 'Breaking Away: The Formation of the Canadian Auto Workers,' *Studies in Political Economy* 29 (Summer 1989).

53 Interviews with Tony Clarke and Dennis Howlett.

54 While Dialogue '86 did make a major contribution towards reprioritizing labour's goals, the labour bureaucracy never entirely abandoned hope for a consultative alternative with state and business. See Smith, 'The Canadian Labour Congress,' 40–1. Moreover, the emerging anti–free trade coalition had no assurance of labour's allegiance to the more confrontationalist coalition-building approach, a

weakness that would raise its debilitating head during the federal elections in the fall of 1988.

55 For greater detail on the tensions and difficulties involved in forming this coalition and in producing the Declaration on Social and Economic Policy, see 'A Time for Social Solidarity: Popular Groups' Statement,' *Our Times* (May 1988), 8–9.

56 *A Time to Stand Together, a Time for Social Solidarity: A Declaration on Social and Economic Policy Directions for Canada by Members of Popular Sector* (Toronto: Our Times 1987), 11.

57 For more on the Massey Hall event, see Ross Howard, 'Trade Critics Taking Fight to Grassroots,' *Globe and Mail*, 26 February 1986; and Ellie Kirzner, 'Joining the Foes of Free Trade,' *NOW*, 13–19 March 1986.

58 Beginning in at least 1985 and until the 1988 election period leading cultural journals also frequently entered the free trade debate, often on the side of the opposition. For examples, see *Canadian Forum*, October 1986; *Canadian Dimension*, September 1987. Also see LaPierre, ed., *If You Love This Country*.

59 Margaret Atwood, *Survival: A Thematic Guide to Canadian Literature* (Toronto: House of Anansi 1972), 18–19.

60 Quoted in Bernard Ostry, 'The Plain Truth: Talking to Americans about Culture and Power,' *Canadian Forum*, October 1986, 7.

61 Quoted in McAdam, *Political Process*, 44.

62 Quoted in ibid., 45.

63 Ibid.

64 Ibid.

65 The original set of groups that first became formally part of the PCN included the COC, the Assembly of the First Nations, the Alliance of Canadian Cinema, Television and Radio Artists (ACTRA), the Canadian Teachers' Federation, NAC, and the National Farmers' Union.

66 Quoted from a interview with John Trent. The path to the creation of the PCN was not without its share of roadblocks, however. The CLC hierarchy continued to be sceptical of a national coalition that might impinge upon its control and its direction of anti–free trade activities by labour; popular-sector groups, especially those involved in the Working Committee for Social Solidarity, were suspicious of the COC, regarding it as an organization of individuals who were without experience in the traditional issues of social solidarity of leftist circles and uncommitted to those issues; and in Quebec many of the popular-sector and labour groups were suspicious of the Pan-Canadian, English-Canadian nationalism that appeared to be most strongly mobilizing COC stalwarts.

67 A Council of Canadians press release, dated 1 April 1987, illustrates the range of formal participants in the 4 April Canada Summit: Alliance of Canadian Cinema, Television and Radio Artists (ACTRA), Canadian Apparel Manufacturers Institute,

Canadian Artists' Representation, Canadian Chicken Marketing Agency, Canadian
Coalition Against Media Pornography, Canadian Conference of the Arts, Canadian
Council on Social Development, Canadian Ethnocultural Council, Canadian
Federation of Students, Canadian Labour Congress, Canadian Nature Federation,
Canadian Teachers' Federation, Council of Canadians, La Coalition québécoise
d'opposition au libre-échange, National Action Committee on the Status of
Women, National Anti-Poverty Organization, National Association of Friendship
Centres, National Farmers' Union, National Federation of Nurses Unions,
Operation Dismantle, Playwrights Union of Canada, Pollution Probe Foundation,
and Project Ploughshares, as well as Inuit from the Northwest Territories.

68 Hugh Windsor, 'Free Trade Conference Lets Nationalist Genie Out of the Bottle,'
    Globe and Mail, 6 April 1987.

69 The CATJO was fronted by two highly visible and outspoken free trade supporters,
    former royal commissioner Donald S. Macdonald and former Alberta premier Peter
    Lougheed, and it was sponsored by the Business Council on National Issues, the
    Canadian Manufacturers Association, and the Canadian Chamber of Commerce.

70 This section draws from the following narratives of the free trade negotiation
    process: Doern and Tomlin, *Faith and Fear*, chapters 5–8; Giles Gherson,
    'Washington's Agenda,' in *The Free Trade Deal*, Duncan Cameron, ed., (Toronto:
    James Lorimer 1988); and Robert M. Campbell and Leslie A. Pal, 'A Big Deal?
    Forging the Canada–U.S. Free Trade Agreement,' in Campbell and Pal, eds., *The
    Real Worlds of Canadian Politics: Cases in Process and Policy* (Peterborough,
    Ont.: Broadview Press 1989).

71 Gherson, 'Washington's Agenda,' 4.

72 Ibid., 128.

73 Donna Dasko, 'The Canadian Public and Free Trade, in *The Free Trade Deal*,
    ed. Duncan Cameron (Toronto: James Lorimer 1988), 248.

74 Ibid.

75 Minutes, Coalition Against Free Trade, General Meeting, Toronto, 12 February
    1986.

76 Ibid., 10 July 1986.

77 Maude Barlow interview, 22 April 1992.

78 Gatt-Fly, *Free Trade, Self-Reliance, and Economic Justice, Report of the Ecumeni-
    cal Conference on Free Trade, Self-Reliance, and Economic Justice, February 26–
    March 1, 1987, Orleans, Ontario* (Toronto: Gatt-Fly 1987).

79 Dasko, 'The Canadian Public,' 248.

80 The CATJO included such significant Canadian business organizations as the
    BCNI, the CMA, the Canadian Chamber of Commerce, the Canadian Bankers'
    Association, the Canadian Federation of Independent Business, and Quebec's
    Coneil du patronat. See David Laycock, 'Organized Interests in Canada and the

Free Trade Election,' In Jane Jenson, ed., *The Free Trade Agreement of 1988: Implications for the Future of Canadian–American Relations* (Harvard University: The Center for International Affairs 1989).

81 Ibid., 17.

82 John Whalley and Roderick Hill, eds., *Canada–United States Free Trade* (Toronto: University of Toronto Press for Supply and Services Canada 1985). See especially the appendices to the Introduction, 17–41.

83 House of Commons, *Debates*, 2nd session, 33rd Parliament, 16 March 1987.

84 Campbell and Pal, *The Real Worlds*, 326.

85 For varied perspectives on this view, see Rick Salutin, 'Keep Canadian Culture Off the Table – Who's Kidding Who?' in LaPierre, ed., *If You Love This Country*; many of the issues of the *Canadian Forum* between 1985 and 1988 for references to the dangers posed to Canadian culture by the deal.

86 This position was argued time and again by anti–free trade activists. See for example Majorie Cohen, 'Our Social and Economic Programs Are in Greater Danger than Ever Before,' and Denis Stairs, 'Canada Will Be a Less Relaxed, a Less Gentle, a Less Tolerant Place in which to Live,' in LaPierre, ed., *If You Love This Country*.

4: The Parliamentary Protest Campaign

1 McAdam, *Political Process*, 42.

2 Ibid.

3 Oberschall, *Social Conflict*, 119.

4 From Tony Clarke, *Building the Movement: The Pro-Canada Network* (Ottawa: The Pro-Canada Network 1989).

5 Various coalitions of social activists, some of which had existed before the free trade movement, soon built cooperative links with the anti–free trade forces. These included the British Columbia Coalition Against Free Trade, the Saskatchewan Coalition Against Free Trade, the Manitoba Coalition Against Free Trade, the Prince Edward Island Coalition Against Free Trade, the Nova Scotia Coalition Against Free Trade, and the Social Action Commission of Newfoundland.

6 The PCN precluded individual memberships to ensure, as one member organization put it, that the PCN was not mistaken for a 'party in the making.' CUPE, *The Development of Coalition Politics in Canada in Recent Years* (Ottawa: CUPE 1992).

7 Objectives and strategies gleaned from the minutes of the first PCN National Assembly, held on 17–18 October 1987, Ottawa.

8 One important exception to this rule was the Citizens Concerned About Free Trade, based in Saskatchewan, under the charismatic leadership of David Orchard.

9 Press statement, Pro-Canada Network National Assembly, Ottawa, 19 January 1988.

10 PCN Strategy Committee discussion document, Ottawa, Ontario, 11 February 1988.

11 Pro-Canada Network strategy document, Ottawa, 16 January 1988.

12 The Pro-Canada Network, 'Pro-Canada Network Leaders Present Petitions to Opposition Leaders,' *Pro-Canada Dossier* 12 (1 June 1988), 13.

13 From minutes of the Pro-Canada Network Lobby Action, Coalition Against Free Trade, Ottawa, 30 May 1988.

14 Maude Barlow interview, 22 April 1992.

15 '300 Protest Free-Trade Deal,' *Ottawa Citizen*, 13 June 1988.

16 The Pro-Canada Network, 'June 12th – Canadians Across the Country Show Opposition to Trade Deal,' *Pro-Canada Dossier* 13, 27 June 1988, 5.

17 McAdam, *Political Process*, 44.

18 Neidhardt and Rucht, 'The Analysis of Social Movements,' 444.

19 Ibid., 443.

20 Banting points out that Canada's brand of neo-conservative was mild in comparison to the Reaganite and Thatcherite versions. Nevertheless, it was still a jolt to the post-war political establishment that had been dominated by the Liberal Party's semi-interventionist, welfare state policies. See Keith Banting, 'Neoconservatism in an Open Economy: The Social Role of the Canadian State,' *International Political Science Review* 13 (1992).

21 Clarkson notes that because of Turner's decentralization of the party Liberal MPs from the nationalist-left of the party's ideological spectrum increasingly by the late summer of 1987 rewrote the party's policy agenda. See Stephen Clarkson, 'The Liberals: Disoriented in Defeat,' in Alan Frizzell et al., *The Canadian General Election of 1988* (Ottawa: Carleton University Press 1989), 32.

22 Mel Clark, a former senior trade negotiator in Canada's civil service who became a liaison between the Liberal Party and anti–free trade groups worked extensively for the party on its trade policy. Mel Clark interview, Ottawa, 12 June 1992. Clark's important role as an intermediary was confirmed through interviews with Maude Barlow, Duncan Cameron, and Dennis Howlett.

23 The PCN's research and analysis network had a much broader grasp of the sectoral implications of the impending free trade deal than the caucus did, making the PCN a highly valued resource for the scrambling Liberal Party.

24 Lloyd Axworthy interview, 10 June 1992. Axworthy specifically mentioned the important role played by Mel Clark as a liaison between the Liberal caucus and anti–free trade groups.

25 See, for example, 'Public Doubt about Trade Deal Rises,' *Globe and Mail*, 1 July 1988.

26 Tarrow, *Struggle*, 84.

27 See for example Lawrence LeDuc et al., 'Partisan Instability in Canada: Evidence from a New Panel Study,' *American Political Science Review* 78 (1984).

28 Clarke et al. estimate that over two-thirds of the Canadian electorate can be classified as 'flexible partisans,' and thus lacking a stable and long-term attachment to any political party. See Harold D. Clarke et al., *Absent Mandate: Interpreting Change in Canadian Elections* (Toronto: Gage Publishing 1991).

29 Heather Bird, '52% Back Senate Stall of Trade Bill Gallup Says,' *Toronto Star*, 22 August 1988.

30 Tarrow, *Struggle*, 88.

31 John Trent interview, 2 April 1992.

32 From the minutes of the Pro-Canada Network First National Assembly, Ottawa, 18 October 1987.

33 Laurell Ritchie interview, 18 June 1992.

34 Pro-Canada Network, 'Campaign Suggestions for the Pro-Canada Network' (Ottawa, 16 January 1988), 6.

35 The PCN commissioned Angus Reid Associates to conduct this survey. The study involved telephone interviews with a representative cross-section of 1,212 Canadian adults conducted between 24 and 28 August 1987.

5: The Constraints of Electoral Politics

1 For notable exceptions see McAdam, *Political Process*; Lee Ann Banaszak, *Why Movements Succeed or Fail: Opportunity, Culture, and the Struggle for Woman Suffrage* (Princeton, N.J.: Princeton University Press 1996); and Tarrow, *Power in Movement*.

2 McAdam, *Political Process*, 53.

3 The Pro-Canada Network, *What's the Big Deal: Some Straightforward Questions and Answers on Free Trade* (Ottawa, October 1988).

4 *What's the Big Deal* appeared with the *Vancouver Province, Edmonton Journal, Regina Leader-Post, Saskatoon Star Phoenix, Winnipeg Free Press, Western Producer, Kitchener-Waterloo Record, London Free Press, Ottawa Citizen, Hamilton Spectator, Toronto Star, Sudbury Star, Windsor Star, Ontario Farmer, Kingston Whig-Standard, Montreal Gazette, Moncton Times-Transcript, Saint John Telegraph, Halifax Chronicle-Herald, Sydney Post, St. John's Telegram, Charolottetown Guardian,* and *Atlantic Cooperator*.

5 Terrance Wills, 'Free Trade Foes to Use Flashy Magazine to Fight Deal,' *Montreal Gazette*, 21 September 1988.

6 Salutin, *Waiting for Democracy*, 143. Rick Salutin interview, Toronto, 13 May 1992.

7 Christopher Waddell, 'Pamphlet Attacking Free Trade Shakes Up Voters,' *Globe and Mail*, 26 October 1988.

8 Ibid.

9 For examples of the stir caused by Bowker's critique and how it became a national media obsession, even warranting coverage across the border in the United States,

see Roy MacGregor, 'She's a Free Trade Thinker for the Average Citizen,' *Ottawa Citizen*, 31 August 1988; William Walker, 'Retired Judge Causes a Stir With Plain Talk on Free Trade,' *Toronto Star*, 16 September 1988; Roy MacGregor, 'Modest Author Sparks Debate of the Decade,' *Ottawa Citizen*, 4 November 1988; John Burns, 'A Citizen's Critique Increases Uproar in Canada over Trade,' *New York Times*, 8 November 1988.

10 Marjorie Montgomery Bowker, *On Guard for Thee: An Independent Review of the Free Trade Agreement* (Hull, Que.: Voyageur Publishing 1988).

11 Ibid., 13.

12 Marjorie Nichols, 'Canadians Are Hungry for Facts on Trade Deal,' *Ottawa Citizen*, 6 September 1988.

13 Maude Barlow, interview, 22 April 1992.

14 Brooke Jeffrey interview, Ottawa, 8 June 1992.

15 Richard Johnston et al., 'Free Trade and the Dynamics of the 1988 Canadian Election,' paper prepared for the American Political Science Association annual Meeting, Atlanta, Ga, 31 August–3 September 1989, 19. Over the period of the campaign approximately seventy-seven interviews were conducted on a daily basis from 4 October to 20 November.

16 Clarke et al. *Absent Mandate*, 80.

17 Harold D. Clarke and Allan Kornberg, 'Risky Business, Partisan Volatility, and Electoral Choice in Canada, 1988,' paper prepared for the American Political Science Association Annual Meeting, Atlanta, Ga, 31 August–3 September 1989, 7.

18 Scott, *Ideology and the New Social Movements*, 6.

19 Dennis Howlett, interview, 30 April 1992.

20 Ken Traynor interview, Toronto, 18 June 1992.

21 Corroborated in interviews with several members of the Liberal Party elite and with activists, including Lloyd Axworthy interview, 10 June 1992; Michael Kirby interview, Ottawa, 22 June 1992; Peter Bleyer interview, 19 June 1992; Maude Barlow interview, 22 April 1992.

22 Peter Bleyer interview, 19 June 1992.

23 Lloyd Axworthy interview, 10 June 1992.

24 Michael Kirby interview, 22 June 1992.

25 For a sampling of the diverse interpretations, see André Blais and M. Martin Boyer. 'Assessing the Impact of Televised Debates: The Case of the 1988 Canadian Election,' *British Journal of Political Science* 26, no. 2 (April 1996), 143–64; Richard Johnston et al., *Letting the People Decide: Dynamics of a Canadian Election* (Montreal and Kingston: McGill-Queen's University Press 1992), especially chapter six; Winter, ed., *The Silent Revolution*, especially chapter 3; and Frizzell et al., eds., *The Canadian General Election of 1988*.

26 For insight and analysis on the impact of the PCN on the movement in public opinion against the deal, see Winter, ed., *The Silent Revolution*, 46–9.

27 Lawrence LeDuc, 'Voting for Free Trade? The Canadian Voter and the 1988 Federal Election,' in Paul Fox, ed., *Politics: Canada* (7th edition, Toronto: McGraw-Hill Ryerson 1991), 362.

28 Blais and Boyer, 'Assessing the Impact of Televised Debates.'

29 Alan Frizzell, 'The Perils of Polling,' in Frizzell et al., eds., *The Canadian General Election of 1988*.

30 Alan Christie, '50% Oppose Trade Deal Gallup Says,' The *Toronto Star*, 8 November 1988.

31 Maude Barlow interview, 22 April 1992. An interesting conference was subsequently held at the University of Windsor in the summer of 1989 to consider the role played by the media in the 1988 federal election, with particular reflections on the impact that the PCN had on the change in public opinion against the FTA. See Winter, ed., *The Silent Revolution*, 46–9.

32 Ibid., 63

33 Ibid., 57.

34 David Meyer and Suzanne Staggenborg, 'Movements, Countermovements, and the Structure of Political Opportunity,' *American Journal of Sociology* 101, no. 6 (May 1996), 1652.

35 Klandermans, 'Linking the Old and the New,' 128.

36 McAdam, *Political Process*, 57.

37 Of course it is crucial to note that the business community in the United States had a keen and supportive interest in the successful outcome of the FTA in Canada. The BCNI is hardly composed solely of Canadian 'national' companies – its list of members includes some of the world's largest multinational corporations, many of them based in the United States. American Express, a BCNI member, for example, was one of the earliest and strongest proponents of free trade with the United States. See McQuaig, *The Quick and the Dead*, and Merrett, *Free Trade: Neither Free nor about Trade*, for elaborate discussions of the influential role played by U.S. business in promoting free trade to Canadians.

38 Separate studies and observations have corroborated that the business community had, until the drop in the standings for the FTA and the Tories after the debates, intended maintaining a relatively low-key presence during the electoral campaign. See Canadian Alliance for Trade and Job Opportunities, Canadian Alliance for Trade and Job Opportunites, *Report of Activities March 1987 to March 1989* (1989).

39 Doern and Tomlin report that by 1987 CATJO had already run full-page pro-FTA advertisements in major newspapers across Canada and that between its formation and the election its members had been active in more than 500 free trade conferences,

meetings, and press conferences held across the country and had spent roughly over $3 million on pro–FTA materials between March 1987 and April 1988. Doern and Tomlin, *Faith and Fear*, 220.

40 Tony Van Alphen, 'Group Defending Free Trade Begins Ad Blitze in 35 Papers,' *Toronto Star*, 3 November 1988.

41 Meyer and Staggenborg, 1638.

42 Alan Freeman, 'Canadian Business Lobbying Its Workers,' *Wall Street Journal*, 14 November 1988.

43 Tony Van Alphen, 'Fight for Free Trade, Business Urged,' *Toronto Star*, 4 November 1988.

44 Van Alphen, 'Group Defending Free Trade,' 4 November 1988.

45 From Janet Hiebert, 'Interest Groups and Canadian Federal Elections,' in F. Leslie Seidle, ed., *Interest Groups and Elections in Canada*, vol. 2 of the research studies of the Royal Commission on Electoral Reform and Party Financing (Ottawa: Minister of Supply and Services Canada 1991).

46 Ibid., 23.

47 See Johnston et al., *Letting the People Decide*.

48 John Foster interview, 8 June 1992.

49 Further evidence of the constraints that the discrepancy of available resources placed on the anti–free trade forces was revealed when *Maclean's* magazine attempted to sell advertising space to the PCN for a final issue on free trade immediately before election day. Owing to a shortage of cash the PCN was forced to decline the offer but was nevertheless given a complimentary two-page advertisement in the magazine, compared to the five-page advertisement paid for by CATJO.

50 Ken Traynor interview, 18 June 1992.

51 Peter Bleyer interview, 19 June 1992.

52 Mary Boyd, in Ronnie Leah, ed., *Taking a Stand: Strategy and Tactics of Organizing the Popular Movement in Canada*, (Ottawa: Canadian Centre for Policy Alternatives 1992), 39–40. For further corroboratory evidence regarding the Liberal cooperation and NDP distancing, see Cy Gonick and Jim Silver, 'Fighting Free Trade,' *Canadian Dimension*, 23, no. 3 (April 1989), 6–14.

53 Many of the anti–free trade activists interviewed conveyed this perception. Interviews with Peter Bleyer, Maude Barlow, and Art Kube.

54 Art Kube interview, 30 June 1992.

55 For evidence see Alan Whitehorn, 'The NDP Election Campaign: Dashed Hopes,' in Frizzell et al., eds., *The Canadian General Election of 1988*; Steven Langdon interview, 19 May 1992.

56 For varying reports of the deteriorating relationship between the NDP and the anti–free trade movement during the election campaign, see Leah, ed., *Taking a Stand*;

Gonick and Silver, 'Fighting Free Trade'; Howlett, 'Social Movement Coalitions';
Mel Watkins, 'The Ed Scare: A Very False Alarm,' *This Magazine* 22 (February
1989); and Bob White, 'From Defeat to Renewal,' *This Magazine*, 23 (May–June
1989).

57 Howlett, 'Social Movement Coalitions,' 47.
58 Cohen, 'The Anatomy of the Decision,' 27.
59 Watkins, 'The Ed Scare,' 14.
60 Reg Whitaker, 'No Laments for the Nation: Free Trade and the Election of 1988,'
   Canadian Forum, March 1989, 11.
61 Duncan Cameron, in Leah, ed., *Taking a Stand*, 69.
62 Yvon Poirier, in Leah, ed., *Taking a Stand*, 71.
63 Peter Bakvis, quoted from the Pro-Canada Network, 1988 National Assembly,
   Montreal, August 1988.
64 Daniel Latouche, 'Free Trade and all that Jazz,' in Philip Resnick, *Letters to a
   Québécois Friend*, 112–13.
65 Clarke, in Leah, ed., *Taking a Stand*, 72.
66 Christian Dufour's comments that Quebec is likely to be significantly affected by
   the 'inevitable' increased continentalism of the FTA stand out in marked contrast
   to the much of the pro–free trade commentary that came from Quebec's nationalist
   community during the campaign. See Christian Dufour, *A Canadian Challenge/Le
   défi québécois* (Lantzville, B.C.: Oolichan Books 1990).
67 See, for example, Rae Murphy and Robert Chodos, 'Most Canadians Voted against
   Free Trade so Why Do We Have a Pro–Free Trade Government?' *This Magazine*
   22 (February 1989).
68 For a sample of the still undecided debate, see John Pammet, 'The 1988 Vote,' in
   Frizzell et al., eds., *The Canadian General Election of 1988*; Johnston et al.,
   Letting the People Decide; and LeDuc, 'Voting for Free Trade?'

6: NAFTA and the Structuring of Domestic and Transnational Protest

1 At the National Assembly held on 3–5 December 1988 the representatives of
  participating organizations reached a consensus in deciding that the PCN should
  continue to build an opposition movement against the FTA 'and related aspects of
  the larger neo-conservative agenda.' The National Assembly on 11–12 March 1990
  thus developed a working instrument designed to lead the PCN in that direction.
  'The Next Four Years? A Working Instrument on the Future Directions of the
  Pro-Canada Network,' PCN Assembly, 1989 March 11–12.
2 The Pro-Canada Network changed its name to the Action Canada Network at the
  14th Annual Network Assembly, held in Ottawa on 5 April 1991. In making the
  name change the organization sought to appeal to Quebeckers alienated by the

symbolism in the 'Pro-Canada' name. Elias Stavrides, 'Network changes name at April 5 event,' *Action Canada Dossier* 31 (May–June 1991), 9.

3 'Coalitions from Coast to Coast,' *Pro-Canada Dossier* 20 (May 1989), 9.

4 CCPA studies on free trade included Matthew Sanger, 'Free Trade and Worker's Rights'; Pat Armstrong and Hugh Armstrong, 'Health Care as a Business: The Legacy of Free Trade'; Bruce Campbell, 'Hard Lessons: Living with Free Trade'; and Bruce Campbell, 'Ten Reasons Why Canada Should not Enter into a Trilateral Free Trade Agreement with the U.S. and Mexico.'

5 Peter Bleyer, 'Coalitions of Social Movements as Agencies for Social Change: The Action Canada Network,' in Carroll, ed., *Organizing Dissent.*

6 Paul Koring, 'Coalition to Ride the Rails in Fight against the Budget,' *Globe and Mail,* 15 May 1989.

7 'Extraparliamentary Protest Activities and Coalition Building' (PCN strategy memo, fall GST Campaigns, 21 September 1990).

8 Pro-Canada Network memorandum, Finance Committee hearings on the GST, 16 September 1989.

9 Ingrid Peritz, 'Liberal Senators Propose Fourth Amendment to GST,' *Ottawa Citizen,* 13 November 1990; and Jeffrey Simpson, 'A More Democratic Route for the Liberals: Promise an Alternative Tax,' *Globe and Mail,* 3 October 1990.

10 Linda McQuaig, 'Keeping the Public in the Dark,' *Globe and Mail,* 17 October 1990.

11 'November the Time to Stop the GST: Network Actions to Coincide with Senate Struggle,' *Pro-Canada Dossier* 28 (5 November 1990), 1; Murray Dobbin, 'Putting the Pressure on the GST,' Pro-Canada Dossier 28 (5 November 1990), 10. See also Julia Schneider, 'Rally Protests GST, other Tory Policies,' *Whig Standard* (Kingston, Ont.), 12 November 1990; and 'Scores Brave Cold to Denounce GST,' *Calgary Herald,* 11 November 1990.

12 *Globe and Mail,* 3 October 1990.

13 William Thorsell, 'Populism is the Tune to which Tomorrow's Politicians will have to Dance,' *Globe and Mail,* 6 October 1990.

14 Randy Robinson, 'At the Federal Constitutional Conferences: ACN Groups Push Alternative Views,' *Action Canada Dossier* 35 (January–February 1992).

15 For a more precise statement of the position of both the COC and the ACN on the three nations thesis, see 'Option Three: Nationhood Revisited,' in Maude Barlow and Bruce Campbell, *Take Back the Nation* (Toronto: Key Porter Books 1991), 157–63.

16 For further insight into the ACN's contributions on unity, see Linda Hossie, 'Grassroots Groups Altered Content of Unity Debate,' *Globe and Mail,* 25 February 1992.

17 Two key figures in the COC's fight against the FTA published important critiques of the accord and the damaging impact that they discerned on the Canadian economy and social programs in just a few years after its implementation. They were both popularly accessible volumes, with Mel Hurtig's staying on the Toronto *Globe and Mail's* best-seller list for weeks. See Maude Barlow, *Parcel of Rogues: How Free Trade Is Failing Canada* (Toronto: Key Porter Books 1990), and Mel Hurtig, *The Betrayal of Canada* (Toronto: Stoddart 1991).

18 The rallying cry of the COC and other popular-sector groups was articulated in the book *Take Back the Nation*, in which COC national chairperson Maude Barlow and CCPA researcher Bruce Campbell spell out steps to be taken to generate greater citizen empowerment in the face of the weakened national political parties.

19 For an accurate overview of the emergence of new community action groups that had begun to articulate alternatives to the Mulroney free trade approach, see Virginia Galt, 'Why Canadians Turn to Grassroots Groups,' *Globe and Mail*, 17 February 1993.

20 The book *Crossing the Line* was a tri-national collective critique published in the summer of 1992 of the NAFTA texts that had been negotiated up to that point. It is a useful reference work for those seeking critical contributions by Canadian, U.S., and Mexican activists involved in the tri-national countermobilizing against NAFTA. See Jim Sinclair, ed., *Crossing the Line: Canada and Free Trade with Mexico* (Vancouver: New Star Books 1992).

21 See Reg Whitaker, 'No Laments for the Nation,' for a flavour of the post-election criticism directed against the NDP.

22 'Pick Leader Who'll Scrap FTA, Liberals Urged,' *Pro-Canada Dossier* 24 (2 March 1990), 4.

23 Randy Robinson, 'Liberals Backing Away from Stance on Abrogation,' *Action Canada Dossier* 33 (September–October 1991), 3.

24 Hugh Windsor, 'Liberal Conference Tests Icy Economic Waters,' *Globe and Mail*, 26 November 1991; and Randy Robinson, 'Abrogationist Liberals at Odds with Leadership,' *Action Canada Dossier* 34 (November–December 1991), 5.

25 For an excellent overview on research into the effects of globalization on the mobilization of social movements and on political opportunities, see McAdam, Tarrow, and Tilly, 'To Map Contentious Politic.'

26 For broad perspectives on this dynamic, see David Elkins, *Beyond Sovereignty: Territory and Political Economy in the Twenty-First Century* (Toronto: University of Toronto Press 1995); Warren Magnusson, *The Search for Political Space: Globalization, Social Movements, and the Urban Political Experience* (Toronto: University of Toronto Press 1996); and Gary Teeple, *Globalization and the Decline of Social Reform* (Toronto: Garamond Press 1995).

27 See various selections from John D. Whyte and Ian Peach, *Re-Forming Canada? The Meaning of the Meech Lake Accord and the Free Trade Agreement for the Canadian State* (Kingston, Ont.: 1989). Institute of Intergovernmental Relations, Queen's University.

28 McAdam, Tarrow, and Tilly, 'To Map Contentious Politics,' 30.

29 The steering committee of Common Frontiers included such organizations as the CLC, CAW, the United Steelworkers, the Canadian Environmental Law Association, the Latin American Working Group, the Ecumenical Coalition for Economic Justice, Oxfam Canada, and the Solidarity Works/Maquila Network.

30 Many Mexican groups looked to Canadian activists as mentors in the lead up to the mobilization against NAFTA, seeking to emulate the coalition-building strategies developed by Canadian groups in the fight against the FTA. See Teresa Gutierrez-Haces, 'Globalization from Below: The Awakening and Networking of Civil Societies in North America,' paper presented to ACSUS in the Canada Colloquium, North America in the 21st Century: Perspectives on Autonomy, Exchange, and Integration, Toronto, 8 November 1996.

31 'Canada Should Keep Out of Continental Trade Deal: PCN Chair,' *Pro-Canada Dossier* 26 (18 June 1990), 1.

32 Randy Robinson, 'Canadian Visit Ignites Debate in Mexico,' *Pro-Canada Dossier* 28 (5 November 1990), 2.

33 Matt Witt, 'Mexico–U.S.–Canada FTA: Free Workers, Not Free Trade,' *Canadian Dimension*, April–May 1991, 28–31.

34 Ken Traynor, quoted in 'These Talks Will Be Different, Groups Vow: Round Two Begins,' *Action Canada Dossier* 31 (May–June 1991), 1.

35 Randy Robinson, 'June 1 Events Mark Start of Round Two,' *Action Canada Dossier* 31 (May–June 1991), 8–9.

36 This coalition included the Confédération des syndicats nationaux, the Centrale de l'enseignement du Québec, the Fédération des travailleurs et travailleuses du Québec, CUSO-Quebec, Development and Peace, and university research organizations.

37 Randy Robinson, 'June 1 Events Mark Start of Round Two,' *Action Canada Dossier* 31 (May–June 1991), 8–10.

38 Randy Robinson, 'U.S. May Delay NAFTA Through '92,' *Action Canada Dossier* 34 (November–December 1991), 3.

39 'More Time Means More Work: ACN Chair,' *Action Canada Dossier* 34 (November–December 1991), 6.

40 See Tony Clarke, 'Alternative Proposals for Development and Trade,' *Action Canada Dossier* 34 (November–December 1991), 13; and 'International Forum Highlights,' *Action Canada Dossier* 34 (November–December 1991), 6, for samples of alternative proposals and resolutions passed by the tri-national working groups.

41 'International Forum Highlights, Continental Development Alternative, Zacatecas Mexico, October 25–27,' *Action Canada Dossier* 34 (November–December 1991, 6. See also Tony Clarke 'Alternative Proposals for Development and Trade,' *Action Canada Dossier* 34 (November–December 1991), 13–15, for insights into the alternatives proposed by the ACN and the Common Frontiers project.

42 Randy Robinson, 'Event Puts Mexican Opposition on Map,' *Action Canada Dossier* 34 (November–December 1991), 4.

43 'Guides to N.A. Solidarity Are Out!' *Action Canada Dossier* 36 (March–April 1992), 11.

44 Lynda Yanz, 'Learning Solidarity: Women Make the Links,' *Action Canada Dossier* 36 (March–April 1992), 7–9; and 'Fighting Free Trade, Mexican Style,' by Fronteras Comunes/COCOPE, translated by Nick Keresztesi, in *Crossing the Line: Canada and Free Trade with Mexico* (Vancouver: New Star Books 1992), 128–36. For a lucid account of the tensions and challenges that present barriers to the expansion of women's mobilization in response to NAFTA, see Christina Gabriel and Laura Macdonald, 'NAFTA, Women, and Organizing in Canada and Mexico: Forging a Feminist Internationality,' *Millennium: Journal of International Studies* 23, no. 3 (1993), 535–62.

45 The major inter-sectoral coalitions opposed to the NAFTA accord by 1993 included the ACN and COC in Canada, the Citizen's Trade Campaign based in the United States, and the Mexican Action Network on Free Trade.

46 Drew Fagan, 'NAFTA Fight Draws on Canadian Experience: American, Mexican Anti–Free Coalitions Look North for Ammunition, Inspiration,' *Globe and Mail*, 15 February 1993.

47 See 'Mexican Workers Protest Free Trade,' *Action Canada Dossier* 38 (December 1992), 42; and John Warnock, 'Workers' and Union Rights Brutally Repressed in Mexico,' *Action Canada Dossier* 38 (December 1992), 40.

48 See for example Bob Davis, 'U.S. Grassroots Coalition Unites against NAFTA,' *Globe and Mail*, 26 December 1992; and Peter Kilborn, 'Opposites in California Join to Fight Trade Pact,' *New York Times*, 13 October 1993.

49 The discrepancy in attendance figures reported by the *Globe and Mail* and by organizers of the event was typical of the running ideological and verbal battle between Canada's self-proclaimed 'national newspaper' and the COC and ACN. See for example Scott Feschuk, 'Protestors Bash Rae as well as Mulroney,' *Globe and Mail*, 17 May 1993, and Maude Barlow, 'Rally Was Focused,' letters to the editor, *Globe and Mail*, 20 May 1993.

50 'Council of Canadians Campaign for Canada,' *Canadian Perspectives*, Special Campaign Issue, Autumn 1993, 4–5.

51 Tarrow, *Power in Movement*, 99.

52 Chrétien successfully straddled the anti-FTA fence well in the period of the election campaign, bridging his party's internal divisions with his 'renegotiate'

stance, while hammering the Tories for not representing Canada's interests more forcefully during the NAFTA round of negotiations. See Jeffrey Simpson, 'Don't Bet Your Sombrero on the Liberals Scrapping Free Trade with Mexico,' *Globe and Mail*, 15 December 1992.

53 A survey of the ACN and of COC documents during this period illustrates that the popular sector had again amassed an impressive information campaign against NAFTA. See in particular, 'Setting a People's Agenda,' *ACN Action Dossier*, no. 39 (Autumn 1993), and 'Campaign for Canada: Stop Free Trade,' *Canadian Perspectives*, Special Campaign Issue, Autumn 1993.

54 James Laxer, *In Search of a New Left: Canadian Politics after the Neoconservative Assault* (Toronto: Viking 1996), 135.

55 Howard Pawley, 'The Crisis in Social Democracy: How the New Democratic Party Has Fared,' paper presented to the conference of the Midwest Association for Canadian Studies, Madison, Wisconsin, October 1996; and Duncan Cameron, 'Campaign Strategy: The NDP Now Carries the Dead Weight of Three Provincial Governments,' *Canadian Forum*, May 1993, 3.

56 Some of the early reflections in the press that was oriented towards the popular sector reveal the high hopes pinned on Bob Rae's electoral victory. See for instance Duncan Cameron, 'That Summer Election,' *Canadian Forum*, October 1990, 2; Kerry McCuaig, 'Keeping the NDP Honest: Social Movements Crucial Factor in Ontario Election,' *Canadian Dimension*, November–December 1990, 8–9; and 'Giving the People a Shot at Governing,' *Pro-Canada Dossier* 28 (5 November 1990), 9.

57 See Thomas Walkom, *Rae Days: The Rise and Follies of the NDP* (Toronto: Key Porter Books 1994); Patrick Monahan, *Storming the Pink Palace* (Toronto: Lester 1995); and Stephen McBride, 'The Continuing Crisis of Social Democracy: Ontario's Social Contract in Perspective,' *Studies in Political Economy* 50 (Summer 1996), 66.

58 See Virginia Galt and Martin Mittelstaedt, 'NDP Chief Quits as Labour Rift Widens: OFL Private Sector Unions Walk Out before Historic Vote to Stop Backing Party,' *Globe and Mail*, 23 November 1993; Virginia Galt, 'CUPE Members to Grapple with NDP Link: President Urges Delegates to Back Party Despite Grievances,' *Globe and Mail*, 20 November 1993; and Pawley, 'The Crisis in Social Democracy,' 23.

59 See Susan Delacourt, 'MP Blasts Rae Policies: Langdon Risks Ire of NDP Caucus in Partisan Battle,' *Globe and Mail*, 29 April 1993; and Geoffrey York, 'Langdon Slapped Down: MP Loses Job as Critic for Assailing Rae Policies,' *Globe and Mail*, 30 April 1993; and 'From Great Expectations to a Family Feud,' Globe and Mail, 15 May 1993.

60 Tarrow, *Power in Movement*, 99.

7: From National Sovereignty towards Popular Sovereignty?

1 The emergence of a wider North American community has been an area of increasingly productive research by scholars. For a selective list of works falling under this domain, see Ronald Inglehart, Neil Nevitte, and Miguel Basanez, *The North American Trajectory: Cultural, Economic, and Political Ties among the United States, Canada, and Mexico* (New York: Aldine de Gruyter 1996); Charles F. Doran and Alvin Paul Drischler, eds., *A New North America: Cooperation and Enhanced Interdependence* (Westport, Conn.: Praeger 1996; Donald Barry, ed., *Toward a North American Community? Canada, the United States, and Mexico* (Boulder, Colo.: Westview Press 1995); and Jean Daudelin and Edgar J. Dosman, eds., *Beyond Mexico: Changing Americas* (Ottawa: Carleton University Press 1995).

2 Bruce Magnusson has written widely on this interesting theme; see for example, 'Decentring the State, or Looking for Politics,' in Carroll, ed., *Organizing Consent*, 69–80; and 'De-centring the State,' in James P. Bickerton and Alain-G. Gagnon, eds., *Canadian Politics*, 2nd edition. (Peterborough, Ont.: Broadview Press 1994), 567–86.

3 Magnusson, *The Search for Political Space*, 279.

4 Ibid.

5 See Elkins, *Beyond Sovereignty.*

6 For an excellent overview of the contending strands and of the stronger and weaker positions of the thesis regarding the globalization of social movements, see Sidney Tarrow, 'Fishnets, Internets, Catnets: Globalization and Transnational Collective Action,' in Michael Hanagan et al., eds., *Challenging Authority: The Historical Study of Contentious Politics* (Minneapolis and St Paul University Press 1998).

7 For an excellent study of the parallels between globalization and the constraints facing social welfare programs globally, see Temple, *Globalization and the Decline of Social Reform.*

8 For a prescient views of Canada's trajectory towards becoming the world's 'first postmodern nation,' see Daniel Drache, 'The Post-National State,' Bickerton and Gagnon, eds., *Canadian Politics*, 2nd edition 549–66; and Richard Gwyn, *Nationalism without Walls: The Unbearable Lightness of Being Canadian* (Toronto: McClelland and Stewart 1995).

9 See Jeffrey M. Ayres, 'National No More: Defining English Canada,' *American Review of Canadian Studies* (Summer/Autumn 1995), 181–201, for an overview of the impact of such political events on the splintering identities across Canada.

10 See Philip Resnick, *Thinking English Canada* (Toronto: Stoddart 1994), and Gordon Gibson, *Plan B: the Future of the Rest of Canada* (Vancouver: Fraser Institute, 1994), for good examples of this trend.

11 See 'The Liberals and Free Trade: A Two-Faced Policy,' *Canadian Perspectives*, Special Election Issue, Autumn 1993, 6.

12 Telephone interview with Mandy Rocks, Action Canada Network, 6 November 1996. See also Action Canada Network, 'Annual Report 1995/96' (Ottawa), 1.

13 The sectoral struggle against social welfare cuts and the impact they have had had on the pan-Canadian work of the ACN is evident in one of the last full-scale ACN Dossier. See the 'Keep Canada Caring: Speak Out for Social Programs,' *ACN Action Dossier* 40 (Fall 1994).

14 Tony Clarke, 'Setting a People's Agenda,' *Action Canada Dossier* 39 (Fall 1993), 2.

15 Telephone interview with Peter Bleyer, Council of Canadians, 1 November 1996.

16 Kathleen O'Hara, 'Building for the Long Term: Maude Barlow and the Council of Canadians,' *Canadian Dimension*, July–August 1996, 17–20.

17 Maude Barlow, 'The Road Ahead: Politics as Usual Won't Restore Democracy,' *Canadian Forum*, July and August 1997.

18 'A Citizen's Agenda for Canada: Building a Movement and Renewing the Council,' *Canadian Perspectives*, Winter 1995, 12–13.

19 'Reclaiming Our Sovereignty: A Citizen's Agenda for Canada,' *Canadian Perspectives*, Winter 1995, 10–11.

20 Tony Clarke, 'Community-Based Resistance: The New Battle Front,' *Canadian Perspectives*, Winter 1994, 9.

21 The Spring 1997 issue of *Canadian Perspectives* presents a thorough critique of the Liberal record on social, cultural, and economic programs. However, noticeably absent from this 'guide to campaign '97' and indicative of the political vacuum and unavailability of viable political allies is a clear statement of support for any national political party. See 'Another Term? Inside: Your Guide to Campaign '97,' *Canadian Perspective*, Spring 1997.

22 See for example, the Council of Canadians *Action Alert* 1, no. 1 (May 1994), that introduces the COC's anti–Wal-Mart campaign, 'Up Against the Wal: A Campaign Primer.'

23 'Building a Movement and Renewing the Council,' *Canadian Perspectives*, Winter 1994, 12–13.

24 Pharis Harvey, 'North-South Organizing and Hemispheric Free Trade,' *Canadian Perspectives*, Autumn 1994, 22.

25 See Common Frontiers, 'Challenging Free Trade and Standing Up to Corporate Power,' *Canadian Perspectives*, Spring 1996, 11.

26 The Canada–Chile Coalition for Fair Trade is composed of the Canadian Labour Congress, Central Unitaria de Trabajadores, Red Nacional de Acción Ecológica, Environmental Mining Council of B.C., Red Chilean para una Iniciativa de los Pueblos, National Office of the United Steelworkers of America, Confederación Minera de Chile, Canadian Auto Workers, Communication, Energy and

Paperworkers, CONSTRAMET-Chile, Canadian Environmental Law Association, Canadian Union of Public Employees, Fédération des et travilleurs du Québec, British Federation of Labour, and Common Frontiers.

27 Maude Barlow, 'How Transnational Corporations Have Replaced Governments and what Canadians Can Do about It,' Third Annual Peter McGregor Memorial Lecture on Social Concerns, 4 November 1996, Sault Ste Marie, Ont.

28 See the web sites of the COC, Common Frontiers, and Citizen's Trade Watch for information and access to hundreds of other groups and related activities mobilizing against globalization.

29 However, perhaps the work of Neil Nevitte, Miguel Basanzy, and Ronald Inglehart, suggests some movement among the broader public in that direction as well, as research suggests attitudinal convergence along a variety of civic measures. See 'Directions of Value Change in North America,' in Stephen J. Randall and Herman W. Konrad, eds., *NAFTA in Transition* (Calgary: University of Calgary Press 1995), 343.

8: Political and Theoretical Implications

1 Gordon Laxer makes a similar point when criticizing those involved in movement politics who desire to 'wish away the state,' an unrealistic goal in light of the enduring strength of party politics. See Gordon Laxer, 'Social Solidarity, Democracy, and Global Capitalism,' *Canadian Review of Sociology and Anthropology* 32, no. 3 (August 1995).

2 Tarrow, *Power in Movement*, 99.

3 Familiar images of a Canadian public and political system conditioned by an elitist, statist political culture are being revised in other forums as well. For a scholarly attempt, see Neil Nevitte, *The Decline of Deference: Canadian Value Change in Cross-Cultural Perspective* (Peterborough, Ont.: Broadview Press 1995); and Paul Sniderman et al., *The Clash of Rights: Liberty, Equality, and Legitimacy in Pluralist Democracy* (New Haven, Conn.: Yale University Press 1996). For a more popular view see, Peter Newman, *The Canadian Revolution, 1985–1995* (Toronto: Viking 1995).

4 Sylvia Bashevkin, 'Reflections on the Future of English Canadian Nationalism,' paper prepared for the ACSUS in the Canada Colloquium, North America in the 21st Century: Perspective on Autonomy, Exchange, and Integration, Toronto, 8 November 1996.

5 Mildred Schwartz, 'NAFTA and the Fragmentation of Canada,' paper prepared for the ACSUS in Canada Colloquium, North American in the 21st Century, 8 November 1996.

6 See Banaszak, *Why Movements Succeed or Fail*, and McAdam, McCarthy, and Zald, *Comparative Perspectives on Social Movements*.

7 J. Craig Jenkins, 'Social Movements, Political Representation, and the State: An Agenda and Comparative Framework,' in J. Craig Jenkins and Bert Klandermans, eds., *The Politics of Social Protest: Comparative Perspectives on States and Social Movements* (Minneapolis: University of Minnesota Press 1995), 34.

8 See for example Sidney Tarrow, 'The Europeanization of Conflict: Reflections from a Social Movement Perspective,' *West European Politics* 18, no. 2 (1995), 223; Gary Marks and Douglas McAdam, 'Social Movements and the Changing Structure of Political Opportunity in the European Community,' *West European Politics* 19, no. 2 (1996), 249–78; and Robert Ladrech, 'Europeanization of Domestic Politics and Institutions: The Case of France,' *Journal of Common Market Studies* 32, no. 1 (1994), 69–88.

Bibliography

Books and Articles

Amenta, Edwin, and Yvonne Zylan. 'It Happened Here: Political Opportunity, the New Institutionalism, and the Townsend Movement.' *American Sociological Review* 56 (1991), 250–65.

Atwood, Margaret. *Survival: A Thematic Guide to Canadian Literature.* Toronto: House of Anansi 1972.

Ayres, Jeffrey. 'From Competitive Theorizing towards a Synthesis in the Global Study of Political Movements: Revisiting the Political Process Model.' *International Sociology* 12 no. 1 (1997), 47–60.

– 'From National to Popular Sovereignty: The Evolving Globalization of Protest Activity in Canada,' in *International Journal of Canadian Studies* 16 (1997).

– 'National No More: Defining English Canada.' *American Review of Canadian Studies* 24, nos. 2/3 (1995), 181–201.

– 'Political Process and Popular Protest: The Mobilization against Free Trade in Canada.' *American Journal of Economics and Sociology* 55, no. 2 (1996), 473–88.

Ayres, Jeffrey, and Robert Geyer. 'Rethinking Conventional Wisdom: Political Opposition towards Integration in Canada and Denmark.' *Journal of Commonwealth and Comparative Politics* 31, no. 3 (1995), 377–99.

Balthazar, Louis. *French-Canadian Civilization.* Washington, D.C.: Association for Canadian Studies in the United States 1989.

Banaszak, Lee Ann. *Why Movements Succeed or Fail: Opportunity, Culture, and the Struggle for Woman Suffrage.* Princeton, N.J.: Princeton University Press 1996.

Banting, Keith. 'Neoconservatism in an Open Economy: The Social Role of the Canadian State.' *International Political Science Review* 13 (1992), 149–70.

Barlow, Maude. *Parcel of Rogues: How Free Trade Is Failing Canada.* Toronto: Key Porter Books 1990.

Barlow, Maude, and Bruce Campbell. *Take Back the Nation.* Toronto: Key Porter Books 1991.

Barry, Donald, ed. *Toward a North American Community? Canada, the United States, and Mexico.* Boulder, Colo.: Westview Press 1995.

Bashevkin, Sylvia. 'Free Trade and Canadian Feminism: The Case of the National Action Committee on the Status of Women.' *Canadian Public Policy* 15 (1989), 363–75.

– *True Patriot Love: The Politics of Canadian Nationalism.* Toronto: Oxford University Press 1991.

Bickerton, James P., and Alain-G. Gagnon, eds. *Canadian Politics.* 2nd edition. Peterborough, Ont.: Broadview Press 1994.

Blais, André, and M. Martin Boyer. 'Assessing the Impact of Televised Debates: The Case of the 1988 Canadian Election.' *British Journal of Political Science* 26, no. 2 (1996), 143–64.

Bleyer, Peter. 'Coalitions of Social Movements as Agencies for Social Change: The Action Canada Network.' In *Organizing Dissent: Contemporary Social Movements in Theory and Practice,* edited by William K. Carroll, 102–17. Toronto: Garamond Press, 1992.

Bowker, Majorie, Montgomery. *On Guard for Thee: An Independent Review of the Free Trade Agreement.* Hull, Que.: Voyageur Publishing 1988.

Brimelow, Peter. *The Patriot Game: National Dreams and Political Realities.* Toronto: Key Porter Books 1986.

Brockett, Charles. 'The Structure of Political Opportunities and Peasant Mobilization in Central America.' *Comparative Politics* 23 (1991), 253–74.

Calvert, John. *Government Limited: The Corporate Takeover of the Public Sector in Canada.* Ottawa: Canadian Centre for Policy Alternatives 1984.

Cameron, Duncan. 'Political Discourse in the Eighties.' In *Canadian Parties in Transition: Discourse, Organization, and Representation,* edited by Alain-G. Gagnon and Brian Tanguay, 64–82. Scarborough, Ont.: Nelson Canada 1989.

– *The Free Trade Papers.* Toronto: James Lorimer 1986.

– ed. *The Free Trade Deal.* Toronto: James Lorimer 1988.

Cameron, Duncan, and Daniel Drache, eds. *The Other Macdonald Report: The Consensus on Canada's Future that the Macdonald Commission Left Out.* Toronto: James Lorimer 1985.

Campbell, Robert M., and Leslie A. Pal., eds. *The Real Worlds of Canadian Politics: Cases in Process and Policy.* Peterborough, Ont.: Broadview Press 1989.

Canel, Eduardo. 'New Social Movement Theory and Resource Mobilization: The Need for Integration.' In *Organizing Dissent: Contemporary Social Movements in Theory and Practice*, edited by William K. Carroll, 22–41. Toronto: Garamond Press 1992.

Carroll, William K. 'The Solidarity Coalition.' In *The New Reality*, edited by Bruce Magnusson et al., 94–118. Vancouver: New Star Books 1984.

– ed. *Organizing Dissent: Contemporary Social Movements in Theory and Practice*. Toronto: Garamond Press, 1992.

Carroll, William K., and R.S. Ratner. 'Social Democracy, Neo-Conservatism, and Hegemonic Crisis in British Columbia.' *Critical Sociology* 16 (1989), 30–53.

Clarke, Harold D., et al. *Absent Mandate: Interpreting Change in Canadian Elections*. Toronto: Gage Publishing 1991.

Clarkson, Stephen. 'The Liberals: Disoriented in Defeat.' In *The Canadian General Election of 1988*, edited by Alan Frizzell, 27–41. Ottawa: Carleton University Press 1989.

– 'Yesterday's Man and His Blue Grits: Backward into the Future.' In *The Canadian General Election of 1993*, edited by Alan Frizzell et al., 27–41. Ottawa: Carleton University Press, 1994.

Cohen, Marjorie. 'The Anatomy of the Decision: The Efforts of Coalitions.' In *The Free Trade Agreement of 1988: Implications for the Future of Canadian–American Relations*, edited by Jane Jenson, 23–28. Harvard University: The Center for International Affairs 1989.

– Discussions about Coalition-Building.' In *Taking a Stand: Strategy and Tactics of Organizing the Popular Movement in Canada*, edited by Ronnie Leah, 32–4. Ottawa: Canadian Centre for Policy Alternatives 1992.

– 'Our Social and Economic Programs are in Greater Danger Than Ever Before.' In *If You Love This Country*, edited by Laurier LaPierre, 91–7. Toronto: McClelland and Stewart 1987.

Crispo, John, ed. *Free Trade: The Real Story*. Toronto: Gage Publishing 1988.

Cuzan, Alfred G. 'Resource Mobilization and Political Opportunity in the Nicaraguan Revolution: The Theory.' *American Journal of Economics and Sociology* 49 (October 1990), 401–12.

Dalton, Russell, and Manfred Kuechler. 'New Social Movements and the Political Order: Inducing Change for Long-Term Stability?' In *Challenging the Political Order: New Social and Political Movements in Western Democracies*, edited by Russell Dalton and Manfred Kuechler, 277–300. New York: Oxford University Press 1990.

Dasko, Donna. 'The Canadian Public and Free Trade,' In *The Free Trade Deal*, edited by Duncan Cameron, 246–54. Toronto: James Lorimer 1988.

Daudelin, Jean, and Edgar J. Dosman, eds. *Beyond Mexico: Changing Americas.* Ottawa: Carleton University Press 1995.

Doern, Bruce, and Brian Tomlin. *Faith and Fear: The Free Trade Story.* Toronto: Stoddart 1991.

Doran, Charles F., and Alvin Paul Drischler, eds. *A New North America: Cooperation and Enhanced Interdependence.* Westport, Conn.: Praeger 1996.

Drache, Daniel. 'The Post-National State.' In *Canadian Politics*, edited by James Bickerton and Alain-G. Gagnon, 549–66. Peterborough, Ont.: Broadview Press 1994.

Eder, Klaus. 'The "New Social Movements": Moral Crusades, Political Pressure Groups, or Social Movements.' *Social Research* 52 (1985), 869–90.

Eisinger, Peter. 'The Conditions of Protest Behavior in American Cities.' *American Political Science Review* 67 (1973), 11–28.

Elkins, David J. *Beyond Sovereignty: Territory and Political Economy in the Twenty-First Century.* Toronto: University of Toronto Press 1995.

Fantasia, Rick. *Cultures of Solidarity: Consciousness, Action, and Contemporary American Workers.* Berkeley: University of California Press 1988.

Frizzell, Alan, et al., eds. *The Canadian General Election of 1988.* Ottawa: Carleton University Press, 1989.

– *The Canadian General Election of 1993.* Ottawa: Carleton University Press 1994.

Gabriel, Christina, and Laura Macdonald. 'NAFTA, Women, and Organizing in Canada and Mexico: Forging a Feminist Internationality.' *Millennium: Journal of International Studies* 23, no. 3 (1993), 535–62.

Gamson, William A. *The Strategy of Social Protest.* Homewood, Ill.: Dorsey Press 1975.

Gherson, Giles. 'Washington's Agenda.' In *The Free Trade Deal*, edited by Duncan Cameron, 1–15. Toronto: James Lorimer 1988.

Gibson, Gordon. *Plan B: The Future of the Rest of Canada.* Vancouver: The Fraser Institute 1994.

Ginden, Sam. 'Breaking Away: The Formation of the Canadian Auto Workers,' *Studies in Political Economy* 29 (Summer 1989).

Gold, Marc, and David Leyton-Brown, eds. *Trade-Offs on Free Trade: The Canada–U.S. Free Trade Agreement.* Toronto: Carswell 1988.

Gonick, Cy, and Jim Silver, 'Fighting Free Trade.' *Canadian Dimension.* April 1989, 6–14.

Griffin, R.W. 'Political Opportunity, Resource Mobilization, and Social Movements: The Case of the South Texas Farm Workers.' *Social Science Journal* 29 (1992), 129–52.

Grinspun, Ricardo, and Robert Kreklewich. 'Consolidating Neoliberal Reforms: Free Trade as a Conditioning Framework.' *Studies in Political Economy* 43 (Spring 1994), 33–61.

Gwyn, Richard. *Nationalism without Walls: The Unbearable Lightness of Being Canadian.* Toronto: McClelland & Stewart 1995.

Hiebert, Janet. 'Interest Groups and the Canadian Federal Elections.' In *Interest Groups and Elections in Canada,* edited by F. Leslie Seidle, Volume 2 of the Research Studies, Royal Commission on Electoral Reform and Party Financing, 3–76. Ottawa: Ministry of Supply and Services Canada 1991.

Howlett, Dennis. 'Social Movement Coalitions: New Possibilities for Social Change.' *Canadian Dimension,* November–December 1989.

Hurtig, Mel. *The Betrayal of Canada.* Toronto: Stoddart 1991.

Inglehart, Ronald. *Culture Shift in Advanced Industrial Society.* Princeton, N.J.: Princeton University Press 1990.

– *The Silent Revolution: Changing Values and Political Styles among Western Publics.* Princeton, N.J.: Princeton University Press 1977.

Inglehart, Ronald, Neil Nevitte, and Miguel Basanez. *The North American Trajectory: Cultural, Economic, and Political Ties among the United States, Canada, and Mexico.* New York: Aldine de Gruyter 1996.

Jeffrey, Brooke. *Breaking Faith: The Mulroney Legacy of Deceit, Destruction, and Disunity.* Toronto: Key Porter Books 1992.

Jenkins, J. Craig. *The Politics of Insurgency: The Farm Worker Movement in the 1960s.* New York: Columbia University Press 1985.

– 'Resource Mobilization Theory and the Study of Social Movements.' *American Review of Sociology* 9 (1983), 527–53.

– 'Social Movements, Political Representation, and the State: An Agenda and Comparative Framework.' In *The Politics of Social Protest: Comparative Perspectives on States and Social Movements,* edited by J. Craig Jenkins and Bert Klandermans 14–34. Minneapolis: University of Minnesota Press 1995.

Jenkins, J. Craig, and Charles Perrow. 'Insurgency of the Powerless: Farm Worker Movements (1946–1972).' *American Sociological Review* 42 (1977), 249–68.

Jenson, Jane. 'Naming Nations: Making Nationalist Claims in Canadian Public Discourse.' *Canadian Review of Sociology and Anthropology* 30 (1993), 337–58.

– ed. *The Free Trade Agreement of 1988: Implications for the Future of Canadian–American Relations* (Harvard University: The Center for International Affairs 1989).

Johnston, Richard, et al. *Letting the People Decide: Dynamics of a Canadian Election.* Montreal and Kingston: McGill-Queen's University Press 1992.

Katzenstein, Mary, and Carol Mueller. *The Women's Movements of the United States and Western Europe: Consciousness, Political Opportunity, and Public Policy.* Philadelphia: Temple University Press 1987.

Kerbo, Harold R., and Richard A. Shaffer. 'Lower Class Insurgency and the Political Process: The Response of the U.S. Unemployed, 1890–1940.' *Social Problems* 39 (May 1992), 139–54.

Kitschelt, Herbert. 'Political Opportunity Structures and Political Protest: Anti-Nuclear Movements in Four Democracies.' *British Journal of Political Science* 16 (1986), 57–85.

Klandermans, Bert. 'Linking the Old and the New: Movement Networks in the Netherlands.' In *Challenging the Political Order: New Social and Political Movements in Western Democracies*, edited by Russell Dalton and Manfred Kuechler, 122–36. New York: Oxford University Press 1990.

Klandermans, Bert, and Sidney Tarrow. 'Mobilization into Social Movements: Synthesizing European and American Approaches.' In *From Structure to Action: Comparing Social Movement Research across Cultures*, edited by Bert Klandermans, Hanspeter Kriesi, and Sidney Tarrow. Greenwich, Conn.: JAI Press 1988.

Klandermans, Bert, et al. *From Structure to Action: Comparing Social Movement Research across Cultures*. Greenwich, Conn.: JAI Press 1988.

Kriesi, Hanspeter. 'Local Mobilization for the People's Petition of the Dutch Peace Movement.' In *From Structure to Action: Comparing Social Movement Research across Cultures*, ed. Bert Klandermans et al., 41–81. Greenwich, Conn.: JAI Press 1988.

– 'The Political Opportunity Structures of the Dutch Peace Movement.' *West European Politics* 12 (1989), 295–312.

Kriesi, Hanspeter, et al. 'New Social Movements and Political Opportunities in Western Europe.' *European Journal of Political Research* 22 (1992), 219–44.

Ladrech, Robert. 'Europeanization of Domestic Politics and Institutions: The Case of France.' *Journal of Common Market Studies* 32, no. 1 (1994), 69–88.

Languille, David. 'The Business Council on National Issues and the Canadian State.' *Studies in Political Economy* 24 (1988), 41–85.

LaPierre, Laurier, ed. *If You Love This Country*. Toronto: McClelland & Stewart 1987.

Laxer, Gordon. 'Social Solidarity, Democracy, and Global Capitalism.' *Canadian Review of Sociology and Anthropology* 32, no. 3 (August 1995), 287–313.

Laxer, James. *In Search of a New Left: Canadian Politics after the Neoconservative Assault*. Toronto: Viking 1996.

Laycock, David. 'Organized Interests in Canada and the Free Trade Election.' In *The Free Trade Agreement of 1988: Implications for the Future of Canadian–American Relations*, edited by Jane Jenson, 15–21. Harvard University: The Center for International Affairs 1989.

LeDuc, Lawrence. 'Voting for Free Trade? The Canadian Voter and the 1988 Federal Election.' In *Politics: Canada*, edited by Paul Fox. 7th edition. Toronto: McGraw-Hill Ryerson 1991.

LeDuc, Lawrence, et al. 'Partisan Instability in Canada: Evidence from a New Panel Study.' *American Political Science Review* 78 (1984), 470–83.

Magnusson, Warren. 'De-centring the State.' In *Canadian Politics*, edited by James P. Bickerton and Alain-G. Gagnon, 567–86. 2nd ed. Peterborough, Ont.: Broadview Press 1994.

– 'Decentring the State, or Looking for Politics.' In *Organizing Dissent: Contemporary Social Movements in Theory and Practice*, edited by William K. Carroll, 69–80. Toronto: Garamond Press 1992.

– *The Search for Political Space: Globalization, Social Movements, and the Urban Political Experience*. Toronto: University of Toronto Press 1996.

Magnusson, Warren, et al., *The New Reality: The Politics of Restraint in British Columbia*. Vancouver: New Star Books 1984.

Marks, Gary, and Douglas McAdam. 'Social Movements and the Changing Structure of Political Opportunity in the European Community.' *West European Politics* 19, no. 2 (1996), 249–78.

Mayer, Margit. 'Social Movement Research and Social Movement Practice: The U.S. Pattern.' In *Research on Social Movements: The State of the Art in Western Europe and the USA*, edited by Dieter Rucht, 47–119. Boulder, Colo.: Westview Press 1991.

McAdam, Douglas. *Political Process and the Development of Mass Insurgency, 1930–1970*. Chicago: University of Chicago Press 1982.

McAdam, Douglas, John D. McCarthy, and Mayer N. Zald. *Comparative Perspectives on Social Movements: Political Opportunities, Mobilizing Structures, and Cultural Framings*. Cambridge: Cambridge University Press 1996.

McAdam, Douglas, Sidney Tarrow, and Charles Tilly. 'To Map Contentious Politics.' *Mobilization: An International Journal* 1, no. 1 (1996), 17–34.

McBride, Stephen. 'The Continuing Crisis of Social Democracy: Ontario's Social Contract in Perspective.' *Studies in Political Economy* 50 (Summer 1996), 65–93.

McCarthy, John, and M. Zald. 'Resource Mobilization and Social Movements.' *American Journal of Sociology* 82 (1977), 1212–41.

McClintock, Cynthia. 'Why Peasants Rebel: The Case of Peru's Sendero Luminoso.' *World Politics* 37 (1984), 48–84.

McQuaig, Linda. *The Quick and the Dead: Brian Mulroney, Big Business, and the Seduction of Canada*. Toronto: Viking 1991.

Melucci, Alberto. 'The New Social Movements: A Theoretical Approach.' *Social Science Information* 19 (1980), 199–226.

Merrett, Christopher D. *Free Trade: Neither Free nor about Trade*. Montreal: Black Rose Books 1996.

Meyer, David, and Suzanne Staggenborg. 'Movements, Countermovements, and the Structure of Political Opportunity.' *American Journal of Sociology* 101, no. 6 (1996), 1628–60.

Midlarsky, Manus, and Kenneth Roberts. 'Class, State, and Revolution in Central America: Nicaragua and El Salvador Compared.' *Journal of Conflict Resolution* 29 (1985), 163–93.

Monahan, Patrick. *Storming the Pink Palace.* Toronto: Lester Publishing 1995.

Morris, Aldon. *The Origins of the Civil Rights Movement.* New York: The Free Press 1984.

Morris, Aldon, and Cedric Herring. 'Theory and Research in Social Movements: A Critical Review.' In *Annual Review of Political Science*, edited by S. Long. 2 (1987), 138–98.

Mueller, Carol. 'Building Social Movement Theory.' In *Frontiers in Social Movement Theory*, edited by Aldon Morris and Carol Mueller, 3–25. New Haven, Conn.: Yale University Press 1992.

Neidhardt, Friedhelm, and Dieter Rucht. 'The Analysis of Social Movements: The State of the Art and Some Perspectives for Further Research.' In *Research on Social Movements: The State of the Art in Western Europe and the United States*, edited by Dieter Rucht, 421–64. Boulder, Colo.: Westview Press 1991.

Nevitte, Neil. *The Decline of Deference: Canadian Value Change in Cross-Cultural Perspective.* Peterborough, Ont.: Broadview Press 1995.

Nevitte, Neil, Miguel Basanez, and Ronald Inglehart. 'Directions of Value Change in North America.' In *NAFTA in Transition*, edited by Stephen J. Randall and Herman W. Konrad, 329–43. Calgary: University of Calgary Press 1995.

Newman, Peter. *The Canadian Revolution, 1985–1995.* Toronto: Viking 1995.

Oberschall, Anthony. *Social Conflict and Social Movements.* Englewood Cliffs, N.J.: Prentice-Hall 1973.

Offe, Claus. 'New Social Movements: Challenging the Boundaries of Institutional Politics.' *Social Research* 52 (1985), 817–68.

Palmer, Bryan, D. *Solidarity: The Rise and Fall of an Opposition in British Columbia.* Vancouver: New Star Books 1987.

Pammet, John. 'The 1988 Vote.' In *The Canadian General Election of 1988*, edited by Alan Frizzell et al., 115–30. Ottawa: Carleton University Press 1989.

Piven, Frances Fox, and Richard Cloward. *Poor People's Movements.* New York: Vintage Books 1977.

– *Regulating the Poor: The Functions of Public Welfare.* New York: Pantheon 1971.

Resnick, Philip. *The Land of Cain: Class and Nationalism in English Canada, 1945–1975.* Vancouver: New Star Books, 1977.

Resnick, Philip. *Letters to a Québécois Friend.* Montreal, Kingston: McGill-Queen's University Press 1990.

– *Thinking English Canada.* Toronto: Stoddart 1994.

Rochon, Thomas. *Mobilizing for Peace. The Antinuclear Movements in Western Europe.* Princeton, N.J.: Princeton University Press 1988.

– 'Political Movements and State Authority in Liberal Democracies.' *World Politics* 23 (1989), 299–313.

– 'The West European Peace Movement and the Theory of New Social Movements.' In *Challenging the Political Order: New Social and Political Movements in Western Democracies,* edited by Russell Dalton and Manfred Kuechler, 105–21. New York: Oxford University Press 1990.

Salutin, Rick. 'Keep Canadian Culture Off the Table: Who's Kidding Who?' In *If You Love This Country,* edited by Laurier LaPierre, 205–10. Toronto: McClelland & Stewart 1987.

– *Waiting for Democracy: A Citizen's Journal.* Markham, Ont.: Penguin 1989.

Schennk, Ben. 'From Peace Week to Peace Work: Dynamics of the Peace Movement in the Netherlands.' *International Social Movement Research* 1 (1988), 247–79.

Scott, Alan. *Ideology and the New Social Movements.* London: Unwin Hyman 1990.

Siisiainen, Martti. 'Social Movements, Voluntary Associations, and Cycles of Protest in Finland, 1905–1991.' *Scandinavian Political Studies* 15 (1992), 21–40.

Sinclair, Jim, editor. *Crossing the Line: Canada and Free Trade with Mexico.* Vancouver: New Star Books 1992.

Skocpol, Theda. 'What Makes Peasants Revolutionary?' *Comparative Politics* 14 (April 1982), 351–75.

Smith, Miriam. 'The Canadian Labour Congress: From Continentalism to Economic Nationalism.' *Studies in Political Economy* 38 (1992), 35–60.

Sniderman, Paul, et al. *The Clash of Rights: Liberty, Equality, and Legitimacy in Pluralist Democracy.* New Haven, Conn.: Yale University Press 1996.

Snow, David, et al. 'Frame Alignment Processes, Micromobilization, and Movement Participation.' *American Sociological Review* 51 (1986), 464–81.

Stairs, Denis. 'Canada Will Be a Less Relaxed, Less Gentle, a Less Tolerant Place in Which to Live.' In *If You Love This Country,* edited by Laurier LaPierre, 212–16. Toronto: McClelland & Stewart 1987.

Tarrow, Sidney. 'The Europeanization of Conflict: Reflections from a Social Movement Perspective.' *West European Politics* 18, no. 2 (1995), 223–51.

– 'Fishnets, Internets and Catnets: Globalization and Transnational Collective Action.' In *Challenging Authority: The Historical Study of Contentious Politics,* edited by Michael Hanagan et. al. Minneapolis and St Paul: University of Minnesota Press 1998.

– 'National Politics and Collective Action: Recent Theory and Research in Western Europe and the United States.' *Annual Review of Sociology* 14 (1988), 421–40.

– 'The Phantom at the Opera: Political Parties and Social Movements of the 1960s and 1970s in Italy.' In *Challenging the Political Order: New Social and Political*

Movements in Western Democracies, edited by Russell Dalton and Manfred Kuechler, 67–83. New York: Oxford University Press 1990.

–   *Power in Movement: Social Movements, Collective Action, and Politics.* Cambridge: Cambridge University Press, 1994.

–   'Social Movements in Contentious Politics: A Review Article.' *American Political Science Review* 90, no. 4 (1996), 874–83.

–   *Struggle, Politics, and Reform: Collective Action, Social Movements, and Cycles of Protest.* Western Societies Program Occasional Paper, no. 21. Center for International Studies, Cornell University, Ithaca, N.Y. 1989.

Teeple, Gary. *Globalization and the Decline of Social Reform.* Toronto: Garamond Press 1995.

Tilly, Charles. *From Mobilization to Revolution.* Reading, Mass.: Addison-Wesley 1978.

Touraine, Alain. *Anti-Nuclear Protest.* Cambridge: Cambridge University Press 1983.

Traugott, Marc, ed. *Repertoires and Cycles of Collective Action.* Durham, N.C.: Duke University Press 1995.

Useem, M. *Protest Movements in America.* Indianapolis: Bobbs-Merrill 1975.

Walkom, Thomas. *Rae Days: The Rise and Follies of the NDP.* Toronto: Key Porter Books 1994.

Warnock, John W. *Free Trade and the New Right Agenda.* Vancouver: New Star Books 1988.

Whalley, John, and Roderick Hill, eds. *Canada–United States Free Trade.* Toronto: University of Toronto Press for Supply and Services Canada 1985.

White, Randall. *Fur Trade to Free Trade: Putting the Canada–U.S. Trade Agreement in Historical Perspective.* Toronto: Dundurn Press 1988.

Whitehorn, Alan. 'The NDP Election Campaign: Dashed Hopes.' In *The Canadian General Election of 1988*, edited by Alan Frizzell et al., 43–53. Ottawa: Carleton University Press 1989.

Whyte, John, and Ian Peach. *Re-Forming Canada? The Meaning of the Meech Lake Accord and the Free Trade Agreement for the Canadian State.* Institute of Intergovernmental Relations, Queen's University, Kingston, Ont. 1989.

Wilson, James Q. *Political Organizations.* New York: Basic Books 1973.

Winter, James P., ed. *The Silent Revolution: Media, Democracy, and the Free Trade Debate.* Ottawa: University of Ottawa Press 1990.

Government Documents

Department of External Affairs. *Canadian Trade Policy for the 1980s: A Discussion Paper.* Ottawa, 1983.

–   *Competitiveness and Security: Directions for Canada's International Relations.* Ottawa 1985.

- *How to Secure Access to Export Markets.* Ottawa 1985.
- 'New Climate for Investment in Canada.' Speech by the Right Honourable Brian Mulroney, prime minister, to members of the Economic Club of New York, 10 December 1984.
Department of Finance. *A New Direction for Canada: An Agenda for Economic Renewal.* Ottawa 1984.
Department of Industry, Trade, and Commerce. *Major Canadian Projects, Major Canadian Opportunities: A Report by the Major Projects Task Force on Major Capital Projects in Canada to the Year 2000.* Ottawa 1981.
House of Commons. *Committee on External Affairs and International Trade.* 33rd Parliament, 2nd session. Issue no. 35 1987.
- Issue no. 38 1987.
House of Commons. *Committee on Labour, Employment, and Immigration.* 33rd Parliament, 2nd session. Issue no. 2 1988.
- *Debates.* 33rd Parliament, 2nd session 1987.
Privy Council Office. *Foreign Ownership and the Structures of Canadian Industry: Report of the Task Force on the Structure of Canadian Industry.* Ottawa: Queen's Printer 1968.
Royal Commission on the Economic Union and Development Prospects for Canada. *Report.* Ottawa: Ministry of Supply and Services 1985.

Newspapers and Periodicals

Calgary Herald	*New York Times*
Canadian Dimension	*North Bay Nugget*
Canadian Forum	*Ottawa Citizen*
Globe and Mail	*This Magazine*
Halifax Chronicle Herald	*Toronto Star*
Monthly Review	*Wall Street Journal*
Montreal Gazette	*Whig Standard*

Popular-Sector Movement Publications

Action Canada Dossier.
Canadian Alliance for Trade and Job Opportunities. *Report of Activities March 1987 to March 1989.* 1989.
Canadian Labour.
Canadian Perspectives.
Clarke, Tony. *Building the Movement: The Pro-Canada Network.* Ottawa: The Pro-Canada Network 1989.

- 'Coalition-Building: Towards a Social Movement for Economic Justice.' *Policy Alternatives.* Spring–Summer 1983, 29–32.
- 'The Pro-Canada Network: Building a Coast-to-Coast Movement to Block the Deal.' In *The Facts: Canada, Don't Trade It Away.* Ottawa: Canadian Union of Public Employees 1988.
Cohen, Marjorie. 'Undressing Macho-Economics: The Macdonald Report's Implications for Women.' *Our Times,* June 1986, 18–21.
Council of Canadians. *Newsletter.*
'Dialogue '86.' *Canadian Labour,* February 1986, 11–14.
Finn, Ed. 'Church, Labour Agree on Need for "New Social Movement."' *Policy Alternatives,* Spring–Summer 1983, 11–16.
Gatt-Fly. *Ah-Hah! A New Approach to Popular Education.* Toronto: Between the Lines 1983.
- 'Churches Urged to Oppose Free Trade with the U.S.' *Gatt-Fly Report* 7, March 1986, 1–6.
- *Free Trade, Self-Reliance, and Economic Justice, Report of the Ecumenical Conference on Free Trade, Self-Reliance, and Economic Justice, February 26 – March 1, 1987, Orleans, Ontario.* Toronto: Gatt-Fly 1987.
New Democratic Party. 'An Alternative Strategy: Fair Trade vs. Free Trade.' Ottawa, March 1985.
Our Times.
Pro-Canada Dossier.
Social Solidarity. 'A Time for Social Solidarity: Popular Groups' Statement.' *Our Times,* May 1988, 8–9.

Unpublished Materials

Bashevkin, Sylvia. 'Reflections on the Future of English Canadian Nationalism.' Paper prepared for the ACSUS in Canada Colloquium, North American in the 21st Century: Perspectives on Autonomy, Exchange, and Integration. Toronto, 8 November 1996.
Clarke, Harold D., and Allan Kornberg. 'Risky Business, Partisan Volatility, and Electoral Choice in Canada, 1988.' Paper prepared for the American Political Science Association Annual Meeting, Atlanta, Georgia, 31 August–3 September 1989.
Coalition Against Free Trade. Minutes. Toronto.
Council of Canadians. Correspondence; Press Releases; Statement of Purpose. Ottawa.
della Porta, D. 'Political Opportunities and Terrorism. The Italian Social Movement Sector during the Seventies.' Paper presented to the ECPR workshop on New Social Movements and the Political System. Amsterdam, 10–15 April 1987.

Gutierrez-Haces, Teresa. 'Globalization from Below: The Awakening and Networking of Civil Societies in North America.' Paper prepared for ACSUS in the Canada Colloquium, North America in the 21st Century: Perspectives on Autonomy, Exchange, and Integration. Toronto, 8 November 1996.

Howlett, Dennis. 'Social Movement Coalitions: Reflections on the Pro-Canada Network Experience.' Unpublished Manuscript. Toronto, April 1989.

Johnston, Richard, et al. 'Free Trade and the Dynamics of the 1988 Canadian Election.' Paper prepared for the American Political Science Association Annual Meeting. Atlanta, Georgia, 31 August–3 September 1989.

Pawley, Howard. 'The Crisis in Social Democracy: How the New Democratic Party has Fared.' Paper prepared for the Conference of the Midwest Association for Canadian Studies. Madison, Wisc., October 1996.

Pro-Canada Network. Minutes. Ottawa.

Schwartz, Mildred. 'NAFTA and the Fragmentation of Canada.' Paper prepared for ACSUS in the Canada Colloquium, North America in the 21st Century: Perspectives on Autonomy, Exchange, and Integration. Toronto, 8 November 1996.

Trent, John, E. 'Unique? Canada? An Essay on Political Identity.' Paper prepared for the Conference of Administrators of Programmes of Canadian Studies, Mount Allison University. Sackville, N.B. September 1990.

List of Persons Interviewed

Lloyd Axworthy	Herb Gray	Rose Potvin
Maude Barlow	Dennis Howlett	Mark Resnick
Sylvia Bashevkin	Brooke Jeffrey	Nancy Riche
Peter Bleyer	Pat Kerwin	Laurell Ritchie
Duncan Cameron	Michael Kirby	Mandy Rocks
Bruce Campbell	Art Kube	Rick Salutin
Michael Cassidy	Pierrette Landry	Sandra Sorenson
Mel Clark	Steven Langdon	Brian Tomlin
Tony Clarke	Lawrence LeDuc	Ken Traynor
Deborah Dunville	Michael McBane	John Trent
John Foster	Katherine Morrison	Kenneth Wardroper

Index

STUDIES IN COMPARATIVE POLITICAL ECONOMY AND PUBLIC POLICY

Editors: MICHAEL HOWLETT, DAVID LAYCOCK, STEPHEN MCBRIDE
Simon Fraser University

Studies in Comparative Political Economy and Public Policy is designed to showcase innovative approaches to political economy and public policy from a comparative perspective. While originating in Canada, the series will provide attractive offerings to a wide international audience, featuring studies with local, sub-national, cross-national, and international empirical bases and theoretical frameworks.

EDITORIAL ADVISORY BOARD

Isabel Bakker, Political Science, York University
Colin Bennett, Political Science, University of Victoria
Wallace Clement, Sociology, Carleton University
William Coleman, Political Science, McMaster University
Barry Eichengreen, Economics, University of California (Berkeley)
Wynford Grant, Political Science, University of Warwick
John Holmes, Geography, Queen's University
Jane Jenson, Political Science, Université de Montréal
William Lafferty, Project for Alternative Future, Oslo
Gordon Laxer, Sociology, University of Alberta
Ronald Manzer, Political Science, University of Toronto
John Ravenhill, Political Science, Australian National University
Peter Taylor-Gooby, Social Work, University of Kent
Margaret Weir, Brookings Institution, Washington, DC

PUBLISHED TO DATE